500 MORE PRAYERS
for All Occasions

Sandy,

with my profound
thanks and best
wishes.
Every blessing,

Geoff

500

MORE PRAYERS
for All Occasions

DAVID CLOWES

David C Cook®
transforming lives together

500 MORE PRAYERS FOR ALL OCCASIONS
Published by David C. Cook
Kingsway Communications LTD
Lottbridge Drove, Eastbourne BN23 6NT, England

David C. Cook
4050 Lee Vance View, Colorado Springs, CO 80918 U.S.A.

David C. Cook Distribution Canada
55 Woodslee Avenue, Paris, Ontario, Canada N3L 3E5

David C. Cook and the graphic circle C logo
are registered trademarks of Cook Communications Ministries.

The Web site addresses recommended throughout this book are offered as a
resource to you. These Web sites are not intended in any way to be or imply an
endorsement on the part of David C. Cook, nor do we vouch for their content.

ISBN 978-1-84291-375-8

The Team: Richard Herkes, Jaci Schneider, Sarah Schultz, and Karen Athen
Cover Design: Amy Kiechlin
Cover Image: iStockphoto, royalty-free

Printed in the United States of America
First Edition 2010

2 3 4 5 6 7 8 9 10

083110

Contents

INTRODUCTION

I have always believed that the leading of public prayer should not be seen as the same as private prayer. Leading the people of God in conversation with their Maker is both a serious and a challenging task. It is too easy to slip into time-worn phrases that lull the congregation into ever deeper slumbers.

In writing this book of prayers I set myself a series of guidelines. First, I have aimed for simplicity of language and for a direct style of writing. This is important if they are to be prayed and not simply read out. Second, I restricted the choice of congregational responses. A simple straw poll revealed that the main dread of most congregations is not the length of the prayers but if they will be able to remember the latest complicated response the preacher has dreamt up! The first book included a selection of alternative responses for those bold enough to use them. Responses in this book are in **bold italics.** Third, I have never used any book of prayers just as they were written, and I do not expect this book will be used any differently. In some sections I have deliberately given a larger number of prayers than should really be used on any one occasion, to provide options. This book is a mine in which to dig, not a building plan to be slavishly followed.

It was Christmas 1967 when I took my first extremely tentative steps in leading worship, when I read a lesson in the carol service. Shortly afterwards I discovered the joy and the responsibility of leading the people of God in conversation with their Maker. My church background at that time was firmly in the camp of extemporary prayer. The very thought of using a prayer written by someone else was quite foreign to me.

I started to write my prayers down for two reasons. First was my shyness and the nervousness I experienced then (and still do) of standing in front of an expectant congregation. Second was the challenge from an experienced lay preacher who was my mentor. He insisted on careful preparation not only of the hymns, readings and sermon, but also of the prayers.

I came to realise that in relying solely on extemporary prayer I was in danger of 'vain repetition' born out of a lack of forethought and a refusal to listen and learn from my fellow preachers. I soon discovered that, though I could trawl to good effect through the prayers written by different people, I didn't need to allow myself to become enslaved by them. I could use the prayers as they were given, or pick and mix and amend at will. This was real freedom, and I am certain my congregations benefited from my journey in prayer.

The first book of prayer, *500 Prayers for All Occasions*, was itself a journey, albeit through the Christian year. This meant that there was a sense of following a path along a clearly defined, well-worn and well-known way. This new collection is intended to be more like a patchwork quilt. It is varied in the areas it covers and in the style of prayers that are included.

Besides the usual prayers of praise, thanksgiving, intercession, commitment and dismissal, you will also find those for more specific facets of prayer life in worship. Some prayers, such as those of adoration and the ones for all-age worship, have been included in response to specific requests. Sadly, while we concentrate our minds on praising God, his adoration is an aspect often missing from our worship. I have focused the prayers for all-age worship around various biblical characters in an attempt to provide a link with those whose names we find in the pages of Scripture.

Most of the prayers have been used publicly before being added to this book. These include prayers for special services such as services of healing, weddings and funerals. You will also find prayers for use as an annual memorial service, which have been well received by all the ecumenical partners involved.

One new section focuses on the use of meditation in worship. Some of these are linked to specific Scriptures. Others explore the call to service, the value of each day, our longing for stillness, the horizons of life, the excuses we make to God and how God allows us to catch a glimpse of him in our daily lives. There are two Christmas meditations which enable us to realise again our need of the Saviour coming to be God with us.

The prayers of intercession cover special moments in the Christian year: Mothering Sunday, Education Sunday, Maundy Thursday, Good Friday, Remembrance Sunday, Harvest and One

World Week. Others explore the fruit of the Spirit, what it means to be anxious, our broken images, the Week of Prayer for Christian Unity, deliverance, the hungry, those with power, those who are rich and those who are facing times of stress.

Many of the prayers of intercession are responsive. Some invite the members of the congregation to 'think of someone', while others provide a thumbnail sketch in the first person followed by a period of silent reflection.

There is a whole section of prayers for use before a service. These can be used with the preacher prior to the service, or made available to the congregation as they prepare for worship.

We are living in the day and generation of the visual. For instance, we are conditioned by the presentation of the news on television in a highly visual, immediate and challenging format. I have tried to outline some ideas for prayers using visuals. They can be pictures for the congregation to see, either in small groups as in café-style worship or by use of projection equipment.

I haven't included the images themselves as these will naturally vary according to the current situation. The BBC News Web site and Google Images are often good places to start your search. I generally use music to accompany the prayers. These tend to work best with either 'prayer captions' which appear on the screen or short 'sound-bite' prayers using one or more voices. I believe that this is a format worth exploring, as many people find this way of praying not only moving but also an enriching experience.

As before, the prayers are set out in verse form. Line breaks have been considered carefully, and punctuation used judiciously, to guide the spoken word.

You will find the prayers listed in sections on the contents page. The Index should lead you to the areas of prayer and the subjects for which you are seeking material.

It may seem strange, but some of the most moving moments in my prayer life have been as I have clicked away with two fingers on the keyboard of my computer. I fully expect that those prayers which you will find most helpful and meaningful are the very ones which for me were gifts I received through the grace of God. And although public prayers are not the same as private devotions, it is true to say that many of the prayers included in this second volume have indeed 'found life' during those precious moments in God's presence. They have come in the early morning before the day began, or when the house was silent, or in the stillness at the end of the day.

My first book of prayers was conceived and written during a sabbatical study period. That it finally came to birth was the result of the encouragement of Malcolm and Elizabeth Pittam and Sheila Smith, who tried to bring some kind of order to my informal style of writing. I have been overwhelmed by the responses I have received from people all over the world to the prayers in that volume. I am grateful for the guidance, help and support of Richard Herkes and to the team at Kingsway and David C. Cook, who provided the opportunity to share my prayers with a far wider congregation than I ever imagined possible.

Once more I am grateful to my wife, Angela, who patiently allows me time and space, and a great deal of 'midnight oil', to set out in the written word those thoughts and prayers with which the Lord bombards my mind. Along with my longsuffering congregations, she is always ready to be the first to sample my latest offering.

David Clowes
Wigan, June 2009

Prayers for a Call to Worship

1 THE LORD IS HERE

The Lord is here, and we will praise him.
The Lord is here, and we will worship him.
The Lord is here, and we will trust him.
The Lord is here, and we will honour him.
The Lord is here, and he has called us to give him all the
glory. Amen.

2 COME AND WORSHIP

Come and worship the living God—and the Saviour of the
world.
Come and worship the one who died—and was raised again.
Come and worship the Spirit who renews and empowers us
to be God's people and to offer him our thanks, our praise
and our worship. Amen.

3 HIS NAME IS ALMIGHTY

His name is Almighty and he is the Lord.
His name is Creator and he makes all things new.
His name is Sustainer and he holds us in the palm of his
hand.
His name is the Saviour and he died in our place.
His name is Forgiveness and he can be trusted to heal and to
bless.
His name is Holy and he is the one that we have come to
worship.
His name means he is worthy to receive all we have and all
we are,
for ever and ever. Amen.

4 YOUR PEOPLE HAVE COME

Lord, we are your people
not because we are worthy but by your grace alone.

We are your people who have come in joy and thankfulness.
We are your people and we have come to praise you.
We are your people and we have come to give you the
worship you deserve.
We are your people and we have come in the name of Jesus.
Amen.

5   WE COME AS YOUR FAMILY

Lord, we do not come as guests but as members of your
family;
we do not come in fear but with joy and thanksgiving;
we do not come alone but with all your people
of every age and in every place.

Lord, we come as your family, for you are our heavenly
Father,
and Christ is our Brother, our Saviour and Lord. Amen.

6   IN JOY AND GLADNESS

Our loving, heavenly Father,
we come because we must;
we come because we ought to;
we come because we need to;
we come because we long to;
we come because in you we have a joy and a gladness we
have never known before;
we come because you are the Lord. Amen.

7   WE HAVE COME TO SING

Lord, we have come—to sing, to pray and to meet with you.

Lord, our songs are for you,
our prayers are in Christ's name
and our meeting is in the power of the Spirit.

Lord, accept our songs, receive our prayers
and make your presence felt, that we may worship you.
    Amen.

8   KING OF ALL CREATION

Almighty God, King of all creation, Sovereign over all
    things,
you hold the universe in the palm of your hand.
Enable us to keep our hearts fixed on you
and our minds on your truth,
for we have come to worship you as Lord of all. Amen.

9   LORD, WE HAVE COME

Lord, we have come because you have called us.
We have come in the name of Jesus.
We have come to declare the Father's love.
We have come because you are worthy.
We have come because you are here.

Lord, empower us with your Holy Spirit to truly
    acknowledge your presence
and to worship you alone. Amen.

Prayers of Adoration

10   THIS IS OUR GOD

love—overwhelming; mercy—releasing;
joy—uplifting; grace—enabling;
faith—demanding; goodness—challenging;
judgement—warning; forgiveness—liberating;
trust—outreaching; kindness—enriching;
compassion—inspiring; sacrifice—cleansing;
resurrection—beginning.
Father, Son and Holy Spirit, this is our God and we will
    adore him. Amen.

11 YOU ARE HERE

Lord, here we are and you are here.
You are here and you have called us.
Here we are and you are worthy.
You are here and we will adore you. Amen.

12 LORD, YOU HAVE GIVEN

Lord, you have given us laughter and song;
work and leisure; hope and anticipation;
faithfulness and peace; praise and thanksgiving.

You have filled our days with journeys and discoveries;
with striving and succeeding; with energy and stillness;
with solitude and togetherness; with silence and celebration.

You have offered us hope and new beginning;
cleansing and renewal; comfort and deep satisfaction;
forgiveness and mercy; yourself, your love and your Son as
       our Saviour.

We come to offer our heartfelt thanks
and the adoration that comes
from lives made new by the power of the Spirit.

We bring our gift in the name of Christ,
the source of all your gifts of grace. Amen.

13 PETER AND CORNELIUS

Lord, as with Peter and Cornelius, you never cease to amaze
       us;
you break into our days, our plans and our dreams.
You refuse to be blocked by our petty thoughts and our rigid
       ideas.
We have come to give adoration,
for you break down our walls and destroy all the barriers
we have carefully guarded and are slow to let go.
Now touch our hearts by your Holy Spirit
that we may be empowered to adore your holy name. Amen.

14 WHAT SHALL WE CALL HIM?

Wonderful—forgiving; beautiful—creative;
holy—overwhelming; merciful—patient;
gracious—understanding; loving—trusting;
incarnate—eternal; crucified—risen;
all-powerful—gentle; all-knowing—faithful.
Almighty, King of creation, Sovereign over all things.

We can't find the right words when all we long to say is
you are our Saviour and you are our Lord, and we will adore
you. Amen.

15 BREAD OF HEAVEN—ADORATION

Lord, we have come, bringing the baggage
that we have carried with us for most of our lives.

We have come, bringing our concerns and our worries
and the questions for which we still have no answer.

We have come, with the frustrations and emptiness
that cripple our lives and encompass our days.

We come, bringing all that we have and all that we are
into the presence of the one who is the bread of life,
that, as we adore you, you may bring
healing to us and glory to him. Amen.

16 OUR GRACIOUS GOD

Lord, you are more gracious than we can imagine.
You are more holy than we will ever grasp.
You are overflowing in majesty that leaves us breathless.
You are almighty in ways beyond our comprehension.
You are all-loving beyond our expectations.
You require us to seek justice in ways that challenge us.
You demand that our lives and our lifestyle
always bring you honour and glory.
You alone are our Saviour, our Lord and our Master,
and there is no other.

We offer you here and now
not mere words, but lips of praise;
not only songs of worship,
but the adoration of hearts that long to know you in Jesus.
    Amen.

17   HOLDING OUR BREATH

Lord, we scan the horizon and search for signs of life.
But nothing moves—
the cool, crisp air freezes our breath and we know we are
    alone.

But it is an aloneness that speaks of space to think, to
    reflect—
the freedom just to be.
And we are overwhelmed by it.

Lord, we have come into your presence
and it makes us want to hold our breath;
to remain utterly still and simply enjoy
the freedom that comes as we step out of our world.
And, for a brief moment, we are overwhelmed by the
    knowledge
that the King of kings, the Lord of time and eternity,
the Sovereign of all things is here—with us.

Lord, we have no words to express just how we feel.
We have come to adore you
and will do so now and for all eternity. Amen.

18   ONE TRUE GOD

Lord, we praise you for creating, healing and loving us.
We thank you for seeking—and finding us;
for holding us and renewing our lives.
We honour you for all you have done
for us, in us and through us.
But we adore you for who you are: the one true living God.
    Amen.

19 GREAT AND GLORIOUS

Great and glorious; powerful and wonderful;
holy and mighty; majestic and sovereign;
helper and carer; Creator and Sustainer; Saviour and Lord.
What else can we add?
We simply run out of words, when all we want to say, Lord,
is that we adore you. Amen.

20 YOU ARE THE KING

You are the King and we will praise you.
You are holy and we will bow before you.
You are the Saviour and we will trust you.
You are almighty and we will serve you.
You are the Lord and we will adore you. Amen.

21 OUR GOD IS HERE

Our God is our Creator
and we will adore him.
Our God is our Saviour
and we will adore him.
Our God is our King
and we will adore him.
Our God is our Master
and we will adore him.
Our God is our Lord
and we will adore him.
Our God is here
and we will adore him.

22 ADORATION—THE TRUE WORTH

Lord, your world looks more wonderful
when we try to see it through your eyes,
but we see more of its pain when we stand next to you.
We begin to recognise the true value of earthly wealth and
    status

when first we look to Christ.
We discover the meaning of hope, peace and love
when we walk hand in hand with our Lord.
We see the true worth of every man, woman and child,
and know that this doesn't depend on who they are or what
they do,
only when we see them held in the arms of your grace.
Lord, all the sights and sounds; all the things we have and
hold;
all our plans and dreams; all our gifts and skills;
all we are and all we will be
only receive their true worth at the foot of your cross.
Lord, source of all that was, all that is and all that will be,
we offer you our adoration. Amen.

23   ADORATION OF THE KING

King of creation, Lord of all history, Sovereign all-powerful,
Master so tender, Saviour for all.
Friend of the poor, Spirit enabling.
Son from all eternity, the Alpha and Omega, beginning and
end.
We offer you our adoration and praise. Amen.

24   LORD, SO GREAT

Lord, so great, so high, so holy,
we lift our hearts to give you glory.
Father, so gentle, so understanding, so full of grace,
we raise our voices and declare that you are worthy.
Holy Spirit, so mighty, so overwhelming, so empowering,
we seek your presence and desire your infilling.
We long to offer worship that is not focused on ourselves—
not on our needs but on your glory.
Lord, your love holds us, heals us and renews us;
we will adore you, here and everywhere, now and for ever.
Amen.

25   COME, LET US ADORE HIM

For God's faithfulness to his people and mercy when we go
     wrong:
Come, let us adore him.
Come, let us adore him.

For his power in creation and his grace in re-creation:
Come, let us adore him.
Come, let us adore him.

For the beauty of our world and the capacity to enjoy it:
Come, let us adore him.
Come, let us adore him.

For the journey of life which we do not make alone:
Come, let us adore him.
Come, let us adore him.

For the command to love our neighbour and the challenge
     to love ourselves:
Come, let us adore him.
Come, let us adore him.

For the path of faith you call us to follow, and for Christ
     who walks with us:
Come, let us adore him.
Come, let us adore him.

For the love of God the Father, the grace of Christ the Son
     and the power of God's Spirit:
Come, let us adore him.
Come, let us adore him.

Christ the Lord. Amen.

26   WE COME TO WORSHIP

Lord, we have not come to sing hymns;
we have not come to say prayers;
we have not come to be with each other.

Lord, we have come simply to worship;
we have come to acknowledge your worth;
we have come to offer adoration, thanksgiving and praise.

Lord, please listen to our songs, receive our prayers
and enjoy your children being together—
but these are only the vehicles of our heartfelt praise and
    adoration
as we worship you. In Jesus' name. Amen.

27 HOW CAN WE NOT ADORE YOU?

Lord, we simply can't help ourselves.
Every time we come into your presence
we are bowled over by the experience of being loved.

Lord, we want to hold our breath
and in the stillness to wonder at the grace, the undeserved
    love,
with which you utterly overwhelm us.

Lord, how can we not adore you—our King, our Prince of
    Peace
and the source of all our hope?
Our hearts, minds and lives are touched by your grace
and healed by your love.

Wonderful, wonderful God, for all that you are
we offer you heartfelt adoration. Amen.

28 MAJESTY

Majesty, majesty, majesty!
Lord, we adore you and proclaim your majesty.
Holy, holy, holy!
Lord, we adore you and worship you in your holiness.
Glory, glory, glory!
Lord, we adore you and celebrate your glory.
Father, Son and Holy Spirit!

Lord, we adore you for all that you are, and all that you
    will be.
O come let us adore him, Christ the Lord! Amen.

29   LET US PRAISE GOD

Let us praise God, for he is glorious.
Let us give thanks, for he is the source of all good things.
Let us worship him now, for he is the Lord of glory.
Let us adore him, for he is the Lord. Amen.

Prayers of Preparation

30   ONE WORLD WEEK

Lord, this is your world and we are your people.
This is your time and we have come to give you our worship.
You have called us by name and we have come to give you
    thanks and praise,
in Jesus' name. Amen.

31   A CALL TO PRAYER

Lord, you are here, waiting for me—
longing to hear me pray, wanting me to be here in your
    presence.

Lord, I am here, waiting for you—
longing to hear you speak, wanting to worship you with all
    that I am.

Lord, we are here, ready to go—
to live a life of prayer, to serve in your name, so that others
    might know you.

Lord, by your grace alone can I enter your presence.
Fill me with the power of the Holy Spirit,
that I may pray without ceasing
and bring glory to the name of my Saviour. Amen.

32 YOU HAVE CALLED US HERE

Lord, we believe that you have called us here
to bring the pain of our neighbour to the throne of grace,
to offer the brokenness of your world
that healing may come on the earth
and to celebrate all that is good in life,
for all good things come from the living God.
Now send us out as witnesses to the love of the Father,
to the grace of the Son
and to the renewing power of the Holy Spirit. Amen.

33 OUR GOD IS WORTHY

Lord, from the busyness of our lives
we have come to be still, in the hush of your quietness.
From the noise of our questions we have come to hear your
      voice.
From the anguish of our hearts we have come to receive your
      peace.
From the emptiness of our struggles we have come to be
      filled.
Lord, we have come.
Meet with us, that we may not have come in vain. Amen.

34 LIFE

Lord, we come as your people; we come as your friends.
We come together.
We come as we are.
We come to be made one.
We come to worship, that we might go in your name. Amen.

35 PRISONERS

Lord, we come with the things that bound us hard and fast,
the things that limit our hope, our joy, our peace and our
      service.
We come to worship you,
because in Christ you came to set us free. Amen.

36   MISSION

Lord, though you are everywhere, we have come here to
    praise you.
Though your love is for all people, we have come to enjoy
    your presence.
Though your truth is for everyone, we have come to receive
    your word for us.
Though your power holds the universe, your love fills our
    lives.
Lord, we ask you to fill us with your Holy Spirit,
that our worship may be worthy of you. Amen.

37   ASH WEDNESDAY

Lord, we have come to confess your strength and our
    weakness,
your light and our darkness,
your infinite fullness and our finite emptiness,
your holiness and our sinfulness.
Lord, we confess your truth and your glory,
your majesty and your mercy, your patience and your love.
We confess our need of your healing, your life-transforming
    grace.
We freely confess that you are Lord of all. Amen.

38   MAUNDY THURSDAY

Lord, we have come because you have called us.
We have come because you have made everything ready for
    us.
We have come because, by your grace, you will make us
    whole.
We have come because you are worthy.
We have come because you first came to us. Amen.

39   GOOD FRIDAY

Father, in the stillness we wait at the foot of the cross,
and in awed expectation we watch to see what you will do.

The Son of God dies, and the heart of the Father is broken.
We come because you know how we feel and what we must
  face.
We come because, in Christ,
you opened the door to your presence and invited us home.
We have come in the name of the Saviour of the world.
We have come to give you heartfelt thanks and praise. Amen.

40   HARVEST THANKSGIVING

Lord, we have come with praise and thanksgiving,
with joy and celebration, with worship and acclamation.
We come because you are the Lord of the harvest
and you are worthy of our glory and adoration.
We come because you have filled us with thankfulness.
We come in the power of the Spirit
to honour your name and give thanks for your glory. Amen.

41   REMEMBRANCE SUNDAY

Lord, we have come to remember you and your great love.
We have come to remember your mercy and your truth.
We have come to remember your grace and your power.
We have come to remember to give you thanks and praise.
We have come to remember.

42   SOCIAL CONCERN

Lord, your presence humbles us, your grace lifts us,
your mercy challenges us, your truth inspires us,
your Spirit enables us and your love amazes us.
Lord, your almighty power and sovereign presence
demand that we offer ourselves as a living sacrifice of praise
  and thanksgiving
and we have come with thankful hearts to worship you.
  Amen.

43 THE WORLD CHURCH

Lord of all the world, we have come to worship you.
Lord of all creation, we have come to give you thanks and
    praise.
Lord of life, we have come to offer you all that life means
    to us,
knowing we shall receive from you
hope, joy, peace and grace in abundance. Amen.

44 CHRISTMAS EVE

'And the Word became flesh and dwelt among us, full of
    grace and truth.'
Lord, we come to prepare for your coming.
We come to stand amazed at the manner of your coming.
We come to acknowledge your supreme act of grace
and the unfathomable riches of your truth.
We come to receive your mercy, your healing, your love,
and to be made whole.
We come, but we are utterly overwhelmed that you came at
    all! Amen.

45 THE STARKNESS OF LIFE

Lord, we had no wish to withdraw, to leave the world
    outside,
but its demands and expectations drown your still, small
    voice
We have come to meet you in the vibrancy of worship,
that we may be better equipped to hear you
here and in the world that Christ died to save. Amen.

46 OLD AGE

Lord, we come with our memories, and we come with our
    experience,
we come a little slower than we used to,
but we come knowing you will be here, ready to receive our
    praise and thanks.

We come, sometimes sad and often a little weary.
We come, aware that many we have known will no longer be
    here.
We come because, in this busy, noisy world,
you are here and you call us to meet with you.
We come in the name of Jesus. Amen.

Prayers of Praise

47   ONE WORLD WEEK—THE ENVIRONMENT

Lord, all creation bears its witness to your glory;
every corner of the world announces your praise;
every tree and every flower, every hill and every valley,
every lake and river, every sea and ocean,
joins in the chorus of praise to our Creator God.
Lord, Creator and Sustainer of all we see and hear,
we too offer you our worship and praise.
We praise you for One World Week
and for the reminder it provides
not only of your glory
but of the challenge of your command to love our
    neighbour.
We praise you not only for giving us eyes to see and ears to
    hear,
but also for the ability to enjoy your world
and for the gift of being thrilled and uplifted
by the beauty of all that you have made.
We praise you, Lord, and we honour your name.
We praise you for Jesus Christ, who gave himself as a
    sacrifice
so that the whole world might be made whole.
We sing our hymns to your praise and glory,
our one, great, powerful and almighty God.
We bring our praises in the name of Christ who is Lord of all
    the world. Amen.

Lord, we praise you for those who, like William Wilberforce,
have made people listen
and whom you have used to change people's minds.

We praise you for those who have taken important decisions
that have enabled other people to be set free;
to live their lives in the way that you intended;
to be treated as human beings;
to walk in hope; to know your peace;
to be free from all that robs them of their humanity.

We praise you for those who, today, work alongside
the lost, the broken, the homeless and the despairing.

We praise you too for those who give of their time,
their energy, their commitment and their love
as they seek to set free all who are trapped in a web of
      poverty;
of drug or alcohol addiction; of depression;
or of mindless aggression from those they have sought to
      love.

We praise you, Lord, who through your life, death and
      resurrection
are, even now, offering a hope, a joy and a freedom
that can be paid for in no other way.

Come, Lord Jesus, and set all people free! Amen.

49   THE LORD IS GOOD—A LITANY

The Lord is good, and the Lord is holy: let us praise his
      name.
Let us praise his name.

The Lord is great, and the Lord is sovereign: let us praise his
      name.
Let us praise his name.

The Lord is Saviour, and the Lord is loving: let us praise his name.
Let us praise his name.

The Lord has died, and the Lord has risen: let us praise his name.
Let us praise his name.

The Lord is here, and the Lord is with us: let us praise his name.
Let us praise his name.

The Lord who came is the Lord who's coming: let us praise his name.
Let us praise his name.

The Lord has called us, and the Lord will send us: let us praise his name.
Let us praise his name.

The Lord is good, and the Lord is holy: let us praise his name.
Let us praise his name. Amen.

50   SO MANY WORDS

Lord, we use so many words,
but our voices cannot offer you the praise that you desire.
We sing so many songs,
but our worship can never scale the heights of heaven.
We offer so many prayers,
but too often our hearts are far from you
and our lives betray what is heard from our lips.

Lord, by your Holy Spirit alone can we sing your praises,
and only through his power can we declare your glory.

Lord, touch our lips and our lives,
transform our prayers and our songs,
and we will give you the glory that you deserve. Amen.

Lord, we think we are so very important.
Though we would deny it, we long to be considered
    irreplaceable;
if we didn't give or serve or support
we imagine the whole edifice of your church
would simply come tumbling down or crumble away.

Lord, we think we are so very important.
Yet in reality we are just your little people.

We say little prayers, and forget that we are conversing
with the King of creation and the Lord of the universe.

We make our meagre assessments
of what you are calling us to do and to be,
and we totally neglect the challenge
that echoes from the voice of your Spirit and the truth of
    your Word.

We consider ourselves to be good, holy, more worthy than
    others,
so long as we choose a role model that is smaller than us.
For when we stand next to Christ, and think of his glory;
when we kneel at the foot of his cross
and measure ourselves against his glory and love;
then, and only then, are we, your little people, truly cut
    down to size.

Yet, Lord, it is also when—and only when—we acknowledge
    our smallness
that we can be lifted up by arms that long to hold us and to
    heal us;
arms that can raise even us to the heights of your glory
and bring praise to your name. Amen.

52   LORD, OPEN OUR EYES

Lord, we fill our days with so many words,
but few of them matter as much as when we turn to you
and simply say, 'Thank you.'

We clutter our minds with an endless supply of meaningless
        thoughts,
but none of them has more value
than when we consider your glory, your worth and your love.

We allow ourselves to become obsessed with the details of
        our existence,
with the small page of each day,
but we completely overlook the vast canvas of your eternity.

We permit our minds to become focused on what we think
        we have achieved,
or exhaust ourselves with regret over failures that haunt us
        each day;
but we are utterly blind to nail-printed hands that now, even
        as we pray,
are reaching out in love, mercy and grace.

Lord, open our eyes to your presence and our ears to your
        voice;
speak into our minds and break into our thoughts;
take hold of our hands and fill our hearts with your grace.
Only then can we give you the praise that your love deserves.
        Amen.

53   WE HAVE A SONG

Father, we have a song to sing
of your creative power that brought all things to be.

We have a song to sing
of your sustaining grace that has touched us and held us,
that has fed us and guided us each step of the way.

We have a song to sing of a Saviour who lived our life,
walked our earth and died in our place.

We have a song to sing
of a Lord who was raised on Easter's third day
and is alive and here now in the midst of our singing.

We have a song to sing
of the Holy Spirit who empowers us for worship
and enables us all to sing our song of praise. Amen.

54   WE PRAISE YOU IN CHRIST

Lord, we praise you that in Christ
all our 'ends' become his 'new beginnings'
and all our weaknesses are clothed in his strength.

Lord, we praise you that in Christ
our times of emptiness are filled with hope
and our brokenness has found the only source of peace and
    wholeness.

Lord, we praise you that in Christ
your damaged world can be restored
and its prisoners of drugs, abuse and hate
can find that freedom of which they dreamed.

Lord, we praise you that in Christ
the joy of heaven bursts into our days and hours
and by your Holy Spirit the things of earth find their centre
    and purpose in him.

Lord, we praise you that in Christ
our lives receive a purpose vast and wide.
Each time we spread the table of bread and wine
we meet with him who gave himself for all. Amen.

55   PETER AND CORNELIUS

Lord, we praise you for the way you burst the bubble of our
    prejudices and pride;

you drain the stagnant pools of our encrusted ideas
and bring crashing down our edifices of power,
our patterns of worship and serving
which through the long years we have so carefully built.

We praise you for being greater than the sum of our
    thoughts;
for giving us hopes and dreams that leave us breathless and
    amazed,
and for giving us Jesus, through whom we are offered peace
    and love
and a sense of belonging we can never deserve.

We praise you for Christ
whose arms on the cross reach out to greet us and hold us,
as you draw us together and as we focus on him.

We praise you, our Father, that Jesus is Lord;
he is the way and the life both now and for all.
He is the source of all truth
and freely offers to each of us the joy of new birth.

We praise you now; we will praise you for ever;
we praise you on earth; and we will praise you in heaven.
    Amen.

56   ALL THINGS IN CHRIST

All things in Christ seem darker now.
The reflection from his glorious light
reveals the emptiness of much we grasp
and shows the way that we should walk.

All things in Christ are brighter now.
His mighty love illumines all;
his presence transforms the darkest hour
as he walks with us, our Saviour and Lord.

All things in Christ are hopeful now.
His grace sets free what once was bound.

With joy unleashed we face each day.
In him the price of peace is paid.

All things in Christ are eternal now.
Our God made man has called us home;
the door with which we locked him out
in Christ alone is opened wide.

All things in Christ are challenged now.
His living presence heals our blindness;
at last we see his broken world
to which he sends us to prove his love. Amen.

57   SOVEREIGN LORD

Sovereign Lord, we live in a world that each day tears itself
    apart;
it breaks what was meant to be whole;
accepts as normal that which was never part of your plan;
and hides its face in the presence of its Maker.

Sovereign Lord, each of us floods our days with nothing of
    real worth
and allows those things that matter to trickle through our
    sieve-like lives.

No time to worship; no time to pray;
No time for you, Lord—no time today!

Sovereign Lord, all things in Christ are changed, eternally
    made new.
In Christ we are given a whole new experience
of belonging to each other, as we belong to him.

Sovereign Lord, in Christ is the end and the beginning of all
    things. Amen.

58   CALLED TO BE FAITHFUL

Lord, we praise you that you have called us to be your
    faithful people;

to remember the story of our faith; to hold fast to all that is
   true;
to keep you at the centre of all things;
to build each other up in hope and in love;
to sing your praises and to make time for prayer;
to stand firm, no matter the cost.

Lord, we praise you that you have *not* called us to be your
   faithful people
within the safety of the closed doors of the church,
or inside locked minds or barricaded hearts.

Each day you require us, your people,
to live out our faith beyond the doors of protection.
You have appointed each of us to speak of Christ
and to do so in words and ways that everyone, anywhere, can
   understand.

We praise you that you are calling us now to be
always listening, always pilgrims, always relying on your
   Spirit
to enable us to be faithful to Christ.

By your grace and for your glory
may we live for him in our fast-changing world. Amen.

59   HOW CAN I NOT PRAISE YOU?

How can I not praise you, Lord of my life,
for in Christ you have given me all things?
In Christ you have given me hope,
In Christ you have given me faith.
In Christ you have given me love.
In Christ you have given me peace.
In Christ you have given me sisters and brothers.
In Christ you have given me a new purpose.
In Christ you have given me forgiveness.
In Christ you have given me the Holy Spirit.
In Christ you have given me new birth.

In Christ you have given me yourself.
In Christ you have given me all things.
How can I not praise you, Lord of my life? Amen.

60   WHAT YOU HAVE GIVEN

Lord, we praise you for the gifts with which you flood our
    lives;
for the gift of laughter that lightens the darkest day;
for the tears we can shed as we share the pain of others;
for the smile that offers the stranger a welcome;
for the hand of peace that brings hope to our troubled
    world;
for the kiss of love that breathes courage into broken hearts;
for the word of forgiveness that unlocks the way to
    reconciliation;
for the arms that offer security and peace to those who are
    afraid;
for the word of faith that points an uncertain world to Christ;
and for the gift of the Holy Spirit
who enables us to demonstrate
the grace of the Lord Jesus Christ and the love of God
so that eventually the whole of creation
might join in the song of praise to your name. Amen.

61   GIFT-WRAPPED PRAISES

Lord, sublime, outreaching;
sovereign, uplifting;
with joy overwhelming, peace surrounding;
in faithfulness holding, gentleness touching;
with courage challenging, presence guarding.

Moment by moment, hour by hour, day by day
you meet our needs;
you lift us when we fall;
you caress us by your grace;
you love us now, you will love us tomorrow, and every
    tomorrow.

Lord, our praises are gift-wrapped in the love of your Son,
Jesus, our Saviour and Lord. Amen.

62   POWER

Lord, we praise you because you are the God of power.
By your powerful word the whole universe came to be.
Under your watchful eye solar systems took flight
and planets were allotted their orbits.
By your will the earth became our home,
and seas and oceans, hills and mountains, found their place.
According to your grand design
every fish and every bird; every tree and every plant;
every creature that lives under the earth or moves upon it
was given the gift of life.

Lord, we praise you because you are the God of power.
And by that power you fashioned us in your own image.
You made us so that we might know you
and walk with joy in your presence.
We praise you that your love is the source of your power
and you have created all things to speak of your
          unconditional grace.
We praise you that we were conceived to be a reflection
of the love that dwells for ever in the heart of the Father.
Lord, we lift up not only our voices,
but the whole of our lives, to sing your glory. Amen.

63   OUR WORDS

Lord, we fill our days with so many words,
but few of them matter as much as when we say thank you.
We clutter our minds with so many thoughts
but none of them has more value than when we consider
          your glory
and reflect upon your love.
We allow ourselves to become obsessed with the details of
          our existence
and overlook the vast canvas of your eternity.

We permit our minds to focus on what we think we have
    achieved
or on where we know we have failed,
and we are utterly blind to the nail-printed hands
that even now, as we pray,
are reaching out in love, mercy and grace.

Lord, open our eyes and our ears;
speak into our minds; break into our thoughts;
take hold of our hearts;
that we may give you the praise that you deserve. Amen.

64   STUPENDOUS GOD

God, stupendous God; holy, overwhelming God.
You are from eternity to eternity.
You are the source of all life.
You have no beginning and no end.
There never was a moment when you were not God
and there will never be a moment when you cease to be Lord
    of all.

God, stupendous God; above and beyond our every thought;
greater, more majestic than our highest longing;
deeper than our most enthralling experience.

God, stupendous God; not far off, not remote, not out of
    sight.
Every facet of your creation illustrates your real presence
and every day is ripe with the fruits of your loving will.

God, stupendous God; once, long ago, you entered our
    world;
we touched that which is holy and we held that which is our
    Lord.
We saw in him your glory and through him we received your
    grace.

God, stupendous God; not far off, not remote, not out of
    sight.

For a brief moment you entered our world,
compressed into the life of a human being.
In Jesus we saw our God: we give you our thanks and praise.

God, stupendous God; daily we enter your presence
in places we think of as special, as holy or blessed by you,
and also in those we think of as part of every day,
untouched by your being there.
We have yet to learn that there is no godforsaken place,
nowhere from which you can be excluded;
for everywhere can become holy by your grace and through
    your presence.

God, stupendous God; you are full of surprises, always
    coming to amaze us.
Now comes your bombshell
that has the power to shake us to the very core of our being.

God, our stupendous God, you have come
to live in our hearts, to expand our minds,
to heal our wounds, to transform our expectations,
to lift us, to change us, to make all things new.
Yet most of all we thank you that you have come
—our stupendous God—and you will never leave us. Amen.

65   PRAISE AND HONOUR

Lord, we praise you for your power which holds us and holds
    everything;
for your grace which touches and renews us;
for your love that gives us life and makes us whole;
for your sovereign will that maps out our journey
and then gives us the freedom to choose.

Lord, we honour you for your holiness which measures our
    lives
and for your mercy that lifts us up and whispers, 'You can
    begin again.'
Lord, we bow before you in love and adoration.

There is no God like you, no God besides you.
You are our God and we will have no other.
You are our God and we will worship you
with all we have and with all we are, now and for ever.
Amen.

66 FREEDOM

Lord, what a gift you have given; what a treasure we hold.
What a fragile inheritance you have entrusted to our care.
What a blessing is ours, what a responsibility we have,
for freedom is your gift and must be handled with care.

Lord, we praise you for the freedom we have to think and to choose;
for the freedom to learn and to share what we have;
for the freedom to discover just why we are here
and to allow you to use us in ways we never dreamt possible.

Lord, the freedom you give is what makes us what we are,
and the freedom you give makes us responsible for the choices we make.
We praise you for the freedom to worship and to confess you as Lord;
for the freedom to serve and, in all we do,
to be able to demonstrate the love of our God;
for the freedom to speak of our Saviour and Lord,
that others might know the freedom that's ours.

Lord, we praise you for our freedom in Christ;
for his death on the cross where our freedom was paid for
and for his glorious resurrection that brought your gift to our door;
for the renewal of our freedom that the Spirit brings daily
and for the freedom of heaven that is already ours.

Lord, we bless you for the freedom that allows us to confess that Jesus is Lord.
All glory to his name. Amen.

67   DELIVERANCE

Lord, we praise you for knowing who and what we are.
You understand that we are imprisoned in our doubts and fears
and that too often we are content to live in the comfort
    zones of life.

We praise you, our Deliverer—you set us free
from the things that would come between us,
and you remove the barriers of self-centredness and self-
    sufficiency
that would keep us apart.

We praise you for Christ
who on the cross reaches out his arms to embrace all who
    turn to him
and brings a new sense of liberation and renewal
through the power of the Holy Spirit.

We praise you for the length of Christ's love,
the depth of your grace
and the limitless heights to which the power of the Holy
    Spirit will lift us.

Lord, we praise you for the offer of your mercy
and your call to obedience.
Overwhelm our hearts and lives with the experience of your
    deliverance,
that we may live in your freedom and declare your grace
in all we say and do and are.
In the name of Christ, the Liberator of all. Amen.

68   HOPE

God of all grace, you alone are our hope.
Without you and your gracious, understanding love
we would feel lost, isolated and without hope in this dark,
    dark world.

God of all mercy, you alone are our hope.
Day by day our words, deeds and thoughts

add to the emptiness of your world.
Each day our self-centredness and self-interest
build the barrier between us ever higher.

Yet we praise you that it is your gracious love that restores
    our hope
and that through Christ you make it possible for us to begin
    again.

God of love, we fall before you in praise and adoration.
It is your unconditional love that tears down
the barricade that our selfishness has fashioned.
It is your grace that transforms our lives.
It is your power that renews our worship.
It is your love that gives us hope.

God of hope, we thank you that, in Jesus, we hear your word
    of grace.
That, in him, you have promised to hold our hand and to
    show us the way.
It is through the Holy Spirit that your hope is planted in our
    hearts and lives.
Now, by your grace, make us channels of your hope
that the whole world may sing of your glory. Amen.

69   PEACE

Lord, we worship you, the God of peace.
Again and again through the servants of your grace
you touch our troubled world.
When we least expect it
you show us the way to renewal, hope and peace.

Lord, we praise you, the God of peace.
Through your word you promised peace
that would outstrip the totality of our understanding.
In Christ you have made possible a new relationship with you
which is always the ultimate source of renewal, hope and
    peace.

Lord, we give you glory because you are the God of peace.
Through the gift of your Holy Spirit you are offering
a peace we cannot win;
a peace we cannot achieve;
a peace we can never deserve;
a peace that is yours alone to give.

Lord, we praise you, the God of peace.
The peace that you give comes with the touch of your grace.
We are cleansed at the foot of the cross,
your peace poured out freely through the power of the Spirit.

Lord, we praise you now and we will praise you for ever,
and we will do so in the name of the Prince of peace, Christ
the Lord. Amen.

70   THE DAY THAT IS GIVEN

Lord, we praise you for each new day.
Whatever it brings—sun, wind or rain—
it comes gift-wrapped from you.
From our first day, when our infant cry announced our
arrival,
to our last, when our sigh will be a silent farewell—
each day we receive we will never deserve.
They are grace-filled tokens from our Father in heaven
and each comes with the promise of your presence and
power.
Lord, today is your gift, whatever it brings.
Today is your present, given to share.
This day may have more than its share of pain or of pleasure,
of delight or despair,
but we can still praise you,
for you are the Lord of each day, which you will hold in your
care.
Hold us now and hold us for ever;
hold us today, and hold us when earth's days are no more.
Then hold us still, in Christ. Amen.

71 RICHES OF PRAISE

Lord, we praise you for the rich things
with which you fill our days and flood our lives;
for the love and the care of those we trust;
for the riches of friendships that have stood the test
of time and tribulation;
for the riches of laughter that colour each day;
and for the tears of joy that speak
of the riches of hope and peace beyond our deserving;
for the riches we have received as we meet at your table;
for the freedom and joy that is ours as we receive him as
    Saviour
and the exhilaration of confessing him Lord;
for the Spirit's empowering for worship and service
and the way he enriches all we do in your name.

Lord, we come as paupers, with nothing to give you
and nothing we deserve to receive.
We praise you that you long to enrich our lives,
our relationship with you and with each other,
and you will do it in ways we simply can't imagine.
Come, Lord, enrich us by your Spirit
that our lives, our worship and our service
may enrich your glorious name. For Christ's sake. Amen.

72 IMAGES OF PRAISE

Lord, you said, 'No graven images,'
for there is nothing we can use to represent your glory,
no earthly object that can fully reflect
your majesty, your authority and your grace.

Lord, you said, 'No graven images,'
for you are far beyond the reach of our deepest thoughts.
Nothing we can make or design, or picture in our minds,
will ever be worthy of you.

Lord, you said, 'No graven images,'
for you will always outstrip our comprehension
and all our human resources cannot even scratch the surface
    of your being.

Lord, you said, 'No graven images,'
but you have permitted us to use word pictures
of Father, Son and Holy Spirit;
to speak of you and to sing your praise.
You have allowed us to glimpse you in your creation;
to see you in the face of the poor;
to acknowledge your mercy in the empty cross;
to confess your power in the empty tomb;
to find your presence in bread and wine.

Lord, you said, 'No graven images,'
for you alone are our God and there is no other.
You are our Saviour and we have no other.
You are our Lord and there can be no other.
We praise you, our living, sovereign Lord. Amen.

73   NO LONGER PRISONERS

Lord, how great is your power,
how mind-blowing your sovereignty.
No matter how hard we try
we can never plumb the depths of your glory,
we can never hope to fully comprehend your creative authority.
We praise you that
though we are trapped by the limits of our finite lives
your infinite wisdom reaches from one end of time to the other.
We praise you that
though we are imprisoned by time and place
your majesty, peace and love can be experienced by everyone,
    everywhere.
Lord, you are too wonderful to know
and yet too loving to ignore.
We praise you that

in Jesus Christ you are still setting us free from fear and
    doubt.
By your Holy Spirit
open our eyes to your glory,
our ears to your word and our hearts to your love.
In Christ's name we offer our prayer and praise. Amen.

74   FAITHFULNESS

Lord, you are the faithful one,
and it is next to you and your gracious, generous love
that we must measure all that we count faithful and true.

Lord, you are the faithful one,
and we know that we can trust you in all things and for ever.
Your utter reliability is the touchstone
by which we must measure signs of our own trustworthiness.

Lord, you are the faithful one,
and we have discovered that your love reaches out and
    reaches down ·
to meet us where we are and lift us to the heights of your
    grace;
your love is the acid test
of all that we call compassion, understanding and mercy.

Lord, you are the faithful one,
your holiness cannot turn a blind eye to our sin and
    disobedience;
but we know too that your love and forgiveness will always
    be the final word—
now, and when we meet you face to face.

Lord, you are the faithful one,
and every time we look at the cross
it's like looking into the face of God himself.
We praise you for Christ
and for his faithfulness to you and your will;
that in and through him

we can receive the offer of your grace
and the evidence of your faithfulness
that will hold us now, will hold us in the storm
and will hold us to the threshold of eternity—and beyond.

Lord, you are the faithful one, and we praise your name.
  Amen.

75   KINDNESS

Lord, we praise you for your kindness.
No matter who we are, or what we have done, or failed to do,
your kindness, love and understanding has lifted us up,
drawn us back to yourself
and given us the opportunity to start all over again.

Lord, we praise you for your kindness.
You gave us life, and you shared our journey every step of the
    way.
Never once have you left us alone.
Never for a moment have we stepped outside the orbit of
    your grace.

Lord, we praise you for your kindness.
When our lives were in turmoil
and we didn't know which way to turn—you were there.
When our hearts were breaking
and pain and sadness all but overwhelmed us—you were
    there.
When all was dark and we were afraid
and no one seemed to understand—you were there.
When our hearts were filled with joy, and we longed
to break out into songs of praise and celebration—you were
    there.
You are always there.

Lord, we praise you for your kindness
which was so powerfully, so wonderfully made known to us
    through Jesus.

He is the very embodiment of that kindness
which is at the centre of the universe
because it flows from the heart of our God.
Our voice of praise and our words of thanksgiving
can never do justice to who and what you are.
But in the name of Christ, our Lord, we give you thanks
and we praise your name. Amen.

76   GOD'S CALLING

Lord, your name is high and holy
and your ways are endlessly loving.
You hold us and everything in the hollow of your hand
and you are at the heart of all that was, all that is and all that
     will be.

Lord, you are great and glorious
and your majesty, power and authority
are beyond anything that our words can hope to express.
Your presence fills everything, everywhere,
and we know that you are here in the midst of your people
to receive our worship.

Lord, you are the divine communicator
and you have so designed us that we can receive your word.
Down the centuries you have spoken
through those who knew you
and even those to whom you were a stranger.

Father, Jesus Christ is your ultimate word
to all who will hear and also to those who refuse to listen.
You have called us and commissioned us to make that word
     known.

Lord, we praise you that you have seen fit to call us into your
     service.
We stand amazed in your presence that you have chosen
     us
poor vessels for your glory.

You are sending us to declare your word of grace
so that injustice is challenged and broken lives are made
    whole.

We offer you our thanks and praise in the name of Christ the
    Lord. Amen.

77   PENTECOST

Lord of the gentle breeze that ripples the surface of the river
and causes the trees to move calmly as if by the touch of
    some unseen hand:
may the gentle breeze of your Spirit
begin to ruffle our lives and start the shaking
that will reach the foundations of our hopes and dreams.

Lord of the wind that whips up the waves
and causes trees to move in unexpected ways
as they struggle to remain standing as they have for many
    years:
may the wind of the Spirit who came at Pentecost
fill our lives, our service and our worship
with a joy and a freshness we have never known before.

Lord of the powerful wind that moves everything in its path,
whose purposes and will seem utterly irresistible;
This is the wind that breaks off dead branches and uproots
    trees with no root;
that challenges everything in its path
and demonstrates the weakness, the shallowness and the
    temporary nature
of all we thought so permanent;
may the mighty rushing wind of your Holy Spirit
make every moment in your presence a Pentecost
and every confrontation with his coming
a time of re-evaluation of those things we now consider to
    be of great worth;
and every experience of his blessing
a challenge to allow him to control all things, for ever.

Come Holy Spirit,
refresh, renew and remould who we are and what we shall
be. Amen.

78   BREAD

*Arrange for a loaf of bread to be displayed or passed around the
congregation during the prayer.*

Lord, we thank you for our bread, the basic food of life.
It is so ordinary, so normal, and yet so important.

We take our bread for granted
because our eyes are focused on more exciting things.

We thank you that it reminds us that Jesus provides
not what we think we want, or what we desire,
but what he knows we really need.

This bread speaks to us of that which is wholeness
and is full of that which satisfies our hunger.
Christ is himself our bread of life.
He alone brings that sense of fulfilment and satisfaction
for which we hunger and thirst.

Thank you that our bread is a picture of your constant provision
of those things so necessary for life—
our food and drink; our homes and our family;
our work and our leisure; our times of activity and our times
of resting.

Our bread is like a promise of the hope and joy, the love and
the laughter
with which Christ, the Bread of Life, longs to fill our lives.

Lord, as our daily bread enables us to grow,
so may Christ give us the strength
to worship, love and serve you all our days.

Lord, we thank you for this, our bread for life,
but we thank you more for Christ, the Bread of life. Amen.

Father, you are the source of all goodness
and the fountain of all that is worthy.
From you comes light and hope, joy and forgiveness;
and for you we bring our songs of joy and thanksgiving.
We praise you that your goodness is always at the heart of
    your creation
and that all we see and experience, all that is wholesome and
    good,
comes from the heart of your glory
and finds its origin at the centre of your love.

Father, it is your goodness that gave us life
and provides for our needs each day;
it is your essential integrity
that calls us and makes us your own.
It is your honest, demanding and unattainable love
that enriches each day and every corner of life.

Father, we praise you and thank you for the goodness we
    find in your Son.
May our prayers bring him honour and glory
and our lives become a reflection of his love.
In the name of Jesus,
who is himself the very centre of your grace. Amen.

80   THE LORD, WHO IS BEYOND US

Wonderful God, we praise you that you are God beyond our
    imagining.
When we confess that you have no beginning and no end
we do not understand what our words really mean,
but we believe that who and what you are is worthy of all
    our praise.
We praise you because you are our God
and you are almighty, all-knowing and all-loving.
Sovereign Lord, there are no words too high, no thoughts
    too extravagant,

no idea of you too holy to celebrate your glory!
You move our hearts, you fill our minds,
you energise our whole being with your presence.
We bring our praise—not because we must,
not because we are able, not even because we want to—
but because you are worthy!
We bring our praise in the name of Christ, who has shown
   us your glory. Amen.

81   CHRISTIAN AID

Father, we believe that you care for all your creation;
that there is nothing and there is no one
who is beyond your loving compassion.

We believe that you made the world to be good
that you have filled it with enough for everyone—just so
   long as we share.

We believe that you gave us minds to think, choices to make,
opportunities to respond to, others to care for, and gifts to
   give.

We believe that you made us for each other,
to reflect your glory, to demonstrate your gracious loving
   concern
and to love our neighbour as ourselves.

We believe that you are a great and a wonderful God,
that your compassion reaches from one end of eternity to the
   other,
that you have made us responsible for each other
and that one day you will ask why we did not care enough.

We believe that our words of thanks and praise,
our hymns of adoration and our songs of joy, have a hollow
   sound
without a life of daring selflessness and a deep, genuine
   concern
for those sent away empty-handed from our rich tables.

We believe that our affirmations of faith,
our words of trust and our good intentions
are meaningless to you—and to others—
unless and until they are clothed with deeds of caring
and sacrificial giving that truly honour your name.

Father, we believe—help us to display your glory,
to make our praises live and our love for you real
as we love all to whom you send us—
no matter who, no matter where, no matter when.

In the name of Jesus,
who gave himself that we might find ourselves
and in finding then give ourselves to bring you glory. Amen.

82   HOLOCAUST DAY

Lord, we do not understand;
the numbers bounce off our minds—we simply cannot take
    them in.
There is a hollowness inside
as we try to imagine the unimaginable.
Lord, how did those made in your image stoop so low?
How was it possible that those you created to be thoughtful
    towards others,
could manufacture systems of torture and death?
How could they use their creative skills to design new ways
    of murder?
How did it happen that minds became so twisted
that people were killed simply because others decided they
    just didn't fit in?

Lord, we praise you for those who did care
and for those sought to help, at great cost to themselves;
for those who today still help us to listen ·
and for those who are reaching out with hands of
    compassion to offer hope for tomorrow.
Lord, we praise you that, no matter our name, our colour or
    race,

in Christ your love is still offered to all.
We praise you in the name of Jesus,
the Prince of Peace and the hope of the world. Amen.

83   LIFE

Lord, your praises have been sung since the dawn of
    creation,
your name has been exalted by countless generations of your
    people,
and will be until the end of time—and beyond!
We come with joy to add our voices to the chorus of praise
that echoes down the centuries and to every corner of the
    world.
Lord, we have brought our hearts and lives and voices,
and like the instruments of an orchestra
we long to join together in one great symphony of adoration.
We praise you because you are worthy.
We praise you because you are God.
We praise you because there is no one like you.
We praise you because you not only love us,
but you have shown your love in Jesus Christ.
Lord, empower us by your Holy Spirit to worship you as you
    deserve.
We ask this in the name of Christ, who is himself the Lord
    of life. Amen.

84   THE STARKNESS OF LIFE

Lord, we praise you for making us who and what we are—
    and what we are not.
You have given us the ability to do some things—but not
    everything.
You have enabled us to appreciate the beauty of your
    creation
and to recognise the barrenness of life without you.

We praise you that, in Christ,
you have demonstrated all that you intend human life to
        be—
and, through him, you have done everything necessary to
        heal our brokenness.
We praise you that his reflection of your glory throws into
        sharp relief
the reality of our emptiness without you.
Lord, we wonder at your love—its depth, length and
        breadth.
Lord, we wonder at your holiness—
it frightens us, challenges us, heals us.
We praise you, our persistent God, that by your grace
you touch our weaknesses,
gather up our foolishness
and walk with us in our lostness
always whispering, 'My love in Christ has found you.' Amen.

85   THE PEOPLE OF GOD

Lord, we simply cannot hold back the praise that wells up
        within us.
Every time we think of you and your goodness to us
we long to offer praise to your holy name.

Father, we are overwhelmed by the vastness of space and by
        the wonder of your world.
We are filled with joy by the beauty of your creation
and the thrill of discovering its intricate designs.

We rejoice in the gift of friendship
and we praise you for the faith of all your people.

Lord, we praise you
for the hope, joy and sense of purpose with which you fill
        our lives;
for the sense of adventure which meets us each day
and for the sheer pleasure of living in your exciting world.

We praise you
for being the kind of God who loves to give good gifts to all
    your children
and for making us so that we can enjoy good things.

We praise you for the journey of life
and for the journeys we are making each day;
for all those who share the path we are taking
and for the love, encouragement and care we receive along
    the way.

We praise you for Christ
who is the beginning and the end of our journey of faith,
and for the Holy Spirit
who enables us to walk close to you.
Father, receive our praise,
and enable us to give you glory.
We ask this in the name of Christ our Lord. Amen.

86   MAUNDY THURSDAY

Lord, we praise you that,
although your majesty and your sovereignty take our breath
    away,
your overpowering love holds us and keeps us safe;
and although you are the one with authority who inhabits
    eternity,
in Jesus Christ you came to us
and you spoke in words and ways that we could understand.
We praise you for Christ
and for the way he shared that Passover meal with his
    disciples;
though they did not understand what he was saying to them,
he still sought to prepare them for what was to happen.
We praise you that, though he was the King of creation,
the Lord of eternity and the Son of God,
he humbled himself and, as he washed the disciples' feet,
he took the role of a household slave.

We praise you for the example of servanthood
that he has implanted at the heart of the gospel
and infused into our walk with him.
We thank you that he has shown us how true greatness is
found
in putting service to you and the needs of others
before our own expectations and personal satisfaction.
We praise you that,
even at that critical moment in his life and ministry,
his thoughts were for others and his prayers were focused on
your glory.
We praise you for Jesus, and we bring our prayers in his
name. Amen.

87   GOOD FRIDAY

Father, we come together to meet with you on this Good
Friday
to hear again of the cross of Christ.
But because we have heard it so often before
we are in danger of failing to recognise
the enormity of the sacrifice that he made for us there.
We praise you for his love, his commitment to your will and
to our renewal.
Turn our eyes, our ears and our thoughts, we pray,
to remember those things that happened
outside the wall of Jerusalem all those years ago.
Enable us to comprehend
something of the extravagance of the love it represents.
You, Father, know us as we really are,
you know our fear, our doubt, our anger, our hatred and our
self-centredness.
We can hide all these things from each other,
but we can never hide them from you.
Now, as we come to the foot of the cross,
we see, perhaps for the very first time,

the awfulness of the result of our sin that put Christ on the
cross.
We try to convince ourselves that it is simply our human
weakness,
that we are no worse than other people,
but today we have learnt that Christ died for our sin to bring
us back to you.
Today we have discovered that the cross is the sign
not just of how much our sin and our selfish lives matter to
you
but of just how much you want us to be made whole
and to be at one with you.

Father, there are many who have died sacrificially for others,
but we remember that only Christ has died as the Saviour of
the world.
Teach us all again that he died to be our Saviour, our Lord
and our Master.
May this be the day when we not only mourn for Christ
and confess that it was our sin that put him on the cross
but also when we commit ourselves to taking up the cross
as true disciples of Christ, the Lord of the empty cross.
In Christ's name we ask it. Amen.

88   HARVEST THANKSGIVING

Lord, we praise you for the ongoing demonstration
of your creative power and your sustaining authority
over all that you have made;
for the love with which you made all things
and the care which you lavish upon us day by day.
We praise you, Lord of the harvest:
for all the good things with which you fill our lives
and the beauty with which you have filled the world;
for the abundance of your gracious gifts
and for the joy with which you flood our lives;
for the world in which you have placed us
and for the life you have given to us.

We praise you for your sovereignty over all your creation
and for your majesty as it is displayed in your world
and for your glory which is reflected in everything we see
    and hear.
Lord, we praise you and we worship you.
We give you thanks and we honour your name,
for you have not only surrounded us with so many beautiful
    things,
but also you have given us the ability to enjoy them all
and the responsibility of caring for all that you have made.
We praise you for Jesus Christ, your Son, our Lord,
and for the harvest of good things with which he has filled
    our days;
for the coming of the Holy Spirit
and for the harvest of love, joy, peace,
patience, kindness, goodness, faithfulness, gentleness and
    self-control
that are the signs of his presence within.
Lord, we have come to praise you for the harvest of life and
    love
and the joy of knowing Christ as Saviour and Lord.
May our lives continue to bring you a harvest of praise.
We ask this in Christ's name. Amen.

89   REMEMBRANCE SUNDAY

Father, on this Remembrance Sunday
we praise you for every memory we have of your goodness
    and love towards us;
for everything that reminds us of your creative power,
your sovereign will and your eternal glory.
We praise you for the cross of Jesus Christ, your Son, our
    Lord,
and for the way it reminds us of his sacrifice for the sin of
    the world—
its self-centredness, self-sufficiency and self-satisfaction.
We praise you for the Scriptures

which record the story of your dealings with your people
    down the centuries
and for the record of the life, death and resurrection of
    Christ.
We praise you that even in the midst of our broken and
    sinful world
the light of the love of Christ still shines
and is the source and centre of all our hope.
We praise you that
even when our lives and our lifestyles made us your enemies
you took the initiative and broke down the barrier
which our sinful lives had built between us.
We praise you that there is absolutely nothing that we can
    say or do
that will make you stop loving us
or stop you wanting us to know you and to have life in all its
    fullness.
We praise you for the power of the Holy Spirit
who softens hard hearts, opens closed minds and brings
peace, hope, joy and reconciliation where none seemed
    possible.
Help us, we pray, to go on remembering you and your loving
    presence
so that every day may be lived for your praise and glory.
Through Jesus Christ our Lord. Amen.

90   SOCIAL RESPONSIBILITY

Lord, you are a great and a holy God.
You are far, far greater than we could ever imagine
and you are far, far more holy than we have ever understood
and you are also far, far more loving than we could have
    dared to hope.
Mighty God, your authority is over the whole of creation
and your purposes are for the good of all that you have
    made.
In Jesus Christ you have enabled us to comprehend

something of who and what you are.
In him, we have begun to grasp that you are not against us.
In him, we are beginning to realise that you have always
    been
seeking the lost, healing the broken and lifting the fallen.
Now that we know Christ is your mirror image,
we understand that there is not, there never was and there
    never will be
any place or any person that can be called forsaken by you.
We praise you for your love that reaches to the depths of our
    need
and lifts us to the height you always meant us to be.
You are our loving Lord;
your compassion, your kindness and your grace
for everyone in every place
causes us to break out in songs of joyful praise!
May our praises so lift up the cross of Christ
that all people, everywhere, will be drawn to him
and confess him Lord of all.
We ask our prayer in the name of Christ. Amen.

91   THE MUSIC OF LIFE

Lord, we praise you for the music of life;
for the sounds of voices all around us;
for the symphony of conversation that comes from your
    worldwide family;
each thought and every smile adds to the concerto of
    thanksgiving
for the life you have given and the days we enjoy.

Lord, we praise you for the music of those who demonstrate
    your love to their neighbours
and those who share your gifts with the poor;
for those whose lives sing of your glory
and whose honesty, goodness and joy are a hymn of praise to
    your name.

Lord, we praise you for the music of life.
To know you and your love is to know the greatest music
    ever written
and the most precious song ever sung.

In the name of Christ, the composer of our praise
and the author of life that is real. Amen.

92   SEEING IS PRAISING

Flying high above the clouds, we look down in wonder
as we see the earth spread out below like some huge
    patchwork quilt.
The land and the sea seem as if they are etched on our slowly
    spinning world.

We praise you for the lofty mountains that seem to reach up
    to touch us
and the rivers that twist and turn their way
towards the seas and the oceans that stretch as far as the eye
    can see.

We praise you for the sky above us.
Its deep ebony backcloth hints at the endless universe
that lies beyond the reach of our eyes.

We praise you for the stars that shine from distances
too incredible to reach, too vast to imagine,
yet each and every one of them is held in the hollow of your
    hand.

No song is too high or too lowly, no word too majestic or
    too holy.
No worship too traditional, or too informal.
No service to great, or too small.

You gather all things up for your praise and glory.
Everything we see and hear declares the praise
of our all-seeing, all-knowing, all-loving God. Amen.

93   IMMANUEL

The song of your coming rings around the world.
The praises of the Christ child are on all our lips
and in every language of the human race.
The Prince of Peace has come and we shall give him glory.
Immanuel is here and we will make him welcome.

Lord, you have declared your love for the poor
and your grace to those who think they are rich.
In the Christ child you have reached down in order to lift us
    up.
You have come to bring an end to our separation from you.
You have come that we might begin again.
Maranatha! Come, Lord Jesus, come.
Immanuel: our God is with us
and we will give him the praises of our hearts and lives.
    Amen.

94   TRIUMPH

Lord, we praise you, the triumphant God.
Yours is the victory of life which we witness in the dawn of
    each new day.
Every sunrise declares your glory, and each sunset affirms
    your authority.
The song of every bird and the beauty of each flower
speak of your indestructible grace.
The majesty of the mountains and the song of each stream
    and river
declare your victory that never ends.
The gentle breeze and the irresistible tornado
articulate your power that cannot be halted.
The shower of rain and the torrential monsoon
that bring life to the dry earth and hope to the farmer
are signs of your triumph over death
and a reminder of your promise that,
    by your grace, we can begin again.

From frozen glaciers to sunburnt deserts,
from arctic ice storms to equatorial rainforests,
each is a token of the assurance that,
no matter who or what we are,
no matter where we go or what we face,
our triumphant God will lead the way.

Sovereign, Saviour, Lord, we worship you, our triumphant
    God
and ask that by your Holy Spirit we may, through your
    grace,
enter into the heaven of your love,
made possible by Christ's triumph over life and death.
    Amen.

95   LEISURE

Father, we praise you for the skills with which you have
    clothed our lives
and for the gifts that are ours to use for your glory.

Father, we praise you for the life you have given
and for the days, weeks, or years that are ours to enjoy;
for work and for leisure, and for time just to be.

Father, we praise you for opportunities for rest and renewal
when 'being' becomes as important as 'doing' often is;
for time to think and to pray;
for time to reflect and to share;
for the chance to do something different;
to relax and to pause;
for listening and learning, and for discovering—
a new pace of life; a different pattern for the day;
and an opportunity to start living instead of just existing.

Father, we praise you for the joy and the refreshment that the
    Spirit brings;
for the infilling of power his presence ensures
and for the gifts and the fruit that are signs of his touch.

Father, we praise you for times when we relax in your
    presence
and allow you to renew, refresh and remake us;
for times to be still and to know you are here;
for those moments of worship—of praise and thanksgiving
and all we experience as we enter into the flow of your grace
as we wait in Christ's name. Amen.

96   SENSES

Lord, you have placed us in such a wonderful world
and we are surrounded by so many exciting things.
You have granted us the privilege of living in a world
of beautiful sights and sounds
that enrich our lives and colour our days.

We praise you that you have so designed us
that we can enjoy the beautiful things we see and hear,
that our hearts are moved by the wealth of experiences
    received by our senses.

We praise you for the gift of taste and smell
that warn us of dangers and help us to enjoy what we eat;
for our sight that receives the rich variety of colour and shape
with which you have flooded our world;
for the touch of a friend that brings comfort and hope
and for the touch of the Spirit that brings wholeness within;
for the experience of sound that thrills, challenges and
    informs us
and changes our lives.

Father, we praise you for the inner experience of your love
    and your grace;
for the sense of assurance and Christ's promise of peace;
for the way that his presence makes sense of each day.

Father, we praise you for all that you are and for all that you
    give.
We offer our senses to you for your glory and praise. Amen.

Father, we praise you for your limitless power,
your sovereign will and your glory which envelops the whole
    world;
for your utter determination that everyone, everywhere,
should hear and know of your love for them;
for the insistent gentleness with which you reach out
to lift the fallen, heal the broken
and show mercy to those who long to begin again.

We praise you for your truth
which is greater than the mere sum of all human knowledge
and for your wisdom
which is foolish enough to send your Son to seek the lost
and bring freedom to those whose lives are imprisoned
in hatred, fear, despair and self-centredness.

We praise you for your love
which, in Jesus Christ, was prepared to be rejected and
    abandoned,
abused and taken for granted;
for your love which is freely offered to everyone, everywhere,
no matter who they are, or what they have done or failed to
    do.

We praise you for your Son, Jesus Christ,
and that through him you have declared the good news
that, as we place our trust in him, we can begin again.
We praise you that we can claim him as our own personal
    Saviour and Lord.
We praise you even more that we can offer him to everyone
    we meet
because he is Saviour of the world,
the Lord of life and the Conqueror of death.

Father, receive our prayer of praise, and so fill us with your
    Holy Spirit

that the praises we begin to offer here may, by the power of
    the Spirit,
reverberate through all the length of our days and echo
    through all eternity.
We ask this through Christ the Saviour of all. Amen.

98   CHRISTMAS
Lord, we have come to praise you
as we sing our carols and listen again to the story of the first
    Christmas
We have come to remember Mary and Joseph,
the angels and the shepherds, the wise men and the star
and the baby in the manger.
We thank you that the story of Christmas is not just a story.
We thank you that when we have opened all our presents,
    and eaten all the food,
when we have been to all our parties and played all our
    games,
you will still be offering your love to us.
When we feel lost, in Jesus you come to find us,
when we feel alone, in Jesus you have promised to be with
    us,
when we are sad, in Jesus you share our tears,
when we do not know which way to go, in Jesus you show us
    the way.
When we are hurting inside, and no one seems to care,
when we are excited, and there is no one to share it,
when we are full of questions, surrounded by problems,
and no one can give us an answer, in Jesus you show us the
    way.

Lord, we have come to praise and thank you for Jesus
because without him there would be no Christmas to
    celebrate at all.
Help us to keep him at the centre of our Christmas,
knowing that we are at the heart of his love. In Jesus' name.
    Amen.

99 · CHRISTMAS

Father, we thank you for Christmas
and for the coming of Jesus Christ into this world;
thank you that you have taught us to see and know you
through looking to him,
that he has shown us you are a God of love
and that your love is real, strong and very demanding.
We thank you that Jesus has shown us that we need never be
    afraid
of the past, the future or the present.
He has given us the assurance that because he is Immanuel,
he is always with us.
No matter who we are, no matter what we face,
he is Immanuel, always Immanuel;
God with us—always. Amen.

100   CHRIST— THE PROMISE OF HOPE

Lord, we thank you that, in the birth of your Son,
you have made the down payment on your promise
that you will always be with us.
In all the twists and turns of life—you are there, always
    there.
You have promised in Jesus to share the whole of life with us,
and we are thankful—so very thankful.
We thank you too, Father, for the help, care and strength we
    receive
from our families, friends and our fellow Christians.
When we are low, sad, or afraid
your love, through them, enables us to come through
with hope and joy, and our eyes even more firmly fixed on
    him.
Thank you for each time,
when in the midst of our troubles, problems, difficulties,
    anxieties or pain,
we have been made more aware of your love
and our need to trust you in everything;

for each and every opportunity you give us
to share the love and knowledge we have of you
with those who feel unloved, unwanted and unnecessary.
We ask that through your love
we may be enabled to make that love real for others, too.
Forgive our words of fear, our thoughts and feelings of
    uncertainty;
forgive our anger, bitterness, and our refusal to forgive.
Father, forgive us that so easily
we allow the things that crowd into our lives
to crowd you out.
Forgive us and make us new. This we ask in Jesus' name.
    Amen.

101   CHRISTMAS

Lord, we are so highly favoured.
Your love met us at our birth and has come with us
on the journey of our lives to this moment in time.
Your love goes before us, preparing the way.
Your love is with us from this day on.
So often the future appears dark, empty and uncertain.
We do not know what tomorrow will bring.
But we trust that through the darkest hour your light will
    shine,
that it will scatter the darkness and show the way through
    the most fearful day
until that time when we enter the light of the knowledge of
    your love.
Father, we praise you for all that you have done,
and all that you continue to do for us, in and through Jesus
    Christ.
We thank you that he came.
We thank you more that he still comes.
Though there is often still no room, he goes on coming.

Lord, as we hear again the story of that first Christmas,
may we not close our inward ears to what you are saying to
    us.
Tell us again of your power, your rejection of all that is evil
and of the hope that nothing, but nothing, that the world
    can say or do
can ever take away or spoil the wonder of your love and peace.

Lord, give us again that peace that passes all understanding,
the peace that only Christ, the Prince of Peace, can give.
As we sing our carols, help us, we pray, to come to know
the Saviour and Lord to whom they point.
And in knowing him, may we begin to know that life
which is like experiencing Christmas every day.
Father, we have prepared many things this Christmas;
help us, we pray, to allow you to prepare our hearts and lives
to worship him who is Lord of all. Through Christ our Lord.
    Amen.

102   CHRISTMAS EVE

Lord, we have come to prepare for your coming.
In the hurly-burly of our Christmas we have left no time to
    meet with you.
In our crowded lives we have no space left to wait for you.
In the noise of our emptiness and our endless chatter
we have no silence left in which you can speak.
In all our activities, all our comings and goings,
we have left you out of all of our preparations, and we are
    sorry.
Lord, there are times when we feel as if we are living such
    empty, futile lives.
We have existence, but we have heard that you came to give
    us life.
We have lost our way, but we were told that you came to
    show us the way back home.
We have lost hope, but we are discovering that you came to
    be our hope.

We often feel ashamed, ill-prepared, damaged and used.
We are less than the persons you meant us to be,
but we have found that the Christ child came that we might
    begin again.
Lord, there are moments
when you break through our hardened, apathetic defences
and share your love.
Lord, we have heard the story of your coming so many times
    before.
In years gone by, we have sung our carols to celebrate your
    coming.
We have memories of Christmases we once enjoyed.
Lord, come again.
Enable us by your Holy Spirit to make those preparations
that will ensure that the Christ child has room
and that, this year, we will truly celebrate his coming.
    Amen.

103   THE GIFT OF LIFE

Lord, we thank you for the priceless gift that we call life,
for the time to live it, space to explore it,
for dreams that lift us and for hopes that encourage us.
Thank you for those who journey with us and offer to hold
    our hand
and share the mystery, the wonder and the pain of each step.
Lord, we thank you for moments of great activity, and times
    of stillness,
for times of success as well as those that appear to be failure,
for opportunities to serve and to be served,
for the things we are able to do
and for times you call us to be content just to be.
Lord, we thank you for Jesus
and his total understanding of what it means not only to be
    human
but what it means to be me.

Thank you that each day contains another opportunity
to discover new ways in which he transforms what we are
into what he always meant us to be.
We bring our thanks in the name of him who taught us to
    give thanks. Amen.

104   MOTHERING SUNDAY

Lord, you are the source of all life.
It is from you that ultimately we receive our lives
through the power of your grace.
We rejoice that you have chosen to give us life
through the love and the lives of others.
On this mothering Sunday we thank you for our parents;
for those through whom you gave us life;
for those who have been like a parent to us;
for those we called mother, or father, aunt or uncle,
for that is what they became for us.

On this mothering Sunday we thank you for our family;
for those with whom we shared our home
and for those from whom we have received so much love,
    care and friendship;
for those who helped us to understand
just what you meant family life to be like.

Lord, on this mothering Sunday, we thank you for your
    church;
for the sense of belonging to your family
and the hope and the peace this gives us;
for the whole church of Christ
which has been like a mother to your people
as it was a channel of your grace and truth to the world.

Lord, on this mothering Sunday, we thank you for all who,
by their words and deeds, by their lives and lifestyle
and by their hope and their faith,
have made you and your love a living reality for us today.

We thank you and praise you for the hope and faith we have
   received
and ask that we too may be channels of your grace to those
   we meet.
This we ask in the name of our Brother, Jesus Christ the
   Lord. Amen.

105   OLD AGE

Lord, we have found that getting older means
we are losing the ability to see things clearly,
but we are receiving a greater clarity of understanding.
We have lost much of our hearing,
but we find we hear you speaking more clearly than ever.
We are finding it harder to walk as quickly and as easily as
   once we did,
but we have a greater assurance of you walking with us than
   ever before.
We find that we have more aches and pains than we used to,
but we have a peace and a joy in you that nothing can take
   away or spoil.
We praise you for the gifts you give us
that compensate for those things we have lost or are losing.
We praise you that Jesus made time and space for all people,
no matter who they were or where they were from,
no matter their position and no matter their age.
We praise you for his life, death and resurrection
and for the assurance that he has won for us the free gift of
   eternal life.
Lord, we praise you for the hope and comfort Jesus gives
to all who put their trust in him
and for the promise that he has gone to prepare a place for us
in the heaven of his love.
Lord, receive our praise and fill us with your Holy Spirit
that we might sing of the joy that comes from knowing you.
In the name of Christ our Lord. Amen.

106 WHERE IS OUR GOD?

Lord, the fool has said in his heart, 'There is no God.'
Our materialistic generation has no place for you.
Our self-sufficient society has no time for you.
In the face of the world's hunger, pain, sufferings and disasters,
even in our own hearts we begin to wonder, Where is our God?

But when our hearts are hurting we long for your presence;
when we are moved by our neighbour's pain we pray to you;
when our hearts are overflowing with gratitude, joy and hope
we lift up our voices in praise to the God who is always
      there;
the one who is almighty.

Lord, it is the innocent smile on the face of a child that
      warms our hearts;
the joy of friendships, old and new, that make life
      worthwhile;
the beauty of your creation overwhelms us;
the vastness of your universe takes our breath away and
      blows our minds.

But, Lord, it is the wonder of your grace
that heals our lives and restores our humanity;
it is your grace that is the ultimate inspiration
for the praise and thanksgiving we long to give you.

Yet, Lord, it is only through the power of your Holy Spirit
that we can offer you the worship that you deserve.
We bring our Spirit-filled praises in the name of Christ our
      Lord. Amen.

Prayers of Thanksgiving

107 ONE WORLD WEEK—THE ENVIRONMENT

Father, every time we praise you
and remember all that we have received at your hand
our hearts overflow with thankfulness.

There are times when it feels as if our hearts will burst
if we do not give voice to the spirit of thanksgiving that wells
    up within us.
There are moments when our joy and our worship
simply cannot be contained—it breaks out in heartfelt
    celebration
to you our Father and our God.
In this One World Week we give thanks for all agencies
that bring the needs of the world to our doorsteps
and focus our hearts and minds on the concerns of the poor.
We thank you for the challenge of One World Week
and for the way that it breaks down our cosy illusions
and chips away at the veneer with which we have protected
    ourselves
from the injustices and the agony of your world.
We thank you that there is not only one world
but also there is only one Lord of all creation,
to whom we give our thanks and praise. Amen.

108 THE WOMAN AT THE WELL

Lord, thank you for the woman that Jesus met at the well;
for the chat that they had and for the things that she learned.

We thank you for the way that Jesus both welcomed and
    challenged her
and pointed to God's presence and power at the heart of all
    things.

We thank you for the promises he made of the new life she
    could have;
the choice she was given to make a fresh start.

We thank you that Jesus made it clear
that he was sad about the way she was spoiling her life,
about the mess she was making and the way she must
    change;
that she needed to remember what was right and what was
    wrong.

We thank you that your love to us in Jesus is never watery or
    weak
but it comes from his cross and is always full strength.
He holds us and loves us and calls us by name,
always making it clear that now is the time to change.

Lord, by your Holy Spirit, make our lives new,
that we may make a fresh start. Amen.

109   A LITANY OF THANKFULNESS

For the gift of memory and the joy of remembering,
for the memories we share and pictures that fill our minds,
we give you thanks,
and we sing your praise.

For the stories to tell and for the laughter we enjoy,
for the experiences we still treasure and the people we have
    known,
we give you thanks,
and we sing your praise.

For the people that are important to us and the places we
    have visited,
for those who make us feel special and we know will never
    let us down,
we give you thanks,
and we sing your praise.

For those who give of themselves and of their time and
    energy,
for all who open our eyes to discover the God who is real,
we give you thanks,
and we sing your praise.

For the world you have given that is full of good things,
for its beauty and colour, and that we can enjoy it,
we give you thanks,
and we sing your praise.

For the friendships made and relationships blessed,
for Christ and his presence at the heart of all things,
we give you thanks,
and we sing your praise.

For the past and the present and the future yet to be,
for the promise of fellowship in Christ eternally,
we give you thanks,
and we sing your praise.

We bring our thanks in the name of Christ,
who is the heart of fellowship that is real. Amen.

110   SILENCE

Lord, we thank you for times of silence
and for moments when all is still;
for opportunities to be unhurried
and for that sense of tranquillity that brings peace to the
        soul;
for the joy that comes from simply learning 'to be'
and for the inner laughter that brings healing within;
for the oasis of peace when nothing moves and the world
        holds its breath.

We thank you for that renewed understanding that,
somewhere deep inside, this silence is your precious gift to us
and we are here in the presence of our Lord. Amen.

111   FAITHFUL PEOPLE

Father, we thank you for those who have found faith in you;
and for those who have remained faithful
though they have journeyed through long and painful ways.

We thank you for those who through the centuries
have lit the fires of faith and fanned the sparks of hope
into a blaze of trust and worship.

We thank you for those who have spoken your word
to those who have closed their minds to your grace
and also to those who have opened their hearts to your truth.

We thank you for your faithful people who told us the story
of Jesus
and whose whole lives reverberate with the joy of his presence.

We thank you that you have called us
to be your faithful people in our generation.
Make us ready to explore new ways of sharing our faith
and of discovering fresh expressions of being your faithful
people today.

112   TURBULENCE

Lord, we thank you for being there
when life seemed so straightforward and so predictable.
Thank you more for your promise to hold us
when times of turbulence come.
Faithful God, you are present when it seems that
the sun will always shine on our plans and our dreams will
never end.
But you also reveal yourself as the one who can be trusted
even when our lives are marked by clouds of uncertainty on
every side.
Sovereign Lord, we thank you for your gentle hand upon our
lives
and your insistent voice that calms our fears;
for your peace which all but overwhelms us
and your grace which is sufficient for all our needs.
For all these things we give you heartfelt thanks and praise.
Amen.

113   THE GOD WHO IS WORTHY

Lord, there are moments when we simply want to hold our
breath
and do nothing that would spoil the moment,

those moments when an overwhelming experience of
    gratitude
wells up within us—
a gratitude too deep, too real, too all-embracing to put into
    mere words!
Lord, we come and kneel at the foot of the empty cross
and we are moved with a deep, deep sense of sorrow and
    responsibility.
We stoop down and look into the empty tomb
and we are touched by your concern that we should have
    new life.
We witness the 'emptying out' of the Holy Spirit
and we are engulfed by a joy and a peace, a hope and a
    power, beyond words.
Lord, it seems almost too easy,
but all we can do is offer words of thanksgiving,
hearts of thankfulness and lives that are lived in gratitude for
Christ who died, Christ who is risen and Christ who will
    come again!
We pray in the name of Christ, the true source and goal
of all our thanks and praise. Amen.

114   MOTHERS AND TODDLERS

A prayer of thanksgiving and rededication

Children and leaders involved in the group(s) stand.

Lord, we thank you for the vision that led to the start
of [*toddler group*] and [*pre-school playgroup*].
We thank you for every child that has attended these groups
and for all the leaders and helpers who have given of their
    time and energy.

We thank you for the children who have been given the
    opportunity
to discover the joy of learning together with other children,
and we thank you for the preparation this has provided
for the learning that lies ahead.

We now rededicate ourselves to you and the work
of [*toddler group*] and [*pre-school playgroup*],
to the enabling of children to play and learn together in safety
and to the glory of your name.
In the name of Jesus Christ. Amen.

115   GIFT OF GRATITUDE

Wonderful God,
we thank you for the gift of gratitude with which you have
    flooded our lives.
We thank you, not only for the gift of life, but for life made
    new in Jesus Christ.
We thank you that, in him, you took the initiative
and demonstrated the utter enormity of your love for us—
love that is as boundless as eternity.
We thank you that you have not only given us eyes and ears
to witness the beauty of life and the wonder of creation,
but also hearts and minds with which we can enjoy it all.
We thank you not only for physical creation,
but also for spiritual re-creation through the power of your
    Holy Spirit.
We thank you that
though there are times when you and your loving presence
    feel far away
and we feel dull, empty and adrift in life
yet your promise holds true:
you have assured us that you will never leave us or forsake us.
We give thanks that, even in the darkest times, we can look
    to Christ who
through his life, death and resurrection
has plumbed the depths for us
that we might, by his grace, be lifted to the heights.
Lord, by your Spirit, transform our prayers of thanksgiving
into lives overflowing with thankfulness,
that others might be drawn to give you thanks and praise;
in the name of Christ our Lord. Amen.

Father, we thank you for your greatness, your glory and your
        power;
for the desire you have planted within us to worship you;
for making us in such a way that we are for ever reaching out
        and up
to that which is beyond our grasp.
We thank you that, the more we search and the more we
        seek knowledge,
the more fully human we are.
We thank you that you have given us the ability
to think, to plan and to choose,
to laugh and to cry, to give and to share, to encourage and to
        love.
We thank you for the gift of your Son, Jesus Christ our Lord,
for the enriching experience that the presence of Christ
        brings to our lives
and for the enabling power of the Spirit
which transforms our feelings and our service;
for those whose experience of you and your grace
has driven them out to love their neighbour as themselves;
for those who care for others in their need
and for those whose words and deeds demonstrate
the reality of your love within their lives.

We thank you for those who made Christ real for us
and ask that, by your Holy Spirit,
you will make us true witnesses of your life-changing love.
We thank you for those who have loved us, helped us
and enabled us to grow more and more into the people you
        meant us to be;
for those who have shared our pain,
listened to our story and stood by us when we were hurting;
for those who have shared with us as we walked the path of
        life
and for those you have given to us to share our journey of
        faith;

for those who have opened our eyes to your glory,
our ears to your truth, our minds to your will and our hearts
to your grace.
We thank you most of all for Christ
who has kept his promise to be with us always.
It is in his name that we bring our prayer. Amen.

117   GOD'S RICHES

Lord, you amaze us!
Again and again you touch our lives and renew our way of
thinking.
Little by little you chip away at what we have been
that we might be refashioned for your glory.
For all your riches,
we thank you, Lord.

Lord, you amaze us!
You open our eyes to see the colours, shapes and sizes
of everything you have made
and you have granted us the priceless gift of finding joy
in the work of your hands.
For all your riches,
we thank you, Lord.

Lord, you amaze us!
From the roaring torrents to the dried-up creeks;
from mountains that soar beyond the clouds
to the ravines whose depths are lost to sight;
from powerful creatures that earn our respect
to tiny insects whose colours dazzle our eyes.
Each adds to the richness of your creation.
For all your riches,
we thank you, Lord.

Lord, you amaze us!
Your limitless patience and your utterly endless grace;
the daily blessings of home, family and friends
that you permit us to enjoy,

touch us deeply
and your mercy that enriches every step we take.
For all your riches,
we thank you, Lord.

Lord, you amaze us!
Again and again you allow us to catch a glimpse of your
    glory.
You daily grant us an audience with the King of the universe,
and each moment you flood our lives with your love.
Every time we walk in the footsteps of your Son
he enriches our journey with his presence and power.
For all your riches,
we thank you, Lord.

Lord, you amaze us!
When we dare to listen to you, your love heals our blindness
and your Spirit leaps the barriers we build.
Your word comes with irresistible force
as you challenge our faith in the riches we think we hold
and you call us to trust you for riches that were beyond our
    reach.
For all your riches,
we thank you, Lord.

Lord, you amaze us!
Your wonder, your glory, your power and your holiness
are greater, more wonderful, than our words and our praises
    can describe.
Lord, so high and so all-sufficient,
come and enrich our lives and our worship.
By your Holy Spirit, reach down and touch us
that we might reach up and love you.
For all your riches,
we thank you, Lord.

In the name of Christ, the source of all true riches. Amen.

Lord, we thank you that you are not the kind of God
who is content to deal with your creation at arm's length.
In Christ you became part of your creation.
In his life, death and resurrection you tasted life for us all.
We thank you that, in him, you took the initiative
and added our humanity to your divinity,
our weakness to your sovereignty;
you gathered up our foolishness into your wisdom,
our time-based imprisonment to your timeless glory and
    freedom.
How can we not thank you for your gracious hand of love
    and friendship?
How can we not be grateful for the very gift of life itself?
How can we not be filled with gratitude that in Jesus we can,
perhaps for the first time in our lives,
know the freedom that was and is your will for everyone,
    everywhere?
We bring our thanks and offer our praises in the name of
    Christ,
the one in whom all are free. Amen.

119   THIS IS OUR GOD

Lord, you mean so much to us.
Your power, majesty and authority are utterly, totally and
    completely
beyond anything we can picture in our minds.
The wonder and depth of your grace
simply take our breath away and leave us astounded.
We call you Creator, Sustainer and Lord Almighty
as our way of expressing the truth you have revealed about
    yourself
through the sights and sounds of your creation
and through your word in the Bible.
We call you Saviour, Father and Lord
to describe our relationship with you,

a relationship your Son made possible through his life, death
and resurrection.
Today, we bring you our thanksgiving and our praise.
We ask that by the presence and power of the Holy Spirit
all our words, all our days and all our actions
may be evidence of the joy we experience
in giving thanks and praise to you, the one, true, living God.
We ask this through Christ who is the Lord. Amen.

120   VALUES

We thank you, Lord, for the value you place on our worship;
for the importance you give to our songs of praise;
for the joy you have in our fellowship with you
and the blessing that is yours through our fellowship with
each other.

We thank you, Lord, for the value you place on our service;
for the way you honour our feeble attempts to care for others
and those moments when we try to love our neighbour as
ourselves;
for the way you give meaning to our concern for the hungry
and starving
and the value you see in our seeking to witness to your great
name
as we pray for peace and justice for all.

We thank you, Lord, for the value you place upon ourselves;
for the song of love that sings in your heart for all the human
race
and for the price you were willing to pay
to restore each of us as a child of your grace;
for the cross of Christ which declares at full volume your
love
which starts in the heart of the Father and reaches everyone,
everywhere.

We thank you and praise you that the value you see in all
your creatures,

from the greatest to the least, never diminishes
but glows with the fire of the Holy Spirit,
bringing hope to all the world and glory to the name of
    Christ our Lord. Amen.

121   PAIN

Lord, this is a prayer we really don't want to pray.
This is a thanksgiving we really don't want to offer.
But something inside us drives us on
and compels us to say thank you—even for pain!
Pain isn't something we go looking for.
It isn't at the top of the list of the things we most desire.
Yet we need pain and, deep down,
we know it is a vital part of our lives.

Thank you, Lord, for the pain in our bodies that acts like an
    alarm system;
warning of something wrong deep inside; telling us we need
    help and healing.

Thank you, Lord, for the pain in our relationships
that reminds us to say sorry for our unkind words and selfish
    actions,
and, perhaps, for the first time in our lives, to really mean it.

Thank you, Lord, for the pain in our consciences
for those challenges to our wrong choices;
for those warnings of the dangers
when we walk in ways that conflict with your word;
for those moments that are uncomfortable
but gently and firmly seek to guide us daily
into thoughts and deeds that honour your name.

Thank you, Lord, for the pain in our hearts
as we are confronted by the pain and suffering in your world;
for the way the hurt and anguish we see
in the lives and on the faces of our neighbours

tear us apart and make us long to respond with love and
    care;
for the pain we feel as we see others suffering
as the result of war, drought, hunger, or disease;
for the pain we experience in the face of injustice, cruelty
    and abuse,
which drives us to seek to conquer evil with love
and hatred with the peace of Christ.

Thank you, Lord, for the pain Christ suffered for us on the
    cross
and that, through his pain, we can be made whole.
May our response to the pain of others always be a reflection
of Christ's sacrificial, self-giving love.

We ask this in the name of the wounded healer,
who bears in himself all the suffering and pain of the world.
    Amen.

122   WHAT GOD DOES

Lord, you have not only created a world of beautiful sights
    and sounds,
but you have provided us with the ability to enjoy it all.
You have not only given us life,
but you have created us to live in relationship with you and
    with each other.
You have not only made us in your own image
but you have so designed us that we can think, plan and reflect
on who we are and what we might become.
You have not only planned that we should have
the gifts and skills with which you have filled our lives,
but from the first you planned for us to rest,
to make time and space just 'to be'.
You never meant us to be like machines that can work
    incessantly.
You meant us to be human beings
needing times of sleep, refreshment and renewal.

We thank you for every opportunity you provide
to step out of our daily routine
and to take a pause from the endless activity each day brings.
Sovereign Lord, be Lord not only of the things we do,
the service we offer and the activities that control our every
 waking moment,
but also be Lord of our silences,
the moments of stillness and the sense of freedom they
 bring.
Lord, teach us that your love cannot be won
by the incessant activities of our lives
but is your free gift to all who wait upon you
and do so in the name of Christ. Amen.

123   ASH WEDNESDAY

Lord, we thank you that you are always there for us;
that even when we wander away from you
and from the path of your love and truth,
you never leave us and you never let us down.
We thank you for the story of your goodness and love
and for the record of all that you have done
to help, guide and transform the lives of your people down
 the years.

We thank you that you are the kind of God
who does not wait for us to be
good, perfect and always doing the right thing before you
 accept us;
that in Jesus Christ we have been given a picture
of who you are and what you are longing to do in and
 through our lives.
We thank you that you have made us in your own image
and that you have given us the ability
to think, to plan, to choose and to love;
that even when we have used your great gifts
for selfish purposes and in self-centred ways,
you continue to reach out to us in mercy.

We thank you that there is nowhere we can go
that will place us outside the sphere of your love and grace;
that there is nothing we can say or do
that will ever prevent you from loving us to the end and
beyond;
that we can come with the faith and hope that you have
given to us
and put our trust in you,
knowing that we are being held and guided by nail-scarred
hands.

Father, we thank you that we can come at all.
It is your grace that has lit the spark of faith within us,
and it is your Holy Spirit that has drawn us to you in this
time and place.
We thank you for all those whose lives and witness
have made it easier for us to trust you
and for those whose words and deeds
have made real to us your presence, your truth and your
love.

On this Ash Wednesday we turn to you with thankful hearts
and lives
and ask that you will use what we say and do together now
and all we share in the coming weeks
to prepare us for what is to come.
Prepare us to follow the pilgrims into Jerusalem,
to witness Christ's anger as he clears the temple courtyard,
to wait with him as he prays alone in the garden
and comprehend something of the pain of his betrayal.
Prepare us to stand at the foot of the cross
and look up into the face of the one who has loved us
with a love that will never die.
We thank you and praise you for Jesus Christ
and ask that you will prepare us to serve him all our days.
Amen.

Lord, you have so made us that we need each other.
You have designed us not to be self-sufficient but
     interdependent;
not to be isolated islands but those who depend on each
     other.

Lord, we thank you for those on whom we depend for our
     health
and those to whom we turn when we are ill;
for those who teach in our schools and colleges
and those whose task is to protect the community
from the danger of fire and the threats from those who break
     the law.

Lord, we thank you too for those on whom we depend
though we do not see them;
those whose work is largely unseen yet would be missed
if they were not there.
We thank you for those who remove the rubbish from our
     homes
and those who keep the streets clean;
for the ancillary staff on whose labours our hospitals depend;
for those who stock the shelves in the supermarkets
and for those who drive buses, trains and planes;
for those who work behind a desk in an office;
for secretaries, accountants and civil servants
and all those we do not see
but whose work is important in the life of the community.

Lord, we thank you for your unseen hand upon our lives
and your endless love on which we can depend now and for
     all eternity. Amen.

125   MAUNDY THURSDAY

Father, our Father, we thank you for your Son, Jesus Christ
     our Lord;
for his faithfulness to the task that you gave him

and for his obedience to your will for his life;
for his grace and kindness to those around him
and for his love for those who betrayed him, rejected and
    crucified him.
We thank you that he is for us
a picture of your endless loving kindness;
that your love is not something simply to know about,
but to be experienced in our own lives;
that your grace and mercy are not just words in the Bible,
but can be a reality in our own hearts.
We thank you for the way Jesus washed the disciples' feet
and for his example of care, compassion and servanthood;
for his challenge to us to love each other just as he has loved
    us;
for his acceptance even of Judas
and that not even his act of betrayal could prevent Jesus
    from loving him.
We thank you that he took the bread and the wine
and transformed them into symbols of his death for us on
    the cross;
that through the Holy Spirit we can know his presence and
    power
and serve in his name and for his glory each day.
Father, we bring our prayer of thanks in the name of the
    Servant King. Amen.

126 GOOD FRIDAY

Father, we thank you for who and what you are
and for what you have done for us and in us;
that though you are our mighty Creator and sovereign Lord
you are also the God whose nature is love.
We thank you for your holiness;
and for your utter purity which is clothed with love and
    mercy.
You are the righteous one.
You are always in the right and you always do what is right.

There is absolutely nothing that is unrighteous in you.
We thank you that you are not only a God of justice
but also a God of deep compassion
whose understanding knows no bounds.
Sovereign Lord, you reign supreme in eternity
and yet you are never far from us.
You are for ever above and beyond us
and yet in Christ you came and lived our life and died our
    death.
Lord, we thank you for all you have done for us
in and through your Son, Jesus Christ, our Lord.
On this Good Friday, we thank you for his death on the
    cross of Calvary
and that through him we can know our sins forgiven
and be assured that we are accepted.
Father, again and again you astound us with your love
that overwhelms our sin and our self-centredness.
In Jesus you have wiped the slate clean,
you have given us a new page in the book of our lives
and have given us the opportunity to begin again.
We thank you that when Jesus said, 'It is finished!'
he assured us that there is nothing we can do, nothing we
    can add
to what he has already done to open the way to life that is
    real,
life that is lived in the knowledge of your presence.
Father, our Father, we thank you and we praise you
as we stand at the foot of the cross
and confess that he is the Lord and there is no other.
In the name of the Saviour of the world. Amen.

127 TODAY

Lord, in the stillness of the early morning the air is clear,
    crisp and cool.
It is like a pause, as the day waits to begin its journey.
We praise you for the gift of this new day.

It comes fresh from your hand,
ready and waiting to be filled, used and enjoyed.
Thank you for each new day that in your grace you permit
    us to have
but not to hold.
We are like guests in the moments and the hours that in
    truth belong to you.
This day is yours, in which you allow us to be.
We arrogantly assume ownership
of days, weeks, months and years we may not see.
Again and again we misuse and abuse the moments we are
    offered
without a word of gratitude or an acknowledgement
of our utter, total and absolute dependence on you and your
    grace.
May how we receive this day, and how we use it,
how we live it and how we entrust it to you
be in itself an act of thanksgiving and a song of praise to
    your name. Amen.

128   HARVEST THANKSGIVING

Father, we thank you for the harvest of life
and for all the things that bring us great joy
and a sense of satisfaction and fulfilment;
for the harvest of hope
that reminds us that you hold all things in the palm of your
    hand;
for the harvest of our relationships
with friends and family and with our fellow Christians
that adds richness to our days and makes life worth living;
for the harvest of joy
and the delight we receive from the beautiful things we can
    see and hear;
for the harvest of understanding
and for the many things that we learn each day;
for minds that can think and remember

and for a harvest of skills we can develop;
for a harvest of memories we can review every day.

We thank you for the harvest all around us
of trees and forests, of plants and animals,
of creatures that creep and crawl,
those that soar to the heights and those that hover on the
wing.
We thank you, Lord of the harvest,
that we can depend on you for everything
and that true thankfulness is seen when we confess our
dependence on you
and your dependability.
We thank you that you have made us responsible for each
other
and that the harvests you have given
are ours to give to those with no harvest of their own;
that there is plenty for all, so long as we share it.

Father, we thank you for the harvest of love
that we have received through the life, death and resurrection
of Jesus Christ;
and for the harvest of new life with which he has flooded our
hearts.
We thank you for the harvest of the Spirit;
and we ask that his presence and power will direct and
control
what we allow to take root in our minds and in our lives.
We ask this in the name of Christ, the Lord of the harvest.
Amen.

129   REMEMBRANCE SUNDAY

Almighty God our heavenly Father, on this day of
remembering
we bring you our prayers of thanks
for all that you do and go on doing in our hearts and
lives;

that when we take a step of faith you prove to be worthy of
    our trust;
when we sing your praise
you reveal yourself as the one who is worthy of all our
    adoration;
when we bring our confession,
you point us to Christ and his sacrifice for our sin;
when we admit our unworthiness, you offer your cleansing;
when we come lost, alone, empty and feeling broken
you remind us of the Spirit's power and presence within.
We thank you for every memory we have
of those whose words and deeds have reflected your goodness
    and love;
for those who gave their own lives that ours might be full
    and free;
for those whose kindness, compassion and self-denial
have directed our thoughts to the Saviour of the world;
for those today who stand for the truth, no matter the cost
    to themselves;
for those whose honesty, trustworthiness and wholeness
challenge us to step out of the dull routine of existence
and to grasp every opportunity to be truly alive.
We thank you that we can remember, and that, in
    remembering,
the care, love, hope and sacrifice of others are never lost.
We thank you for those whom we are remembering today;
for those whose words and deeds have changed our lives;
for those whose words and deeds led us to Christ
and for those whose words and deeds made Christ real for us.
Father, on this Remembrance Sunday we thank you for the
    assurance
that you remember our names, but not the sin we confess,
and that you remember your love for us.
We pray that you will help us always to remember
to love, honour, serve and worship you. Through Jesus
    Christ our Lord. Amen.

130 GOD'S LOVE FOR ALL

Lord, we thank you for your love, which has no beginning
and knows no end;
that though we cannot see it or prove it, your love, even as
we pray,
is alive and active in the world that you have made.
We thank you for the love which not only gave us life
but also, in Christ, gave us new life, new hope and a new joy;
for every moment when we are once more made aware
of your irrepressible love and your extravagant mercy;
for those who, by their words and deeds,
have made Christ and his love real for us;
for every opportunity you have given to us
to speak of Christ and to name his name.
We thank you for those whose kindness, generosity and
faithfulness
have opened the door of faith and hope to others;
for those whose lives are light in the darkness,
stillness in the storm, strength in weakness, joy in despair
and Christ to their neighbour;
for those who stand with the fallen, wait with the dying,
comfort the grieving, enable the powerless to cope
and are Christ to those to whom you send them.
Lord, how can we not thank you, praise you and worship
you?
For you are our Saviour and our Lord,
in whose name we bring our prayer. Amen.

131 MISSION TO THE WORLD

Lord, we thank you for your love
which again and again simply overwhelms us.
Just when we think we know who and what you are
you break the limits of our understanding.
Just when we feel that we know what you will expect of us
you frighten us again with what seem like your impossible
demands.

We thank you, Lord, that though your demands are high
    and holy,
deep and demanding, long and almost overwhelming, wide
    and far reaching,
you are the one who not only calls us but also equips us
to go and to serve in the way you desire.

Lord, we thank you for every person who has, like Abraham,
set out not knowing where they were going;
for those who have gone the extra mile in love,
in compassion and in offering forgiveness;
for those who have travelled to distant lands
to take the good news of your love for all people;
and, for those who have quietly and consistently shared their
    faith
with their family, their friends and their colleagues at work
    and at school.
We thank you for those who have risked everything
to make certain that the message of your life, death and
    resurrection
is declared throughout the whole world;
for those who have worked tirelessly in the work of mission
    around the world;
for those who have raised money
and those who have raised our awareness of the needs
of our brothers and sisters in Christ around the world;
for those who have come to us
from your church in various places around the world
and for those who have opened our eyes, our ears, our minds
    and our hearts
to the great and mighty things you are doing there.

Lord, we thank you that in you we are one people;
that no matter where we come from,
and no matter our language or our custom,
no matter our way of worship and praise, in you we are
    united.

We thank you for your one church,
your body witnessing on earth and celebrating in heaven.
Take our thanksgiving and, by your Holy Spirit,
transform our words and our deeds into vehicles of your glory.
Through your holy name we ask it. Amen.

132   CHRISTMAS EVE

Lord, we thank you that you have made yourself known to
     us,
and you have done so in a way that we could understand;
that in the coming of your Son, Jesus Christ,
you have brought an end to our empty speculation
as to who you are and whether or not you love us;
that you have not only revealed yourself to us,
but also that in the simplicity of Christ's coming
you have swept away any reliance on ourselves—
our intellectual searchings, or the assumption of our personal
     worth.
We thank you that his being born of an earthly mother
and his entering into our world in the poverty of a stable
speaks to us of the depths to which you are prepared to reach
     down
in order to lift us to the height of your throne of grace;
that his coming teaches us to be open to your coming to us
when we least expect it and in ways we would never have
     dreamt possible;
We thank you that Jesus was born as a human being
and shared all our limitations of time and place;
that though he was King of Kings and Lord of Lords,
he was not born into a life of privilege
but grew in knowledge of you and your purposes for him.
We thank you for all those who, like Mary,
have been prepared to say yes to you and to your will for
     their lives;
for those who, like the shepherds, are so open to you
that they respond with a sense of urgency to do your will;

for those who, like Joseph, are prepared to serve you in the
background,
to remain almost unnoticed and remain faithful at great cost
to themselves.
Lord, we have come to prepare ourselves to celebrate not
only your coming,
but also your living, dying and your rising again.
We come to celebrate the victory of your love,
a victory into which, by your Spirit,
we can enter today and every day of our lives.
Lord, we thank you, and we always will
and we will do so in and through Christ our Lord. Amen.

133   LORD OF ALL AGES

Lord of all ages, we thank you for the days and years of our
lives,
for the precious memories of those we have known and
loved,
and see no more.
Lord of all ages, we thank you for all the knowledge our
years have brought,
for the things we have learnt and the skills we have gathered,
and for the wisdom we have received.
Lord of all ages, we thank you that though we often feel or
are excluded
by the world of today,
you always receive us with open arms and love that never
ends.
Lord of all ages, we thank you for the patience that has come
with the years,
for the ability to be gentle with those with whom we
disagree,
and for the inner confidence that comes from knowing you.
Lord of all ages, we thank you that to you all ages are the
same,

that no one is excluded because of the number of their years,
and that your love is for all, no matter who, no matter what.
Lord of all ages, we thank you for your greatness, your glory
and your power,
for your ageless love and your endless patience with your
wayward children;
for Christ who was crucified without reaching old age,
and for his sacrifice and the offer it gives of eternal life
that cannot be lost by old age or ended by death itself.
Lord of all ages, we thank you that by faith in Jesus
we can know you when all ages are past and life and time are
no more.
Lord of all ages, be our Lord, our Saviour and eternal friend.
Amen.

Prayers of Confession

134   ONE WORLD WEEK—THE ENVIRONMENT

Lord, you made one world, but we have divided it;
You made us to be one, but we have chosen to be separate
from you and from each other.
Forgive us for creating haves and have nots,
rich and poor, privileged and deprived.
Forgive us too that so often we neither think about what we
have done
nor act to change the world.
Lord, forgive us, and by your Spirit disturb us and challenge
us
that the world may be one in you.
In the name of Christ, one Saviour for the whole world.
Amen.

135   WE CONFESS

Lord, we confess that we live in a day and generation
that appears to be hell-bent on doing its own thing.

Each day our lives arrogantly declare
that there are no ultimate rights and wrongs; no final court
of appeal.

We confess that we prefer to make our own rules
and set the bar of life where it suits us
in order to ensure that it causes us no pain
and demands no effort to vault its meagre requirements.

Yet, Lord, the snow-topped hills oversee our fallen world
and set a standard of purity that denounces ours as
inadequate.

The mighty waterfall, the explosive volcano,
the masterful hurricane and the raging torrent
herald a power and authority that demolish our foolish pride
in our temporary achievements.

The vastness of space ridicules our dependence on our
earthly successes;
while the cool mountain stream laughs at our wistful dreams
and our hope that we can change our lives.

Lord, we confess that apart from you we can do nothing;
that apart from you even our highest endeavours are doomed
to failure;
that apart from you we are nothing.

Lord, cleanse, renew, and by your Holy Spirit
enable us to live for your glory, that we may fully live. Amen.

136   BREAD OF HEAVEN—CONFESSION

Lord, we confess that we long for more of the Bread of Life;
that we rarely make time to receive the bread of heaven.

We confess that our grasping at
more than our fair share of your world's resources
is robbing our sisters and brothers of even the crusts we don't
want.

Lord, forgive our foolish, unthinking greed
and refocus our lives on giving instead of getting. Amen.

137   LORD, WE CONFESS

Lord, we confess that we have tried and failed!

We thought we could follow Jesus and do it in our own
        strength;
that we could serve our neighbour without relying on you;
that we could live the Christian life and rarely turn to you in
        prayer;
that we could plan our own lives, make our decisions and
        live each day
never listening for your voice, never opening your Word.

Lord, we confess that we have tried and failed!

Now send the living fire,
that the Holy Spirit may refine, reform and renew—even
        people like us!

Lord, we have made our confession;
come now, that the living fire may make us new. Amen.

138   COUNTING THE COST

Forgive us, Lord, when we do count the cost and find that
        the price is too high;
when we know that you are calling us but we don't want to
        listen;
when you challenge us to trust you but we would rather put
        our faith in ourselves;
when we know we should pray but we have left you no time;
when your word is before us but we are afraid you will speak;
when you tell us to keep no score of wrongs, but we keep
        writing the list;
when you teach us to pray 'forgive us as we forgive others'
but the truth is we don't really mean it!

Yet we need to know that we are accepted, loved and
    forgiven.
By your grace, transform what we are,
and by your Holy Spirit may we live for your glory. Amen.

139   PENTECOST

Lord, we confess that we have tried
to worship you in our own strength and in ways that pleased
    us.

We confess that, though we seek to serve you,
our commitment is stretched to the limit.

We confess that we have relied on ourselves and on what we
    do
and hoped that this would restore our relationship with you.

We confess that we have tried in vain.

Come, Lord, fill us with your Holy Spirit.
Come, Lord, renew our whole lives.
Come, Lord, transform us by your grace.
Come, Lord, come that by your Spirit we may serve you,
know you and love you as our Saviour and Lord. Amen.

140   FORGIVENESS

Lord, we confess that we long to know that we are forgiven;
that the slate is wiped clean and that we can begin again.

Lord, we confess that we find it hard to accept that we are
    accepted,
that the debt has been paid and that your forgiveness is ours.

Lord, we confess that though we long to be forgiven
we find it so hard to forgive others;
that we don't want to share with others the gift which we
    have received
and which like them we simply do not deserve.

Lord, by your grace, apply your forgiveness to our lives
that by your Spirit we might become channels of Christ's
    cleansing and renewal.
In his name and for his glory. Amen.

141   CRITICISING OTHERS

Lord, we confess that we are not the people you meant us to be,
nor are we living the kind of lives that you intended.
We confess that we criticise others for the mistakes we so
    easily excuse in ourselves.
We confess our blindness to our own faults
and our microscopic examination of each other's weaknesses.
We confess our failure to be
the forgiving, accepting people Christ called us to be.
Cleanse, renew and forgive us for Christ's sake. Amen.

142   LACK OF LOVE

Lord, we find it hard to like everyone,
and to love them seems utterly impossible.
Christ told us that your love is for the whole world,
yet our sights are set so much lower and
we still fail to love our neighbour as ourselves.
We confess our indifference to others
and our slavish concern for ourselves.
We have tried to break out of this self-centred imprisonment
and open our eyes and our ears to the cry of the lost and
    despairing.
We ask not simply for you to forgive us our failures
but that the power of your Spirit will empower us
to be like mirrors of your love for the whole world.
In the name of Christ. Amen.

143   OUR BURDEN

Lord, we confess that we are overwhelmed by our sense of
    responsibility.
We bring to you our burden of concern—

for ourselves and for your world, for the way we have lived,
for what we have said and what we have done,
for what we have failed to be and refused to become.
Lord, our burden is too heavy for us,
we cannot carry it alone, we cannot carry it any longer.
By the grace of your forgiveness lift from our shoulders
the despair, the hurt, the weakness and the failures that
    crucify us
and set us free to live again the life you always meant us to
    live.
Through Christ, the true liberator of all. Amen.

144   RELYING ON OURSELVES

Lord, we confess that, despite your offer of free grace,
we still seek to deserve your love;
though you have told us that you have looked in our hearts,
we still try to hide our true selves from you;
though you have given your life for us
we still hold back part of our lives for ourselves;
though you gave everything, we only give something,
and though you are our living Lord
we live as though you are still in the tomb.
Lord, change, renew and set us free
to be the persons you meant us to be from the very
    beginning.
In the name of Christ. Amen.

145   FAILURE TO TRUST

Father, forgive our futile attempts
to make ourselves worthy of your love and mercy;
that we still try to overcome our sin and selfishness in our
    own strength
and that we count ourselves better than others.
Forgive us when we are self-satisfied, or when we think we
    have arrived,

when often we have not really begun the journey of faith to
   which you are calling us.
Forgive us for being content with offering you anything less
   than the best
of our time, our talents, our service and our worship;
for setting ourselves impossible goals
which means our highest endeavours are doomed to failure
through our refusal to trust you.
Forgive us for standing still and not walking and growing in
   Christ.
Forgive us our hard hearts, our stubborn wills
and our failure to accept that we are accepted.
Father, forgive us, and renew our lives, for Jesus Christ's sake.
   Amen.

146   STARKNESS OF LIFE

Lord, forgive us that, even when we have experienced the
   warmth of your love
and the power of your grace in our own lives,
we still turn our backs on our neighbours
and leave them to face the starkness of life
without the knowledge of your presence;
forgive us for allowing your love to reach into our own hearts
but never to flow out to a world in need of hope and joy and
   peace.
Lord, by your Holy Spirit drive us out into the wilderness of
   your world
to demonstrate your extravagant love
to those who are hurting and whose hopes are broken.
May the reality of your grace transform not only our lives
but the lives of our neighbours to whom you send us.
In Christ's name. Amen.

147   PRETENCE OF FREEDOM

Father, though we pretend to be free, we confess that we are
    prisoners of fear.
Though we say we do not care how others think about us,
we are prisoners to their praise.
Though we give the impression of peace, hope and faith,
you see through the prison walls of doubt and despair,
though we have been set free in Christ
we confess that we still are prisoners
to many things that hold us and enslave us.
Lord, set us free to be the people you meant us to be
and for whom Christ died. Amen.

148   OUR MISSION TODAY

Father, we acknowledge that you have given us
everything we need for life and for living.
You have filled our hearts with hope, peace and joy.
You gave us your Son as our Saviour and Lord
and you gave us your Spirit to make our lives new.
Forgive us that we live as though we had received nothing
and deny others the opportunity to know you.
Forgive us for the poverty of our vision
and our failure to share the riches of Christ.
Forgive us whenever we consider
life to be empty, boring, meaningless and futile
and close our hearts and minds to the wonders of your grace.
Forgive us for those times when we fail to live as your people
    of grace.
We ask that you will use our lives to create pictures of your
    love.
We ask this in the name of Christ. Amen.

149   ASH WEDNESDAY

Father, we admit to ourselves and to you
that we have failed to be the people you meant us to be.
When duty called we avoided it

and we defended ourselves with excuses that did not deceive
  ourselves or you.
We confess our failure which has hurt us as well as those
  around us.
We resolve to do all we can to put things right,
to apologise to those to whom we should
and to forgive others even before they ask.
We surrender to you all those mistakes that cannot be
  changed
and which constantly remind us of our weakness and frailty.
We give back to you our selfish anger, our pain, our bitter
  thoughts and words.
We hand over to you our frustrations, our shallowness,
our powerlessness and our hopelessness.
Father, set us free from those things that haunt us from the
  past
and those things that make us afraid of the future.
Release us from the burdens that we foolishly and needlessly
  continue to carry.
Teach us to enter tomorrow in the knowledge that even our
  failure
does not put us beyond the reach of your love.
We ask that we may heed every warning that our experience
  of life brings us
and that we may rediscover
the joy of allowing you your rightful place in our lives
and the certainty of the place your grace claims for us in
  your eternity.
May the offer of your undeserved love which took Christ to
  the cross
give us hope that even we can become your renewed people.
Here and now, Father, we not only accept that we are
  accepted,
but also we respond to the challenge to empty ourselves of
  all that pleases us
in order that we might overflow with those things that are
  pleasing to you.

May we not crucify Christ again, but be crucified with him,
so that by your Holy Spirit we may be raised with him
and live to bring him praise and glory.
This we ask in the name of Christ. Amen.

150   MAKE ME CLEAN

Lord, take my hands, and wipe them clean of every selfish
action.

Lord, take my feet, and change the paths of self-interest they
love to walk.

Lord, take my lips,
and remove every hurtful word that brings division where it
is heard.

Lord, take my ears,
that I may no longer listen to gossip but only to what is
pleasing to you.

Lord, take my eyes, that I may see the suffering of my
neighbour,
and not simply see the things that affect me.

Lord, take my mind and transform my way of thinking,
that your will and the needs of others may take precedence
over my own.

Lord, take my heart, the centre of my being,
and reign in my place as you were always meant to do.
Amen.

151   MAUNDY THURSDAY

Father, we know only too well that, humanly speaking,
we have no right to call you Father.
It is through your grace alone that we have become your
children
and by the power of the Holy Spirit that we have been
adopted into your family.

We confess that we find it hard to put other people first
and their needs before our own;
that we find it easier to expect others to serve us
rather than for us to offer loving service to each other;
that we, like Christ's disciples, are filled with doubts and
 despair;
that there are times when our lives are a denial of the
 commitment we have made
and our words often betray our trust in Christ.
Forgive us that we find it so hard to stand firm for Christ
and that we so often run away from the challenge
to take his name onto our lips and his purposes into our
 lives.
Forgive us and renew us, for we ask this in the name of
 Christ our Lord. Amen.

152   GOOD FRIDAY

Father, we see your forgiveness
for our ignorance, our blind stupidity, our weakness and our
 prejudice.
Forgive us that, so often and so easily, like Pilate we are
 swayed by the crowd.
We do not find it easy to stand out, to be different,
or even to stand up and be counted as your people.
We are like Pilate: we know what is right,
we know what we ought to say and do,
but we find the price of doing it far too high.
We are like the crowd: we know deep down
what our words, thoughts and actions are doing to your
 world,
to other people's lives and to you.
We are like the soldiers: we find it so much easier to stand
 by,
to excuse ourselves by claiming that
all the suffering in your world is not our fault—there is
 nothing we can do.

We are like the disciples: here in the midst of those who
    believe
we have made our proud confessions of faith.
Sunday by Sunday, we have met to praise, thank and
    worship you.
We have gathered for fellowship with the faithful.
But Lord, we, like the disciples, have denied you,
running away in fear of our Christianity being discovered.
Father, forgive us that who and what we are,
and what we are not, cries out against your love;
help us not to crucify again the Lord of glory.
We pray that our experience of your presence may give us
    the power
to become living examples of your grace,
that as we know you more and more as our Father
we may have that conviction that enables us
to place everything into your loving hands,
even our sin and shame.
In the face of all the hatred, hostility and bitterness of his
    enemies,
Christ offered nothing but love in return.
Lord, enable us to do the same
and may we do it in his name, in his strength and for his
    glory. Amen.

153   HARVEST CONFESSION

Those who are the hungry people of the world
wait for crumbs to fall from our rich tables.
Lord, forgive us when we are deaf to their cries.

Those who are the poor of the world
long to share in our harvest of plenty.
Lord, forgive us when we close our eyes to their needs.

Those who are crying in the world
long to feel the love and care of their neighbour.
Lord, forgive us when we refuse to reach out and touch.

Those who are sick and dying want to receive healing and help.
Lord, forgive us when we turn our backs
because the cost of caring is too high for us to bear.

Those who are afraid are waiting for our comfort and support.
Lord, forgive us when we fail to make time to love.

Those who are without hope and without a future
are wanting us to act on their behalf.
Lord, forgive us that we close our minds.

Those who have been hurt or abused
are waiting to know that they are accepted.
Lord, forgive us when we fail to show the unconditional love
    of Christ.

Those who have no harvest to thank God for
are waiting to receive from the harvest he gave us to share.
Lord, forgive us our greed and our fear, our selfishness and
    our neglect.

Those whose homes, lives, families and future
have been destroyed by war and bitterness
are waiting for us to begin to work for peace.
Lord, forgive us that we allow our selfishness to spoil each
    other's lives.

Those who are empty, lost and without hope
are waiting to hear the name of Christ and to learn the love
    of our Father.
Lord, forgive us that we remain silent when we should speak
and that we speak when we should have silently lived out
    your love.
Forgive us and make us new. For Christ's sake. Amen.

154   REMEMBRANCE SUNDAY

Lord, we confess that we remember with shame
the things we have said and done and thought
that have hurt you, each other and ourselves.

We remember with shame
that we have praised you with our lips and denied you with
    our lives,
we have used our voices to offer you thanks and worship
and also to spoil our lives, our relationships and our witness.
We remember with sadness
the pain we have caused our friends and our families,
and the foolishness with which we have filled our days.
We remember the times we have failed to read your word,
to turn to you in prayer, or to seek your will for our lives.
We remember the anger and the bitterness that have clouded
    our thoughts
and the grudges and envy and jealousy that we have
    harboured within.
We confess that we have often failed to remember
to love you with our whole being and our neighbour as
    ourselves.
In the silence of our own hearts
we remember those things which are spoiling our lives,
things we would rather no one else knew anything about.
Forgive us, and forget the sin that we have remembered
    before you,
and make us new and clean again. For Christ's sake. Amen.

155   NO OTHER GODS

Father, you told us to have no other gods;
that there should be no one more important to us than you
and nothing that matters more than giving you honour,
    thanks and praise.
But we have sought honour for ourselves
and we have fed ourselves on the praises of others.
We attempt to find our security in our earthly possessions
and not in being your special possession.
We find our purpose in our achievements
and our joy in the thanks we long to receive.
We confess that we would grieve more over the loss

of our health and wealth, or our family and friends,
than we would if we were deprived of your loving presence.
Father, forgive us for giving room
to the gods we allow to take your place
and to the idols which receive the devotion that is yours by
     right, alone. Amen.

156   OUR LACK OF CONCERN

Father, our Father, we confess that we are often weak when
     we should be strong;
that we live as though we are lost, though we have been
     found;
we remain broken, though Christ has made us whole;
we feel unloved, though your love for us is endless.
We confess that, though you have promised the Spirit will
     empower and enable us,
we often rely on our own strength for our worship and
     service,
our commitment and our praise.
Forgive us our doubts, our fears, our lack of joy and our lack
     of hope;
our insensitivity to the needs of others;
our self-centred concerns in the face of our neighbour's pain;
our times of apathy and indifference to each other's
     successes
and our critical attitude to each other's failures.
Forgive us, cleanse and renew us and make us more like
     Christ,
in whose name we pray. Amen.

157   CHRISTIAN AID

Father, you said that the world was very good
and that there would be food and contentment for
     everyone.
But our greed and our selfishness have spoilt your world
as we have spoilt our lives.

Father, you said that the world should reflect your glory
and that it was designed to bring you thanks and praise.
But we have neglected our neighbour and loved only those
who loved us.

Father, you said you were making us responsible for all your
creation;
you placed it in our hands, to love and care for everything
and everyone.
But we forgot that it is yours
and that one day we would answer to you for everything we
did
or allowed others to do in your world.

Father, we do not simply ask for your forgiveness,
but for a new desire to show your compassion for all
and your care for your creation,
and so demonstrate that we are truly your children. In Jesus'
name. Amen.

158   OUR SMALL-MINDEDNESS

Lord, we confess that we have thought of ourselves
as the ones you love the most
and we have forgotten that your love is for the whole world;
that we have lived careful, risk-free lives
and have ignored your call to walk by faith;
that we have served you within the life of the church and in
the community,
but we have looked too expectantly for thanks and
recognition;
that we have trusted you with the small things in our lives
but that we still find it so hard to trust you completely and
for everything.
We confess that we have often lived
as though you were an old man whom we visit every Sunday
and have forgotten that you are the Sovereign Lord of all
creation;

we have tried to reduce you and your demands to a size
that we can understand and cope with in our own strength,
and we have forgotten that you are greater
than anything our tiny, finite minds can ever comprehend,
and that only through your power can we live for your glory.
Forgive us, renew our minds, our hearts and your hold on
us.
And please do it for Christ's sake, in whose name we ask our
prayer. Amen.

159   CHRISTMAS EVE

Lord, forgive us for our failure to trust you;
a failure we repeat every day of our lives,
a failure we have confessed to you before.
Forgive us the anxieties that cripple our lives
and the words of hopelessness with which we burden ourselves
and our neighbour.
Forgive us that, though we prepare to welcome the Christ
child,
we continue to live as though he had never been born.
Forgive us that we seem to find it easier to depend on each
other
rather than on you and your sovereign grace and your living
presence.
Forgive us that, though we listen to the story of the first
Christmas,
and we rejoice to hear again the message of peace on earth
that the angels brought,
we are still not ready to respond to you as Mary did,
with love, faith and obedience.
Forgive us, most of all, whenever our faithlessness acts as a
barrier
which prevents someone else finding faith in Christ.
Lord, reclaim us as your own, and make our lives a fanfare
for your glory.
We ask this in the name of Christ our Lord. Amen.

160   ONE WORLD WEEK—THE ENVIRONMENT

Lord, we thank you for giving us such a wonderful world in
    which to live.
There is always so much to see, so much to do and so much
    to discover;
so many places to visit and so many people to meet.
You have made our lives so exciting
and each day is a new opportunity to thank you and praise
    you
for all you have done and all you have given to us.
We thank you for Jesus, and that he came to show your love
for everyone, everywhere and for ever.
Forgive us for being so selfish,
for not playing fair and always wanting our own way;
for always wanting the best for ourselves
and not wanting the best for others, too.
Forgive us and make us new, and make us more like Jesus.
In his name. Amen.

161   WE HAVE COME TO SAY WE ARE SORRY

Lord, we have come to say we are sorry for the times
when we were angry; when we wanted our own way;
when we said something that wasn't true;
when we didn't play fair; when we didn't want to share;
when we were unkind, unhelpful or selfish; when we didn't
    want to say sorry.

Lord, we have come to say we are sorry
and to ask you not only to forgive us, but to help us
to be honest; to be caring; to be helpful; to be loving; to be
    forgiving;
so that the way we live will show that Jesus lives in our
    hearts. Amen.

162   BREAD OF HEAVEN

Lord, bread—it's such ordinary stuff, and not a very exciting
    word.
For many people bread means money
and for most of us it's what we make our toast with.
It's ordinary stuff, for everyday people,
but daily bread was the first request in prayer that Jesus gave
    us.

Lord, we thank you for the farmer who sows and reaps;
for the baker who mixes the dough and bakes the loaves;
for those who wrap it and bring it to our table.

Lord, we praise you for Jesus, our daily bread,
who offers us a life of challenge and adventure.
He promises to all who will listen to him
forgiveness and love beyond our deserving.

Lord Jesus, be like bread for us, filling our hearts and our
    minds
with the love of your Father. Amen.

163   THE CALENDAR

Lord, we praise you for the calendars that hang on our walls;
for their pictures of birds and animals;
of people and places; of sea and sky.
They remind us each day of the good things
with which you have filled your world
and which you require us to protect.

Lord, we praise you for the calendars that hang on our walls;
for the months and the weeks; the days and the hours;
for the minutes and seconds.
They are waiting and ready to be used for the glory of your
    name
so that the whole world may know that Jesus is Lord.

Lord, we praise you for the calendars that hang on our walls;
for the time you have given to us

to give and to share, to love and to care, to offer peace and
  forgiveness.
It was your plan from the beginning
that no one be forgotten and peace be restored.

Lord, we praise you for the calendars that hang on our walls;
for the promise of hope that each new day brings
and for the new things we can learn before tomorrow begins;
for the fresh adventure of faith, of which each dawn is the
  herald.
May we so use each new day that tomorrow, for someone,
will be flooded with the joy of your love.

Lord, we praise you for the calendars that hang on our walls;
for the comfort we can offer to those whose days overflow
  with tears;
for the help we can give to those who feel lost and alone;
for the peace we can share with those whose hopes are
  broken.
May we so live that everyone we meet feels the presence of
  your grace
and the power of your love.

Lord, we praise you for the calendars that hang on our walls;
for the times we have been given to share your good news;
to make sure this day doesn't end before
we have spoken to someone of that love which never ends;
to take every opportunity to name Jesus as Lord.
May all we say and do this day
bring peace to our world and hope to our neighbour.

Lord, we praise you for the calendars that hang on our walls;
for they are like life—they have a start and a finish, a
  beginning and end;
they have a plan and a purpose and give direction to our days.
They announce a journey we must make and a goal to be
  reached.
Each day you give us another twenty-four hours
to be used to the full and lived for our Lord.

As we look at the calendar that hangs on our wall
help us to begin each new day
walking in faith, putting our trust in you, Lord,
that, by your grace, we may give you
all the thanks and praise that you deserve. Amen.

164   CREATION

Lord, you give us times of stillness,
and quiet moments of life to remember you and your love.
We give you thanks,
and we sing your praise.

Lord, you made the rippling streams and the mighty
        waterfalls
as signs of your goodness and power.
We give you thanks,
and we sing your praise.

Lord, you built the snowy mountain tops and designed lakes
        of clear water
that fill us with hope and joy.
We give you thanks,
and we sing your praise.

Lord, you created animals of every shape and size and colour
as well as birds and fish and insects.
We give you thanks,
and we sing your praise.

Lord, your creation reflects your beauty and your glory;
it makes us want to worship you and to praise your name.
We give you thanks,
and we sing your praise.

Lord, you gave us eyes to see and ears to hear,
lives to enjoy your creation, and voices to give you glory.
We give you thanks,
and we sing your praise.

Lord, long ago you created glaciers that remind us
that you are the God who has no beginning and no end.
We give you thanks,
and we sing your praise.

Lord, you gave us mighty rushing waters
that speak to us of your life-sustaining power and love.
We give you thanks,
and we sing your praise.

Lord, the light sparkling on the water and sunsets that take
    our breath away
speak to us of the light of the world.
We give you thanks,
and we sing your praise.

In Jesus' name. Amen.

165   WE CAN SING AND WE CAN SHOUT!

Lord, we are so glad that you gave us our voices
and that we can use them to make so much noise—
we can sing and we can shout!

We can use our voices
to say please and to say thank you;
to say something kind to those who are sad;
to give encouragement to those who are hurting inside;
to show the way when someone is lost;
to say something good when others are being nasty;
to speak about Jesus, even when others only laugh.

We can use our voices to sing your praise,
to say our prayers, to speak of your love
and to shout aloud that we think you're wonderful.

We can make sure our voices keep quiet
instead of saying something hurtful or unkind;

we can be silent, instead of getting angry;
gentle instead of being a bully; thoughtful instead of being
  selfish.

We can use our voices to say thank you for all the wonderful
  things
with which you fill our lives, our world and our days;
to say sorry when what we say or do hurts you, other people
  and ourselves;
to shout aloud that we follow Jesus and that we are giving
  our lives to him
whose life, death and resurrection shouts aloud your love for
  all the world.

Lord, we can shout and we can sing;
help us to shout and sing for Jesus. Amen.

166   FOUR FISHERMEN

Lord, what did you see in them? They were just four
  ordinary men:
they were simply fixing their fishing nets and you just said,
  'Come.'

Lord, what did you see in them? They were not very clever;
they'd never been to school or passed an exam and you just
  said, 'Come.'

Lord, what did you see in them? They were not very good
and they didn't have much time for you,
and worship wasn't something that was high on their list.
But you just said, 'Come.'

Lord, what did you see in them—or in us?
Like those four fishermen we are not very good.
But though we are not special in the eyes of the world
you still call people like us to come follow Jesus
wherever he leads and wherever he goes. Amen.

Lord, we don't know her name and we don't know what she
    was like,
we don't know what she did and we don't know if she had
    any family.
All we know is that she had made a mess of her life;
that was the woman at the well.

But Lord, you seemed to know absolutely everything about
    her.
You knew what she had done and how she had lived;
you knew she had no friends and that she trusted nobody;
you knew she was lonely and that she was hurting inside;
you knew just how much she wanted to begin again.

Lord, thank you for the story of the woman at the well.
We now know that, as with her,
you know everything in our hearts and in our lives;
you know the things that spoil our lives
and the good things that mean so much to us.

Lord, thank you for the promise that, like fresh spring water,
you are wanting to make our lives new;
to change who and what we are
and, by the Holy Spirit, enable us to live the kind of lives
that bring you thanks and praise.

Lord, fill us with your love, guide us by your word
and live in us—that we may have life that is real. Amen.

168   NICODEMUS—THE MAN WITH MUCH TO LEARN

Lord, the story of Nicodemus is so amazing.
He was a very religious person;
he certainly believed in God, he said his prayers and read his
    Bible.
But he still had so much to learn about what it means
to become one of your children and part of your family.
He was so shocked when Jesus told him that

if he wanted to become a child of God
then his life needed to be changed so completely
and in such a dramatic way
that being 'born again' was the only way it could be
    described.

Lord, it isn't just Nicodemus who has much to learn!
We want you to show us
not only how much you love each and every one of us
but also just how much you want to change every part of our
    lives.

It is only when we allow you to make us new that we will
    really know,
as if for the very first time, what it means to call you 'our
    Father'.

Lord, touch our lives and make us new;
touch our hearts and make us your own;
touch our voices that we may give you
the thanks and praise that you deserve. Amen.

169   A CHILD'S CONFESSION

Lord, we are sorry for the wrong choices we make;
we are sorry that we are greedy and selfish;
we are sorry that we don't play fair and we cheat;
we are sorry that we like to get our own way.
Forgive us, and help us to make a new start.
We ask this in Jesus' name. Amen.

170   LORD, WE NEED YOUR LIGHT

Lord, we confess that we need your light
to heal our brokenness; to restore our relationships;
to show us the way; to cleanse and renew us;
to enable us to offer forgiveness to those who have hurt us
    most,
and to receive the forgiveness that you give
to those who come confessing their need of your light.

Lord, we confess our need of your light,
trusting that you will light up our lives with your grace.
    Amen.

171   ELIJAH—THE MAN WHO STOOD FIRM

Lord, we want to praise you for all those
who have faced great opposition but stood firm for you;
for those who felt rejected and unwanted but were faithful to
    you.

We want to thank you for the stories about Elijah
and the way he was ready to challenge anyone and everyone
because of his faith in you.

We praise you for his willingness to stand out from the
    crowd;
to be unpopular and to be ready for people to laugh at him
because he trusted in you.

We thank you for his example of what it means to put you
    first
every day, in everything and in every way.

Lord, we praise you because you are so great, so loving
and so worthy of all that we can say and do in your name.
Help us never to be happy just to sing your praise each
    Sunday
or to say a prayer when we are afraid.
Like Elijah, help us to allow nothing and no one
to prevent us living each day for the praise of your name.

We ask this, for Jesus' sake. Amen.

172   ELIJAH—THE MAN WHO WAS READY TO STAND
OUT!

Lord, we thank you for those people who are willing to stand
    out;
to be different; to be faithful—no matter the cost.

We thank you for those who, like Elijah,
are determined to be obedient to you
as they stand firm against all the wrong things
that are being said and done;

for those who refuse to be silent
but speak up for the poor and for those with no voice;

for those who will not close their eyes to the way we are
    living
and the damage it is causing your good earth;

for those who will not shut their ears to the refugees' daily
    cry of despair
but seek to open our minds to the pain and the suffering of
    those with no home.

Lord, we thank you for all who speak the truth
openly and honestly in the power of your name.
We pray: may what they say and do, and how we respond,
bring hope and peace to your world. Amen.

173   MOSES AND ME

I've been thinking, Lord, about Moses and me.
Like me, you gave him life and people who cared about him.
Though he lived in a palace and had more good things
than he really deserved—
he never forgot his people and their needs.

I've been thinking, Lord, about Moses and me.
Like me he could be strong; he could also be weak;
he did some good things and things he knew were wrong.
But he always trusted your love for him.

I've been thinking, Lord, about Moses and me.
Like Moses, each day you are calling me
to trust you, to serve you, to praise you
and to do what you want me to do with my life.

Lord, I want to praise you for all the love and care that I
    receive each day.
I want to thank you that you love me when I'm good and
    when I'm not.

I want to say yes when you ask me to give, to love and to
    share.
Walk with me, Lord, so that I can hold your hand
and follow the path through life you have chosen for me.
    Amen.

174   THE STORY OF TWO BROTHERS

Lord, we have mixed feelings about the story that Jesus told
    of two brothers.
The older one was a model son; he stayed at home;
he did good things; he never did anything wrong;
he did whatever his father wanted and he always worked
    hard.

But his younger brother was quite different.
He was a real disappointment to his father; was he always
    into mischief?
He was selfish and greedy; he wanted his own way;
you couldn't trust a word he said.
And when he left home everyone breathed a sigh of relief –
everyone except his father.

Day after day, Lord, he would just stand there—looking for
    his son;
waiting for him to come home;
longing to reach out with arms of forgiveness and love.

Lord, we praise you that the welcome the father gave
and the love he offered when the son finally returned home
is a picture of the welcome and the love you have for each
    and every one of us.
No matter who we are or what we have done, or failed to do,
you still long for us to come home.

But we still have mixed feelings, Lord, for we know the story
     is really about
the attitude of the elder brother.
We know it is a picture of our hard-heartedness
and our belief that our supposed good lives and our service
will win your love and guarantee our place in the kingdom
     of God.

Lord, we realise that neither of the brothers
had really understood their father's love
and had never entered into the joy of being his son.

We thank you for Christ's story that reveals your total
     understanding
of who we are and what we are capable of.
We praise you for its demonstration that by grace alone
can we know what it means to call you our Father.

Lord, touch us by your grace and fill us with your Holy
     Spirit
that we may be children of our Father in heaven.

We ask this in the name of Christ, your only Son. Amen.

175   THE ELDER BROTHER

Lord, he is the one we always forget;
he appears only at the end of the story of his prodigal
     brother.

He felt it was unfair—he had always tried to please his
     father;
he had never caused the family any bother
and he had always done what his father wanted.

But when his useless brother came home after wasting the
     family fortune
he got the biggest party the family had ever seen.

It was so unfair!

Lord, the elder brother was right, it was unfair—
but then, your love is not about being fair.

We thank you that you love us, though we don't deserve it,
and you offer us a place in your family, though we can never
    be worthy of it.

You want us to understand that just being good, kind and
    believing in you
will never make us into your children.
Now we know that this can only happen by grace alone.
It is through your extravagant love that we become children
    of God.
So touch us with your love and change us by your grace
that as members of your family we may give you thanks and
    praise.

In the name of Jesus, our brother, we ask our prayer. Amen.

176   THE PRODIGAL COMES HOME

Lord, we know the story of the prodigal son,
the young man who made a mess of his life.
He thought of nothing and no one except himself and what
    he wanted.
He was greedy, selfish and rude and he didn't seem to care
who got hurt by his selfishness
or what it cost to clear up the damage his greed had caused.

If he were alive today we would have called him a vandal,
he would have been in trouble with the police and have been
    put on an ASBO.

Yet we thank you, Lord, that this story has a great ending
for the awful young man.
He allowed God to change his heart and to transform his
    attitude
to himself, to other people and to what really matters in life.

We thank you for the story of his welcome home by his
father
and for the way it reminds us that each of us can know you
as father.

We praise you that no matter what we have done or failed to
do
and no matter how far we have wandered away from you—
your incredible love reaches out, and changes the way we
live.
You draw us to yourself and, even though we don't deserve it,
you welcome us home, and you do it for the sake of your
Son,
in whose name we ask our prayer. Amen.

177 JEREMIAH—THE YOUNG MAN WHO MADE EXCUSES

Lord, we praise you that you call all kinds of people to serve
you;
that you can use everyone to do your will
and that there is not one person whom you cannot use
in your great plan to change our lives, our world and
everything in it.

But we were surprised when we discovered
that you had actually chosen Jeremiah!
From what we know of him he had nothing going for him,
nothing that made him stand out from the crowd.

He was just an ordinary person—just a young man
who hardly ever had fun, who never smiled,
was full of excuses and always expected things to go wrong.

He didn't seem to have any special skills;
there was nothing that he was particularly good at,
nothing that made him an obvious candidate
for the most important job in the world.

So why, Lord, did you call Jeremiah to be the one to take
your message

of warning and of hope to the people you loved so much?
Was it because in the end you knew he was ready to trust
    you
and he was willing to say yes?

Lord, we praise you that in the story of Jeremiah
you are calling each one of us
to serve you in ways we never thought possible
and to do those things that will bring you glory.

Lord, we know now that, like Jeremiah, you know us
    completely.
Not one corner of our lives is hidden from you.
Thank you, Lord, that you will ignore all our excuses
and go right on calling us until we say yes.
We ask our prayer in the name of Jesus, who always said yes
    to you. Amen.

178   ISAIAH'S BIG DAY

Isaiah 6:1-8

Lord, you gave me such a surprise!
It was that day when you spoke to me in your temple.
I had been there many, many times before
but I had never, ever heard your voice as I did that day.

I have offered you prayers of thanks and sung songs of praise
but I had never even stopped to think
that you might have been there—listening and enjoying it
    all!

I had read your word
and listened to those who seemed to know what it meant.
But I never knew you wanted me to listen to you
and that through your word you were wanting to speak to
    me.

But now, Lord, everything has changed—
all because of that day in your house.

It was then that I did hear you speak—
and I knew that you were speaking to me.
Now I hear you speaking everywhere and through everyone.
I hear your voice in the most surprising places
and the most unexpected people.
You speak to me through those who know you and through
    those who don't;
through those I like and through those I don't!

Now that I know you are always wanting to speak to me
it makes each day a day of discovery,
and coming to worship is something I really, really look
    forward to—
just because I am meeting with you.

Lord, I want to praise you for opening my mind, my ears
    and my eyes,
to hear and to know you, here and everywhere.
I want to thank you for showing me that you do speak—
but that I will hear your voice only when you know that I
    am ready to say,
'Yes, here I am, send me.' Amen.

179   PETER—THE MAN WHO WAS CHANGED

Lord, how did it happen?
How did Peter become the one who was your spokesperson?
If we remember correctly,
he was for ever saying the wrong thing and letting you down.
He even denied that he ever knew you,
which must have really upset you.
We would never have forgiven him—
but you simply welcomed him back as your friend and
    disciple
and even gave him the important job of feeding your
    sheep—
caring for those who put their trust in you.

Lord, didn't Peter run away?

We know he ran to the tomb on Easter day
but it wasn't Peter who found faith at that moment;
it was John who believed what he saw in the tomb.

But, come the day of Pentecost, everything and everyone was
    changed.
When the Holy Spirit came he overwhelmed them all—
    including Peter.
That's why he could stand up in front of them all
and tell all the people the truth,
that the Jesus who had died on the cross was alive again
and through the Holy Spirit helps us all to speak of him
and to live for him every day. Amen.

180   NOAH—THE MAN PEOPLE LAUGHED AT

Lord, we want to praise you for Noah and for the way that
    he listened to you;
for the way he did what you wanted even when others
    laughed at his plans.

Lord, we want to thank you for Noah, and that he never
    gave up
but trusted you even when it was very hard;
for the way he was willing to obey you when he had only
    your word to trust:

Lord, we want to praise you that you still want to speak to us
    today,
and we thank you that we can trust you completely
no matter what other people may say.

Lord, we thank you for Noah, whose trust in your word was
    rewarded
by your love that was with him each day.
Like Noah we offer you our worship
and we bring our songs of thanks and praise. Amen.

181 SAMUEL—THE BOY WHO LISTENED

Lord, we thank you for the story of Samuel
and how he listened to your voice;
he believed that you were there
and he trusted that you would never leave him.

Lord, we praise you for showing us that though, like Samuel,
we may not be big and strong,
you still want to share our lives and to live in our hearts.

Lord, we thank you for the story of Samuel
and how he did what you told him to do;
that, though you are so very great and a really wonderful God,
you have a place for everyone
in your amazing plan to show your love to all the world.

Lord, we praise you that you still speak today—
if not always in the same way that you spoke to Samuel.
You make your presence felt in our hearts and in our lives.

Lord, we thank you that you speak to us
through the things we see and through the things we hear;
through people we love and through those we trust.

Lord, we praise you for the way you make us uncomfortable
when we say or do the wrong thing;
and you fill us with a sense of fulfilment
when we sing your praise and read your word.

Lord, we thank you for Jesus
through whom you speak loud and clear.
Speak Lord, we really want to know what you want us to do
and how you want us to live.
And speak to us through Jesus,
for his is the name we use when we speak to you. Amen.

182 KING SAUL—THE MAN WHO LET YOU DOWN

Lord, Saul must have been a special person,
someone who had once been open to you

and known what it meant to walk in your love.
He was a big, strong man and everyone looked up to him.
You gave him a very important job when you made him king
　　of Israel.

Lord, Saul must have been a very disappointed man
when everything went wrong and he let you down.
He spent so much time being king for you
he forgot to make time just to kneel before you
and to make sure that you still got all the praise and the
　　glory.

Lord, it is very easy for any of us to let you down
and by being greedy, jealous and angry
to spoil all the plans you have for us.
Forgive us when, as with Saul,
pleasing ourselves becomes more important than pleasing
　　you.

Lord, we are sorry for being selfish and mean.
Fill us with your love and help us to start all over again
so that how we live each day might be pleasing to you.
　　Amen.

183　EZEKIEL—THE MAN WHO OFFERED HOPE

Lord, your people must have been very down.
They had been taken away from their homes
and from the country where they were born.
Their enemies made them their slaves
and life must have come very hard.

Not only were they far from home but they felt all alone
and it must have seemed to them that you were no longer
　　with them.
They felt so bad they couldn't sing and they couldn't pray.

They felt so absolutely hopeless that your prophet, Ezekiel,
said they were about as hopeless and useless as a pile of
　　dried-out bones!

But Ezekiel did something really amazing—he gave them
hope.
They actually began to realise that you were still with them
and that they were not really alone after all.

He helped them to see that no situation is completely
hopeless
and no one is ever really beyond your love.
Ezekiel was saying that if God could give new life to a pile of
dried-out bones
doing something special for his people would be no problem
at all!

Lord, help us to know you are with us
both when things work out just as we planned
and when everything seems to be going wrong.
Help us to know you love us even on the darkest day
and to trust you whether or not the sun is shining on our
lives.

Lord, help us to love you, just as Ezekiel did,
that we might bring hope to the hopeless,
your love to those who feel lost and alone,
and to do it all in the name of Jesus,
the only source of hope and the way home to you. Amen.

184   NEHEMIAH—THE MAN WITH A VISION

Lord, Nehemiah was a man with a mission
because you had first made him a man with a vision.
You showed him the problems that your people in Jerusalem
were facing,
the city in ruins and under attack from all sides.
Nehemiah was a man with a mission;
a task had been given that only he could do.

Lord, we thank you for those who allow nothing and no one
to ever get in the way of working for you
in the way that you wanted and called them to do;

for those who work in hospitals and health centres
and know they have been given a mission of healing;

for those who work in schools or in colleges,
who have received the task of sharing their learning,
whose mission is daily to equip us for life;

for those who work out their service in the police force,
as prison officers or in the courts,
whose task is upholding the law and keeping us safe;

for those who work for the community as social workers,
    care workers,
or collecting our rubbish and keeping our streets clean;
whose mission is the health of our lives;

for those who are parents, or family and friends,
who have a mission of love and forgiveness each day to fulfil.

Lord, we thank you that you have something you have
    planned for us to do.
Help us, like Nehemiah, never to give up or give in
but, each day we are given, to fulfil the task you have placed
    in our hands. Amen.

185   GIDEON—AND HIS AMAZING DISCOVERY

Lord, you are amazing!
Every time we think we know who you are
and we think we know what you can do
again and again you do the most amazing things.

Lord, Gideon discovered just how amazing you are.
He wasn't very brave; he wasn't very strong;
he wasn't very important and he didn't think you could use
    him.
But you amazed him by what you did.

Lord, we want to praise you for being the really amazing
    God that you are;
that you are bigger than the greatest thing we can think of

and more wonderful than anything we have ever seen.
We praise you that, as with Gideon, you can and will use us
in ways that will take our breath away.
We bring our prayers in the name of Jesus, the most amazing
   gift of all. Amen.

186   HEROES OF FAITH

Lord, did we hear you correctly?
For a moment we thought you were wanting us to be heroes
   of faith.
But they were people who were special and lived a long time
   ago;
they were empowered by the Holy Spirit
for the challenging tasks you had given them to do.

We remember their names on the roll call
of those who have done great things and brought glory to
   your name.
We rejoice when we hear of Abraham and Moses,
of Joshua and King David, of Peter and Paul
and of all those whose names the Bible records as heroes of
   faith
in the service of their Lord.

We thank you for your heroes in later history, who
   transformed your world:
those like Luther and Wilberforce, Pankhurst and Fry;
and in our own day Mother Teresa and Nelson Mandela.

Lord, we know that you can't really mean it—
but it seems that you are calling ordinary people like us
to be your heroes of faith for the people we meet.

But perhaps, just perhaps, the heroes of the past were
   ordinary like us
and they simply allowed you to do extraordinary things.

Lord, by your grace and through the power of your Spirit
open our eyes—to see your glory;

open our minds—to discover your truth;
open our hearts—to receive your Spirit
that you may do something unexpected even through us.

187   THE MAN WITH A DONKEY

Lord, we don't know who he was or what he did,
we don't even know what his name was—
he was just the man with a donkey.

We don't know if he was rich or if he was poor;
we don't know if he was old of if he was young;
all we know is that he was the man with a donkey.

We don't know how well he knew Jesus, or if he knew him
    at all.
We don't know if the request for his donkey came as a big
    surprise
or if it had all been planned from the first.
But we do know—he was the man with a donkey.

We thank you, Lord, for the man with a donkey
and that he lent it to Jesus on that Palm Sunday.

We thank you more that, whoever we are and whatever we
    have,
you can still use us like the man with a donkey
in ways we never dreamt of and for things that seem
    impossible.

What we have and what we are may not seem so much,
and others may think we are foolish
for even daring to hope that we might be useful to you.
But thank you, Lord, as with the man with a donkey
you have a purpose for us
and what we have now will be useful to you. Amen.

188   JOSHUA WHO STOOD FIRM

Lord, we want to thank you for the stories of Joshua.
He was a person with limitations just like us.

He didn't always find it easy to do what he knew was right
or to do what you wanted him to do.

Lord, we thank you that Joshua listened to your word
and was ready to trust you even when it was very hard.
You gave him the courage he needed to win the battle
against the temptation to give up and give in,
and to serve you no matter what others said or did.

Lord, help us to be like Joshua,
that we might be able to stand firm; to stand out;
to stand for you. Amen.

189 JONAH, THE MAN WHO RAN AWAY

Lord, sometimes we feel sorry for Jonah.
He was just an ordinary little person
that you called to do something very special for you.

What we don't understand is why you called him
to do what he didn't want to do.
You knew he was all mixed up inside
and that he was full of wrong ideas and bad thoughts.

Lord, we praise you that your love is so very strong
that you call us to help and to care even for those we don't
    like
and you expect us to forgive even those who are very unkind.

We thank you that, as with Jonah, you are always wanting to
    help us
to see everything and everyone as you see them.
Help us to allow you to change the way we think;
to fill our lives with your love
and to offer kindness and friendship to those who are
    lonely
and to those who feel they are not wanted,
and to do it in Jesus' name. Amen.

Lord, we do not find it easy to say what we want to say.
We do not find it easy when we know everyone will be
    listening.
We do not find it easy to talk to you and tell you just how
    we feel.

Lord, we thank you for David
and for the amazing way he wrote such wonderful praise
    songs to you.
He wrote down the songs that we know as his psalms,
and we can use them ourselves
to offer our thanks and our praises to you.

Lord, we know that David sometimes made a mess of his life
and that again and again he needed your forgiveness
so that he could make a new start.
Your love for him means we too can know
that even when we say and do wrong things
when we say we are sorry—and mean it
you are not only ready to forgive us
but to help us to begin all over again
and to use us in the most amazing ways.

Lord, we thank you for David
and for the songs we can use to praise your name. Amen.

191   DANIEL WHO WAS BRAVE

Lord, we like Daniel because he always did what was right.
Daniel was special because he put you first in everything
and trusted you completely.

Lord, we like Daniel because he was so brave,
so strong and so full of love for you.

Lord, we like Daniel because he told others about you
and helped them to know what a wonderful God you are.
He wanted everyone he met to trust you

and showed them all what it means to love you completely.

Lord, we like Daniel; help us to be like him. Amen.

192   BLIND BARTIMAEUS

Lord, sometimes everything seems to go wrong:
we think we have some really big problems and we don't
    know what to do.

Lord, sometimes we feel afraid, and there is no one to help
    us.
We have so many questions and we can't find the answers.

Lord, Bartimaeus was blind, and that made life very hard for
    him.
He must have had lots of questions,
but when he called out to Jesus he found someone
to help, to listen, to heal and to answer his deepest questions.

Lord, though we can't see you, we know that you are always
    with us.
Though we can't touch you, we know you are always ready
to answer our questions and to help us—
when, like Bartimaeus, we call out to you. Amen.

193   BARNABAS—THE MAN WHO ENCOURAGED

He wasn't a great speaker and he wasn't much of a teacher;
he didn't like to be noticed and worked out of sight;
but Barnabas was the man who lived up to his name.

Barnabas's name meant he was the one
who gave encouragement to others
to use the gifts they had been given
and to serve God in the way that he wanted.

Because of Barnabas
Paul set out on his journeys to tell others of the love of Jesus.

Because of Barnabas
thousands and thousands of people put their faith in Jesus.

Because of Barnabas
good news was declared and hundreds of lives were changed.

Because of Barnabas
the soldiers who were guarding Paul in prison heard the story
    of God's love for them.

Because of Barnabas
kings and queens learned more and more of the place they
    had in the plans of God.

Because of Barnabas
an emperor's life was changed as he put his trust in Jesus—
    and so did his people.

Lord, thank you for Barnabas
and for those who have been like Barnabas for us;
for aunts and uncles,
for teachers at church and teachers at school;
for those who told us the story of Jesus
and encouraged us to put our faith in him.

Thank you, Lord, for the encouragement we receive
and help us to be like Barnabas for someone today. Amen.

194   JAIRUS—THE MAN WHO TURNED TO JESUS

He was surely one of your most unlikely followers, Lord.
Jairus was a man with a position in the synagogue—
he was the man in charge;
he was the one who gave the orders;
he was the one everyone looked up to;
he was the one who had everything under control.

Except that day when Jesus came into town—
it was also the day when Jairus's daughter was taken seriously
    ill.
There was nothing he could do; no one who could help him;
everyone was saying that she was beyond help.

But he was her father; she was very precious
and he wasn't for giving up or for giving in.
Did someone say that Jesus was in town?

We praise you, Lord, for Jairus, the man who turned to
  Jesus.
This great man of the synagogue had found one who was
  greater;
this important person in his community
was led to put his trust in the presence and power of a
  stranger.

Lord, we thank you that whenever, like Jairus, we turn to
  you
in simple trust and faith no bigger than a mustard seed,
literally anything can happen—and it did!

We praise you, Lord, that you bring hope to the hopeless;
forgiveness to the sinful; peace to those who are all mixed
  up;
strength to those who are weak; courage to those who are
  afraid;
faith to those who seek your face.

Lord, touch our lives and renew us completely,
that being made whole we may offer you
the worship you truly deserve—as we do it in Jesus' name.
  Amen.

195   THE BOY WITH THE LOAVES AND FISHES

He was just a boy with some loaves and fishes.
He had probably come with his friends and family.
He had heard so much about Jesus
and he wanted to hear just one of his stories.
It had been a perfect day as they sat on the grass
and enjoyed simply being with him.

Kindness and joy were written all over Jesus' face;
what he said and what he did made God's presence so real.

You felt you could reach out and put your hand into God's,
knowing for certain his love had found you.

He was just a boy with some loaves and fishes.
To go on a picnic was nothing new
except that that day was different—he would never forget
how Jesus had fed the five thousand with his loaves of bread.

Lord, we praise you for the story of the boy with some loaves
    and some fishes.
Now we know that whatever we have we can place into your
    hands
and watch you work another miracle
to bring hope, joy and peace to your broken world.

Lord, whatever we have is what you have given
and what you have given is not ours to keep.
But once we place ourselves and our gifts into your hands,
it is then that you can work your miracle of hope, joy and
    healing. Amen.

196 GOD'S LOVE

John 3:16

Lord, you said God loves everyone:
there is not one person in the whole wide world that he
    doesn't love.

We suppose that means that you love even us;
that you love us when we are good and when we are not;
that you love us when we are happy and when we are sad;
that you love us when we are kind and when we hurt others;
that you love us when we forgive others and when we don't.

But Lord, we know that your love means
that you love those we find hardest to like
and those who are unkind to us and have hurt us the most.

Lord, you have promised that when we put our trust in Jesus
there will never ever be an end to your love for all eternity.
Amen.

197   PAUL—THE MAN GOD CHANGED

Lord, you really are amazing!
It doesn't seem to matter who we are or what we have done,
you still want us to know not only that your love is for us
but that you have a plan for our lives.

Lord, you really are wonderful!
It doesn't seem to be important to you
whether we work with our hands or with our minds—
you still want to live in our hearts and work through our lives.

Lord, you are utterly incredible.
It seems that you have room in your love and in your
        kingdom
for those who have done good things
and those whose words and deeds have hurt everything and
        everyone.

Lord, Saul was a very religious person.
He did everything by the book
and he thought he was pleasing you when he put Christians
        in prison.
But you met him on the road to Damascus
and he was never the same person again.

Lord, we praise you for the way you changed
Saul the man of bitterness into Paul the man of hope.
We thank you for the story of Paul
and for the promise that there is no hopeless person
and no hopeless situation that you cannot change.

Lord, we ask you to touch our hearts and lives,
and by your Holy Spirit help us to serve you
in ways that bring hope to others and praise to your name.
        Amen.

198 PAUL—THE MAN WHO USED HIS HEAD

We have heard many stories, Lord,
of those you have called to serve you.
You never seemed to mind that they were not always very
    clever
and sometimes not very good.
It didn't put you off when, like Abraham, they told lies,
or even, like Moses, when they killed someone.
You didn't take any notice when, like Jeremiah, they made
    excuses
or, like Jonah, they tried to run away.

It seems that you always have time and space
in your love and in your kingdom.
You open your arms to those whom everyone else rejects
and you give your promises to those who have wandered far
    from you.

But Paul was a very clever man, ready to use his mind in
    your service.
Thank you, Lord, for Paul and the way he reminds us
that you expect us to use our minds when we have given our
    hearts to you.
Paul shows us that following Jesus means we are to use
the gifts and skills you have given to us.

Like Paul, you have given us your special gift
that means we can think, learn and discover
more and more of what it really means to put our trust in
    you.
Help us to use our minds and to follow Jesus wherever he
    leads. Amen.

199 TIMOTHY—THE TIMID DISCIPLE

Lord, we thank you for inviting us
to join in the great adventure that began with Jesus.
We know you have something really important that you have
    planned for us to do.

But if we are honest—we are a bit worried that we won't be
    able to do it;
that we'll let you down and that people will laugh at us.

Lord, we want to praise you for Timothy
and all that he did in the name of Jesus.
In many ways he was just an ordinary young man
who by your power within him was able to do extraordinary
    things.

We know, Lord, that he could have made lots of excuses to
    get out of serving you.
He could have said that he was too young,
that he wasn't very well or that he didn't know enough.
But you told Timothy, your timid disciple, to trust you
    completely.

Lord, help us to learn from Timothy
and though we may think we are not very clever,
not very strong, not very faithful and not very good disciples,
you can use each one of us in ways we never thought
    possible.

Lord, we praise you that you have all the power we need
to enable timid disciples to be strong and bold for Jesus.
    Amen.

200   PHILIP—GOD'S WILLING WORKER

Lord, Philip had a really exciting life.
He was never bored, because he was following Jesus.
Every day was different—he never knew what was going to
    happen
or where you would send him.
One day he was in the midst of a crowd in a busy, noisy city
    in Samaria,
then the next he was heading off down a dusty, desert road.
Philip wanted to put you first in all things,
all the time, every day and everywhere.

Lord, we praise you for people like Philip
who make God real for us
and show us how exciting everything can be when we follow
    Jesus.

We thank you for those who love you so much
that they want everyone, everywhere to know your love for
    them.

Lord, may what we say and how we say it;
may how we live and the way we show it;
help someone else to know that Jesus is Lord. Amen.

201   A PRAYER FOR ADVENT

Lord, we've been meaning to say
something of how hard we are finding it
to trust you, to pray, to walk the path of discipleship.

Lord, we've been meaning to say
that so often we feel we are walking alone,
that no one else sees things the way we do.
We know deep inside that we have so much to share,
so much good news to give
but it appears that no one wants to listen any more.

Lord, we've been meaning to say
how disillusioned we are becoming;
we feel a dryness within that we have never experienced
    before
and each day we are finding it harder
to find a way out of our prison of emptiness.

Lord, we've been meaning to say
that we always thought we could rely on you—
to make sure that nothing really awful ever happened to us;
that nothing would challenge our faith
or make the way you are leading us seem so dark and
    uncertain.

Lord, we've been meaning to say
that our world has changed.
The picture we once held in our minds of you and your
     power and your love
has been torn from our grasp.
It seems that the time has come when we are having to learn
     all over again
to walk by faith and not by sight;
to trust you, even when the darkness is deepest;
to believe that you will keep your promise—
to be there for us in ways too deep for words.

Lord, we've been meaning to say
though we have treated this world as if it were our own,
in this Advent moment, we are preparing to watch you step
into a world which is yours and which your love has created,
though we have treated it as if it were our own.
Once more, you will remind us that you are
the Alpha and the Omega, the Beginning and the End.
You who had the first word will most certainly have the last.
This is your promise and this is our hope.
By the Holy Spirit—hold our hand, guide us through the
     darkness
to your glorious, overwhelming light
and into the peace that only you can give. In Christ's name.
     Amen.

202   OUR SPECIAL FRIEND

Lord, you are so amazing!
When we are lonely you promise to be with us.
When we are difficult you are patient with us.
When we are hurting inside because of what other people say
     or do,
you are gentle with us.
When we feel like jumping for joy, or want to hide ourselves
     away in a corner;
when we feel sad or afraid or full of excitement;

you share everything with us.
Lord, you are our special friend who never lets us down,
but guides us the way you want us to live.
Help us to give you the thanks and praise that you really
    deserve.
We are sorry for the times we have let you down,
for the ways we have hurt each other
and for the chances we have missed to show your love and
    care.
Forgive us and, by your Holy Spirit, help us to know the joy
    of beginning again.
We ask this in the name of Jesus, our friend and Lord.
    Amen.

203   LORD, SO GREAT

Lord, so great, you made the world.
Lord, so big, you hold it day by day.
Lord, so good, you gave us life.
Lord, so loving, you gave us Jesus.
Lord, so forgiving, you help us to start again.
Lord, so great, you help scientists to make discoveries that
    will change our lives,
Lord, so big, you call us to care for your world.
Lord, so good, you teach us to care for each other.
Lord, so loving, help us to show the love of Jesus each day.
Lord, so forgiving, help us to forgive each other,
knowing that we have been forgiven. Amen.

204   TELLING OTHERS

Father, we praise you because you are so very wonderful
and we thank you because you are so very loving.
We praise you that you have given us so many people
who love and care for us each day,
and we thank you for our family who love us
and for our friends who make life so special for us.
We praise you that you have filled the world

with so many good and exciting things to see and to
    discover,
and we thank you for happy memories to enjoy and new
    challenges to face.
We praise you for the world in which you have placed us
and we thank you for the lives we can live.
We thank you for the things we can learn and the skills we
    can develop;
for time to work and opportunities to rest.
We thank you for those who share our tears and for those
    who make us laugh;
for those who provide our food and for those who keep us
    safe;
for those who love us even when we are not very nice to
    know
and for those who stand by us
and try to understand the things that hurt us and make us
    afraid.

We thank you for Jesus who has shown us
that we can trust him with everything and in every way.
No matter what we are facing, no matter what is happening,
no matter who we are or what we have done or what we have
    failed to do,
we can trust him completely.
Forgive us that so often we say we will trust him
when we would rather trust ourselves;
that we allow him only into part of our lives and never into
    the whole;
that though we say we believe in you
we do not allow you to change how we live;
that we say that we trust you but sometimes we are too afraid
    to begin again.

Forgive us and make our lives new
and help us to live lives that make you happy and bring
    praise to your name.
We ask this for Jesus' sake. Amen.

For centuries and for decades; for days and for hours;
and for every minute and each second that comes from your
hand;
we praise your name,
and we thank you, Lord.

For elephants, lions and tigers; for kangaroos, ostriches and
zebras;
for dogs and cats, and rabbits and gerbils; for every creature
large and small;
we praise your name,
and we thank you, Lord.

For tulips and daffodils; for chrysanthemums and roses;
for dandelions, buttercups and daisies; for every flower that
adds colour to your world;
we praise your name,
and we thank you, Lord.

For beech and for elm; for oak and for sycamore; for pine, fir
and birch;
for the trees of the forest that come in all shapes and sizes;
we praise your name,
and we thank you, Lord.

For grasshoppers and beetles; for bees and for caterpillars;
for butterflies, dragonflies and moths; for tiny things that fly
or crawl;
we praise your name,
and we thank you, Lord.

For ducks and for penguins; for sparrows and for chaffinches;
for eagles, herons and budgerigars;
for the songs they sing and the way they fly;
we praise your name,
and we thank you, Lord.

For Cornflakes and Rice Krispies; for biscuits and cakes;
for breakfast, lunch and our evening meal;
for all the food we eat and for the strength it gives to us;
we praise your name,
and we thank you, Lord.

For mothers and fathers; for brothers and sisters;
for aunties and uncles, and for relatives and friends;
for all the people we meet each day at home, at school, at
    work or at play;
we praise your name,
and we thank you, Lord.

For your love that gave us life; for your love in Jesus that
    gives us new life;
for your love that holds us and guards us each day;
for your love to us as Father, Son and Holy Spirit;
we praise your name,
and we thank you, Lord.

In Jesus' name. Amen.

206   ADVENT

(Each of the headings can be displayed if desired.)

Advent

We pray for those who are Angry, and for those who are
    Alone,
for those who have been Abused by others,
and for those who Ache to be Accepted.
May the coming of Jesus fill them with hope.

aDvent

We pray for those who feel Defeated by all that they face
    each day,
for those who are sick or Dying, and for those who are filled
    with Despair.
May the coming of Jesus fill them with hope.

adVent

We pray for those with a Vision for peace,
and for those who are the Voice of the poor;
for those who teach us to Value each other,
and for those who work with the Vulnerable, the homeless
    and the lost.
May the coming of Jesus fill them with hope.

advEnt

We pray for planet Earth and for those who Encourage us to
    care for it;
for those seeking to Escape the fighting in [*country*]
and for those working to provide Essential food and clothing
    for the world's refugees.
May the coming of Jesus fill them with hope.

adveNt

We pray for our Neighbours—
those who live next door, across the road, or across the
    world;
for those who are seeking to follow the Narrow way,
and for those who Name the name of Jesus
and bring good News of him to others.
May the coming of Jesus fill them with hope.

advenT

We pray for those whose lives have been changed by the
    work of Terrorists;
for those whose faith has been Tested by the things that have
    happened to them;
for those who Teach us about Jesus
and for those who should be the Target of our love.
May the coming of Jesus fill them with hope.

We ask our prayers in the name of Jesus,
the one who comes with hope. Amen.

Those who are hungry

We pray for [*Christian Aid*], [*Tear Fund*] and [*Save the
  Children*]

and all who break new ground

as they make us remember the hungry, the lonely and the
  poor.

Children

We pray for parents, teachers and youth leaders

for the leaders of [*Sunday Club*], [*Crusaders*] and [*the holiday
  club*]

and all who break new ground

as they seek to keep children safe and help them to grow and
  learn.

Doctors

We pray for doctors, scientists and research chemists

and all who break new ground

as they try to find new ways of healing people who are ill.

Peacemakers

We pray for politicians, soldiers, members of NATO and the
  United Nations

and all who break new ground

as they act as peacemakers in a world that has forgotten to
  live in peace.

Floods

We pray for those who break new ground as they risk their
  lives

seeking to rescue people from floods and from drought.

Environment

We pray for [*Friends of the Earth*] and [*Greenpeace*]

and all who break new ground

as they teach us how to care for your beautiful world.

Refugees
We pray for [*the Red Cross*] and [*Amnesty International*]
and all who break new ground
as they work for all true refugees and asylum-seekers longing
   to feel safe and secure.

Rescue services
We pray for firefighters, lifeboat men and deep sea divers
and all who break new ground
as they work in places of great danger.

Other people
We pray for anyone we know
who needs someone to break new ground
for anyone who is sad, angry, lonely or hurting; for ...

Ourselves
We pray for ourselves, that we might break new ground for
   you.
Help us to place our lives in your hands
and to be ready to be used by you anywhere, anytime and
   with anyone.

We ask our prayers in the name of Jesus Christ,
the one who always breaks new ground. Amen.

208   HARVEST THANKSGIVING

Father, we thank you for the world in which you have placed
   us
and for the way you have made us;
for the beautiful things we can see and hear;
and we also thank you that we have eyes to see and ears to
   hear
and that we can enjoy all the good things that you have
   given to us.
We praise you for mountains and for hills; for streams and
   for rivers;
for plants and for animals; for fruit and for flowers;

for the food we like to eat and the things which quench our
    thirst.
We thank you for the different harvests all around us—
for the harvest of the farm and the harvest of the sea;
for the harvest of the garden and the harvest from under the
    ground;
for the harvest of things that are made in huge factories
and for the harvest of power that we use in our homes;
for the harvest of things to learn; and the harvest of
    friendships to enjoy;
for those whose harvest of love and care fills us with
    thankfulness and praise.
We thank you for Jesus and the love that he has given to us
and for the way that he helps us to love one another;
for reminding us that everything we see and hear belongs to
    you
and is the harvest of your loving will.
We thank you for the harvest of worship and praise and
    thanksgiving
that brings you glory and honours your name.
We bring our prayer in the name of Jesus. Amen.

209   PASSION SUNDAY

Lord, we thank you for giving us eyes to see the world
    around us
and for making it a picture of your love and power;
We thank you that you have shown us that it all belongs to
    you;
for ears to hear the songs of birds
and the sounds of laughter, music and life each day.
We thank you that you have made us
so that we can enjoy the things we hear and the music of life;
that you have given us voices so that we can speak and sing;
that we can sing your praise and share your love;
that you have given us lives to live and things to learn;
that you can use us to show your love and care to those we meet

at home, at school, at work and in the world.
We praise you for sending Jesus
who came to show us what you are really like;
that through him we can know that you will love us for ever.
Forgive us that we will follow Jesus when things are easy,
but that we give up and give in
when following him makes too many demands upon us.
Forgive us that, like the crowds, we will follow Jesus on Palm
    Sunday
but we find it hard to follow him when he shows us the price
    of commitment.
Forgive us and change our lives with his love. We ask this in
    Jesus' name. Amen.

210   MOTHERING SUNDAY

Lord, we confess that we have treated
those whom we should have cared for most
with an unkindness we would not have shown to strangers.
The way we speak to each other,
and how we abuse our homes, does not honour you.
Our selfish attitudes and our self-centred behaviour
do not allow others to see Christ in us.
Lord, forgive us and, by your Holy Spirit,
so renew our relationship with you
that those around us and those within our homes
may experience your love in their lives.
In Christ's name we pray. Amen.

211   ALL-AGE CONFESSION

For the wrong things we have said and done;
we have come to say,
we are sorry, Lord.

For the times we have cheated and we have not played fair;
we have come to say,
we are sorry, Lord.

For the times we have been selfish and wanted our own
way;
we have come to say,
we are sorry, Lord.

For the times we have not told the truth, and got others into
trouble;
we have come to say,
we are sorry, Lord.

For the times when our behaviour has hurt you
as we have spoilt things for other people and for ourselves;
we have come to say,
we are sorry, Lord.

For the times we have forgotten to pray to you
and we have not made time to give you our worship;
we have come to say,
we are sorry, Lord.

Quietly, in our own hearts we will now tell God
the things for which we are sorry.

Silence

Jesus died on the cross for us,
and because we trust that you will forgive us
we have come to say,
we are sorry, Lord. Amen.

212   MISSION FOR ALL

(Suitable pictures may be displayed for each prayer.)

The world

Lord, we pray for your world.
When you made it, it was good, beautiful and perfect.
We are sorry for the ways each day we spoil your world
by the things we say and do and choose.

We thank you for those who remind us to care for your world.
Lord, in your mercy,
hear our prayer.

Crowd of people

Lord, we pray for people, for those who feel lost and afraid,
for those who are lonely even in a crowd,
for those who have lost their way in life and do not know
how to find their way to hope, joy, peace and love.
May caring hands reach out to bring your good gifts to
people everywhere.
Lord, in your mercy,
hear our prayer.

On the street

Lord, we pray for those who are struggling,
for little children and young people who are forced to live on
the streets of big cities,
for those with nowhere to live, nowhere to go,
and who sit and beg for help from those who are rich.
May those who see the need open the eyes of those who can
give.
Lord, in your mercy,
hear our prayer.

The debt

Lord, we pray for the leaders of nations, for those with
power to change things
and for those who long to see good things happening,
for those who can make a real difference for the poor nations
of the world,
for those who can act and cancel the debts of hungry nations.
May those with the power hear the challenge,
and may your grace change the hearts of many people.
Lord, in your mercy,
hear our prayer.

Young people

Lord, we pray for young people everywhere;
for those who are at school, college or university,
those for whom life is challenging and exciting,
those who are showing how we can live with people
from different places and of different colours.
May the Holy Spirit help us to see each other
through eyes of love and not hate.
Lord, in your mercy,
hear our prayer.

Little boy with no future

Lord, we pray for those whose future seems bleak,
for those with no hope and little chance to learn new things
or to discover the wonder of your world,
for those who will always be poor, deprived of life's good
        things,
for those who haven't yet heard of the love of God in Jesus.
May what we give, the words we use and the things we do
bring new life and new hope to many people.
Lord, in your mercy,
hear our prayer.

Old and young

Lord, we pray for the young and the old,
for those who are at risk because of their age,
for those who feel left out, unwanted and unnecessary,
for those whose hopes and dreams are spoilt by the actions of
        others,
for those who long to be loved and to know that they matter.
May God's people, everywhere, reach out to all in the name
        of Jesus.
Lord, in your mercy,
hear our prayer.

Those we know

Lord, we pray for those we know to be in any kind of need,
for those who are lonely and alone, for those who feel old
and forgotten,
for those who are sad and uncertain,
for those who are ill, and those who care for them and love
them.
May we all take our share in showing the love of God
to those to whom he sends us each day.
Lord, in your mercy,
hear our prayer.

We ask our prayers in the name of Jesus,
the one who loves us and sends us to care. Amen.

213   HANDS OF PRAYER

*Cut out five large 'hands' with the words WORLD, CHURCH,
PEOPLE and OURSELVES, and one left blank. The younger
children can colour them in during the first part of the service.
They are then brought forward one by one and the following
prayers used as each is placed on the prayer board.*

The World

Lord, we pray for your world which you gave us to live in
and to care for.
We pray for the people of [*current area of need*] and for [*area
of conflict*]
that there will be peace, hope and forgiveness.
This is our prayer.
We put our prayers in the hands of Jesus.

Church

Lord, we pray for the church, for those who belong to your
family here
and all the other churches in this area.
We pray for their ministers and all their members.

We pray especially for [*local congregation*].
This is our prayer.
We put our prayers in the hands of Jesus.

People

Lord, we pray for people.
We pray for those who give a helping hand to others,
for those who reach out to touch those whose lives are in a
    mess,
to hold those who are sad or in pain.
We pray for young people going to college or university and
    for [*local young group*].
This is our prayer.
We put our prayers in the hands of Jesus.

Ourselves

Lord, we pray for ourselves, and all that we will be facing
    this week,
for all the things that are making us happy or sad, angry or
    full of joy.
We pray that we may know the peace and the hope
that comes from placing everything in our lives into your hands.
This is our prayer.
We put our prayers in the hands of Jesus.

[Blank]

In the quietness, we pray for anyone we know to be in need
of God's peace, joy, healing power and love.
This is our prayer.
We put our prayers in the hands of Jesus.

We ask all our prayers in the name of Jesus. Amen.

214   THANK YOU FOR THE WORLD

Lord, we thank you for our world
and we praise you for the gift of life
and for the things that make each day so special.

We thank you for the animals, the birds and the fish,
for flowers and trees, and for everything that makes your
world so special.

Lord, we praise you for mountains and hills, for rivers and
lakes,
for seas and for oceans,
and for all those things that make your world such a special
place.

Lord, we thank you for things to drink to quench our thirst
and for food to eat that helps us to grow
and gives us energy to serve.

Lord, we praise you for everyone with whom we share each day;
each of us—from the youngest to the oldest—is special to
you.

We thank you for music to play and songs to sing,
for holidays to enjoy and games to play with our friends,
for new things to learn and for discoveries to make
that make being alive in your world such a special gift of
your love.

Lord, we thank you for the empty cross where Jesus died for
us all,
so that each of us might experience you and your love for us
all,
for the empty tomb that tells us
that nothing can defeat you and your love—
a love which is always reaching out to make us your special
friends.

Lord, we thank you for the gift of life,
for the promise of new life and the assurance that
wherever we go in your world
we can know that you will be especially near to us
when we put our trust in Jesus.
Thank you for hearing our prayer. In Jesus' name. Amen.

A Litany of Praise

For our homes and our families
where we feel safe, loved and wanted
we praise you, Lord,
and we give you our thanks.

For our parents who love us and care for us
and through whom you gave us life
we praise you, Lord,
and we give you our thanks.

For those who comfort us when we are afraid
and hold us when we are sad
we praise you, Lord,
and we give you our thanks.

For those who are patient with us when we do wrong
and who care for us when we are ill
we praise you, Lord,
and we give you our thanks.

For those we can trust and we know really love us
and for those who teach us to put our trust in you
we praise you, Lord,
and we give you our thanks.

For aunts and uncles, for grandparents and cousins,
for all those who help us to know we belong
we praise you, Lord,
and we give you our thanks.

For whose who adopted or fostered us
and those who taught us to love and to give
we praise you, Lord,
and we give you our thanks.

On this Mothering Sunday
we thank the Lord for our place in his family

and that he died on the cross to show us his love.
we praise you, Lord,
and we give you our thanks.

In the name of Jesus,
our brother and our friend.
Amen.

216   BEGINNINGS

Lord, you were at the beginning of all things,
from you and by your sovereign power everything we see had
    its beginning.
For the beginning of all good things
we thank you, Lord.

Lord, you were there at our beginning.
You knew our names, even before we were born.
Every new step we take is already known to you.
For the beginning of all good things
we thank you, Lord.

Lord, you have watched us as we have grown.
From our first day until the end of our days
our whole lives are held in your hands.
For the beginning of all good things
we thank you, Lord.

Lord, every new skill we have learnt
and all the exciting discoveries we have made
were under your watchful eye.
Every good lesson we were taught was dug from the quarry
    of your truth.
For the beginning of all good things
we thank you, Lord.

Lord, you are at the start of every journey
and we find you waiting at our destination.

Your promise is to walk with us and to love us all our days.
For the beginning of all good things
we thank you, Lord.

Lord, we thank you for every new friend we make
and those whose love and care make each day special,
and for those who show us the way to become friends of Jesus.
For the beginning of all good things
we thank you, Lord.

Lord, we thank you for each new flower
that adds colour and beauty to your wonderful world.
We praise you for the sun and the rain that make things grow.
For the beginning of all good things
we thank you, Lord.

Lord, we thank you for every new song
that points our thoughts and our praises to Jesus,
and we thank you for each time we can meet together for
    worship.
For the beginning of all good things
we thank you, Lord. Amen.

217   CHILDREN'S LITANY OF PRAISE

We can dance and we can sing;
we give thanks to God,
and we give him praise.

We can laugh and we can cry;
we give thanks to God,
and we give him praise.

We can learn and we can play;
we give thanks to God,
and we give him praise.

We can run and we can rest;
we give thanks to God,
and we give him praise.

We can give and we can share;
we give thanks to God,
and we give him praise.

For the food we eat and the strength it gives;
we give thanks to God,
and we give him praise.

For games to play and friends to play with;
we give thanks to God,
and we give him praise.

For songs to sing and praise to give;
we give thanks to God,
and we give him praise.

For God's forgiveness even when we are wrong;
that he loves us and helps us begin again;
we give thanks to God,
and we give him praise.

In Jesus' name. Amen.

218   IT'S WINTER

Lord, it's winter again, and everywhere is cold and still.
When I look out of the window I see the frost and the snow:
everywhere sparkles like diamonds on the grass and the trees.
I can wear my warm coat, my gloves and my hat, and feel
      quite snug,
though my face tingles and my breath looks like fog!
I put out the bread crumbs to make sure the birds have been
      fed.
When I run and jump I can see just where my feet have
      been.
Then it's time to go home where a hot drink is waiting, and
      it's safe and warm.
It's good we have winter so everywhere can rest and get ready
      for springtime.

Lord, you have shown us in Jesus that your love is always
warm
and wherever we go we can be sure you are there. Amen.

219   SPRING IS HERE

Lord, winter has gone, and so has the snow;
each day is just a little warmer and everywhere is brighter.
Lord, when I look at the trees and the hedgerows, the
gardens and the fields,
it makes me think that you have been busy making them all
fresh and clean.
Every year it's the same: your world looks as if it has just
been made!
Spring is here, the lambs are jumping and dancing with joy,
and I feel I want to join in!
Lord, thank you for springtime—it's like a picture that says,
'Like my world, you can begin again.'
Lord, I can't do that on my own
so I'm trusting you to help me—just as you told me to. Amen.

220   SUMMERTIME

Will it always be like this?
Will I look back one day and remember only long, hot
summer days?
Lord, I want to say thank you for all the lovely flowers.
They look so proud as they hold their heads high.
It is as if they are saying,
'Look at me, smell my perfume and enjoy my wonderful
bright colours.'
Summer is the time to play outside with my friends,
to go to the seaside and have lots of fun.
Summer is the time for laughter, for holidays,
and for enjoying just being alive in your world.
Thank you for summertime.
Help me to fill it with wonderful memories
that I can enjoy for the rest of my life. Amen.

221   IT'S AUTUMN AGAIN

Autumn is a unique time of year.
It's neither hurried and hot like summer should be,
nor is it like winter, with its chills and its cold.
It's certainly not spring, for there's little new to be seen.
No, autumn is different—sort of stuck in between.
If the season were traffic lights,
then while winter means stop, and spring and summer say
     go,
autumn is a kind of get-ready—either to stop or to go.
The harvest is gathered, and all seems completed—
but there are the seeds of the new crop that will be sown
     come next spring.
No, autumn is different, and some like it best.
There are leaves on the ground that rustle and snap,
and when you walk through them they get stuck in your
     shoes.
Autumn seems gentle, like nature thinking aloud;
as if, Lord, you are saying, as you look back over the year,
'Well, that went well, just look what was achieved!'
So, Lord, thank you for autumn, its trees and its bright-
     tinted leaves.
No artist could create that—until you showed them how.
Thank you for time to reflect, and prepare. Amen.

222   THE DIFFERENCE

I am so small and you are so great.
Thank you, God.
Thank you, God.

I am so weak and you are so strong.
Thank you, God.
Thank you, God.

I can do so little and you can do everything.
Thank you, God.
Thank you, God.

I need others to help and you are the one who helps
    everybody.
Thank you, God.
Thank you, God.

I have a birthday each year to remember the day I was born,
but you are so great and so wonderful you have no beginning
and your love never ends.
Thank you, God.
Thank you, God.

I know so little about so many things
but you know everything that there is to know about all
    things!
Thank you, God.
Thank you, God.

I am so small that grownups don't see me
but you see everyone, everywhere and for ever.
Thank you, God.
Thank you, God.

Thank you, Lord, for being so different and for loving us all
    so much.
Thank you, God.
Thank you, God. Amen.

223 EDUCATION SUNDAY

We thank you for the world in which we live
which is full of so many good and exciting things
that we can learn and discover.
We thank you, Lord.
We thank you, Lord.

We thank you for our teachers at school
who help us to learn the things we need to know.
We thank you, Lord.
We thank you, Lord.

We thank you that Jesus was a teacher
to the disciples and to the crowds who listened to his stories.
We thank you, Lord.
We thank you, Lord.

We thank you for those who help us to learn about Jesus
and what it means to know him as Saviour and Lord.
We thank you, Lord.
We thank you, Lord.

We thank you for those who teach us to trust God
and show in their lives what it means to know Jesus.
We thank you, Lord.
We thank you, Lord.

Forgive us when we do not want to learn about you
and refuse to open our hearts and lives to your love.
We are sorry, Lord.
We are sorry, Lord.

Forgive us and teach us to be more forgiving and more
    loving.
We ask this in Jesus' name. Amen.

224   REMEMBRANCE SUNDAY

(Ask the congregation to suggest things to thank God for.)

Father, we thank you for everything that reminds us
of your love and goodness to us.
We thank you for the world in which we live,
which reminds us that you are the one who made us.
We thank you for the beauty of the world, which reminds us
    to praise you.

*(Either include a list of suggested things to thank God for, or use
    the following.)*

We thank you for the food we eat; for our family and
    friends;
for games to play and things to learn;

for minds to think, things to discover and remember and
 enjoy.
We thank you for those who help us when we are in need
and for those who love us even when we are in the wrong;
for those teach us at school and for those who care for us at
 home;
for those who help us when we are ill and hold us when we
 are sad.
We thank you for all your love to us in Jesus
and that every time we look at the cross
it reminds us that he lived and, though he died, he rose
 again,
and, though we cannot see him, he is always with us.
We thank you that your Holy Spirit reminds us
to trust you, to praise you and to thank you everywhere and
 every day.
We want you to know, Lord, that we are sorry for the times
when we know we have pleased ourselves and not you,
and when we have done what we wanted to do
and not what you had planned for us.
We want to say that we are sorry
for the things we have said and done
and the things we have forgotten to say and do
that have hurt you and other people and ourselves.
We ask you to forgive us
and help us to forgive other people too. In Jesus' name.
 Amen.

225   CONCERN FOR OTHERS

Lord Jesus Christ, we thank you that you have shown us
just how much we matter to you,
that, though we can never be worthy of your love, it will
 always be there for us.
We live in a world where we often feel ignored, unwanted
 and unnecessary.
We praise you that you have shown us

there is nothing we can do that will ever stop your loving us.
We thank you for the world in which we live
which tells us that your care and goodness are still there for
us.
We praise you for the way you surround us with
those who heal us when we are ill;
those who help us when we feel lost;
those who hold us when we are afraid;
those who accept us even when we don't deserve it;
those who are patient with us when we are unkind;
those who help us to start all over again when everything
goes wrong.
We thank you for those who make us laugh,
those who share our tears and those who give us hope.
Forgive us for those times when we think only about
ourselves
and forget the needs of others.
Forgive us when we are angry with others for hurting us and
spoiling our lives.
Forgive us that we often forget to be angry when others are
hurt
and their lives are spoilt by the selfishness of others.
Forgive us and help us to start again.
We ask our prayer in Jesus' name. Amen.

226   GIVEN BY GOD

Father, we praise you because you are our great Creator.
You not only gave us life but you also hold our lives—
and the lives of everyone in the whole world—in your hands.
We praise you not only because you are a God of love;
but by sending your Son, Jesus, you proved that your love is
real.
In him you have given us life that is real,
life as you always meant it to be.
We praise you for the Holy Spirit. He is the power for life.

It is only with his help that we can care and worship as you
     meant us to.
We thank you for minds to think and things to learn;
for food to eat and strength to use;
for games to play and friends with whom we can enjoy life;
for eyes to see and ears to hear;
for fun and for laughter with family and friends,
for hearts to love, and for words of hope and peace to share;
The whole world is in your care and everyone matters equally
     to you.
You have made everywhere the place where we can serve you,
and each person we can love in your name.
We are sorry for not serving you as we could
and not loving each one around us as you planned.
We are sorry that the things we say and do
make it harder for other people to know you and your love.
Lord, open our hearts, our minds and our lives,
that all we do this week may bring glory to your name.
Through Jesus, the one whose love is for everyone. Amen.

227   CHRISTMAS EVE

Lord, we are preparing to celebrate your birthday
but we find it so easy to forget why you came.
We sing our carols and say our prayers,
but when we open our presents and spend time with our
     family and friends
we find it so hard to make space for you.
We know that Christmas loses its meaning
when we forget to place you at the centre of all we say and
     do.
We have come today, on the eve of Christmas,
to praise you for loving us enough
to be born into our world to make us your new people.
Help us to remember that you came to change our selfish
     ways
and to be the centre of our lives.

We are sorry that even at Christmas we think more about
     what we want,
instead of what you are wanting to give.
We are sorry that, even at Christmas, we think about
     ourselves and our family
and not enough about you, or those who don't know you.
Forgive us, and by your love, change our hearts and change
     our minds.
In Jesus' name. Amen.

228   CHRISTMAS DAY

Heavenly Father, we praise you for Jesus Christ
and for his coming among us at Christmas.
It is so easy to think that we don't count,
that we have been forgotten or that no one cares.
We praise you that in your Son
we have one who assures us of your almighty presence
and proves that your love is truly for each and every one of us.

Father, we praise you for Jesus Christ,
and for the value he gives to our lives
as we live them in faith, hope and love.
It is as we look to him that we know
some things are right and some things are wrong,
some things are against your will,
and some things are within your purposes for our lives.
We thank you for all the fun and laughter,
for the joy and peace, and for time with our families and friends.
We thank you too for the singing of carols
and for listening to the familiar Christmas story—
and that we can know that it is not just a story!
Help us not to lose our hold on Christ this Christmas.
Teach us again to remember
that the baby in the manger is the man on the cross
and the man on the cross is the Lord of the empty tomb
and the Lord of the empty tomb is the one who is Lord of
     eternity.

We bring our prayer in the name of the King of Kings and
the Lord of Lords. Amen.

229   CHRISTMAS DAY

Lord, we praise you that you have shown us in Jesus
that you are not remote, that you are not a long way from us.
Though we cannot see you, or touch you,
you have promised that, no matter who or what we are,
what we have done or failed to do,
you will be very near to each and every one of us.
Today we remember the coming of Jesus:
help us to know the joy of his presence in our lives.
Lord, we praise you that he came as a helpless baby.
We thank you for the story of Mary and Joseph,
the shepherds and the angels, the wise men and the star.
We praise you more that it is all not just a story
but a record of all you have done to open
our hearts to your love and our lives to your power.
We are sorry that we spend so much time preparing to enjoy
ourselves
that we forget those who will have no joy this Christmas.
Forgive us when, as we decorate our homes,
we forget those who have no home.
Lord, help us to remember that
the baby in the manger is the man on the cross,
and the man on the cross is always with us as our living Lord.
We ask our prayer in the name of Jesus, our Immanuel, God
with us. Amen.

Prayers of Intercession

230   ONE WORLD WEEK—THE ENVIRONMENT

Lord, we pray for those who are hungry in a world of plenty,
for those who do not know where their next meal is coming
from
and for those who can only watch as their children die.

Lord, please help us to provide for them.
The Lord hears our prayer.
Thanks be to God.

Lord, we pray for those who have the power to change the
world,
for leaders of nations whose decisions can mean the
difference
between death and life for many
and for those with the power but not the will to cancel the
debts of the poor.
Please help them to hear the cries of the poor.
The Lord hears our prayer.
Thanks be to God.

Lord, we pray for those who work for agencies of relief,
especially [*name*],
that they may have wisdom and courage in the decisions
they must make.
The Lord hears our prayer.
Thanks be to God.

Lord, we pray for those who cry for justice for the poor,
for those who speak out for those whose voices are not heard
and for those who work unselfishly for those who cannot
work for themselves.
Please give them strength in their endeavours.
The Lord hears our prayer.
Thanks be to God.

Lord, we pray for those who do not want our pity—
they simply want a new chance;
for those who do not want our help—they simply want fairness;
for those who need aid, but would rather
be allowed the opportunity to live and to grow for
themselves.
Please open up new opportunities for them.
The Lord hears our prayer.
Thanks be to God.

Lord, we pray for the church, your people throughout the
world.
We ask for the courage to speak for those deprived of a voice,
the willingness to share the pain of those whose hands are
empty
and the power to stand up for the powerless, the lost and
those with no hope—
and to go on standing, no matter the cost.
The Lord hears our prayer.
Thanks be to God.

In the name of Christ, who like his Father is always on the
side of the poor. Amen.

231   WE LIGHT THIS CANDLE
We light this candle for those who remember today
the ones who went to war and never returned;
who set out in the prime of life
and whose bodies and minds and lives were damaged
by all they had seen and heard.
May the light of Christ bring peace to the world.

Silence

We light this candle for those who remember
the high hopes and exciting dreams that once were theirs;
for those whose lives have been wrecked
by addictions that now rule their lives
and for those who are left to ponder their 'if onlys' and their
'might have beens'.
May the light of Christ bring peace to their hearts.

Silence

We light this candle for those who seem unable to remember
people and places that once meant so much;
for those who sit alone with no one to visit them,
no one to brighten their day,
and for those whose memories are all that they have left

but who have no one to share them with.
May the light of Christ heal broken hearts.

Silence

We light this candle for those on fire with the love of God;
for those whose hearts are ablaze with their passion for Jesus;
for those who are committed to working and praying for
    others
to be filled with the Holy Spirit;
but also for those who seem to be losing their love for Christ,
and for whom prayer and worship are becoming a lower
    priority.
May the light of Christ bring renewal and praise.

Silence

We light this candle for anyone we know to be in need of
    our prayers;
for those whose lives have been devastated
by disaster or disease, by depression or despair.

Silence

We also light this candle for ourselves,
and ask that the love of God will melt us and mould us,
touch us and change us, call us and empower us all for his
    glory.

Silence

Lord, in your mercy,
hear our prayer. Amen.

232   LORD, COME AS THE LIGHT

Lord, we pray for those whose lives are trapped by the
    darkness of fear;
for those facing a time of uncertainty, illness and the fear
    that comes from not knowing;

for those in hospital, and those undergoing unpleasant
    treatment;
for those who wait through dark days of anxiety.
Lord in the darkness,
come as the light.

Lord, we pray for those whose lives are filled with the
    darkness of hate;
for those whose words and deeds are the source of much
    pain, sorrow and despair;
for those whose whole way of life is the enemy of peace
and whose attitude to their fellow human beings destroys
    hope;
for those who cause terror and assume the role of the suicide
    bomber.
Lord in the darkness,
come as the light.

Lord, we pray for those in the darkness of loneliness;
for those who are single in a society designed for the family
and for those left alone now the family have gone;
for those who spend their days in the prison of their home
and long for someone to visit, to break into the silence of
    their aloneness;
for those who with the passing years have only their
    memories
and no one with whom to share them.
Lord in the darkness,
come as the light.

Lord, we pray for those in the darkness of doubt;
for those who long to believe, to have faith to trust;
for those with questions they can't answer
and for those whose doubts are simply tearing them apart;
for those whose ability to trust has been damaged by the
    behaviour of others
and for those whose faith is all in their heads

and not in their hearts where you meant it to be.
Lord in the darkness,
come as the light.

Lord, we pray for those in the darkness of emptiness;
for those who have filled their days and their hours
with the passing pleasures of the moment
and are discovering that the security, peace and contentment
    they promised
were but a mirage that could never last in the reality of the
    coming day;
for those whose riches account for nothing of value
and for those whose hollowness is bringing them pain and
    despair.
Lord in the darkness,
come as the light.

Lord, we pray for those in the darkness of sin;
for those who today will destroy a little more of themselves
through the addictions that imprison their days;
for those whose selfishness brings pain to their neighbour
and whose self-centredness is building the wall ever higher
and locking the door to the grace that would heal them.
Lord in the darkness,
come as the light.

Lord, we pray for those whose lives have been darkened by
    disaster,
for those whose lives have been destroyed
by the impact of earthquake, flood or fire;
for those who have lost everything and everyone that
    mattered to them;
and for those facing hunger and starvation through no fault
    of their own;
for those struggling for existence
and for those who know that they are losing the fight.
Lord in the darkness,
come as the light.

Lord, we pray for those who are facing the darkness of the
  years;
for those who are in the twilight of their days
and for those who have only their might-have-beens,
and their if-onlys are still causing them pain;
for those whose memories still haunt them
and those whose memories are darkened and lost;
for those who can hardly remember their names
and for those who have forgotten the faces of those that they
  loved.
Lord in the darkness,
come as the light.

Lord, we pray for those whose lives have been touched by
  your grace
and whose days are set ablaze with your love;
for those whose faith in Christ is daily being renewed
and the light of the Father's presence fills them
with hope, peace and joy from within;
for those for whom the light of the Spirit
is the source of their strength, their compassion and trust,
and for those who are daily committing themselves
to be beacons of light in Christ's name.
Lord in the darkness,
come as the light.

Lord, we pray for those we know by name
that the light of Christ will bring them the joy of renewal
  and refreshment.

Silence

We pray too for ourselves, that the light of Christ will find
  its way
even into the darkest corners of our lives,
that we might walk in the light of his love.
Lord in the darkness,
come as the light.

We bring our prayers in the name of Christ, the Light of the
world. Amen.

233   PETER AND CORNELIUS

Lord, we pray for those who listen to the voice of the poor;
for those who speak out on behalf of those
with no hope, no meaning and no future;
for those with the power to change things
and for those with no vision of what they could do.
Lord of life and time and eternity,
listen to our prayer.

Lord, we pray for those who listen to the cry for justice;
for those imprisoned for their political ideals or their faith in
    Christ;
for those who work tirelessly
for people locked up without trial and for crimes they did
    not commit.
May they share with others their vision of truth.
Lord of life and time and eternity,
listen to our prayer.

Lord, we pray for those who listen to the silent suffering
of the hungry and starving, especially [*name*],
who seek to cross boundaries and reach out today
on behalf of those who may have no tomorrow.
May they challenge us all with their vision of hope.
Lord of life and time and eternity,
listen to our prayer.

Lord, we pray for those who listen to you speaking
through the ones that they meet;
for those who hear you calling through what they can see;
for those who, like Peter and Cornelius, allow you to speak
    to them
in the most unexpected of ways
and go on listening at times and in places
even when they feel unprepared to respond.

May their vision of expectancy encourage us all.
Lord of life and time and eternity,
listen to our prayer.

Lord, we pray for those who don't want to listen
and who pretend you're not there;
for those who reject what you say because they deny your
     existence;
but also we pray for those whose words and deeds
demonstrate your presence to their neighbour
and bearing the pain and the suffering of others
bring the light of Christ to us all.
May their vision of love transform your world.
Lord of life and time and eternity,
listen to our prayer.

Lord, we pray for those who are listening for you to call
     them
and are ready to serve in ways that you choose;
for those who are seeking to be fresh expressions
of what it means to be your people today;
for those who are longing to reach out to the prodigal with
     faith that is real
but are hampered by the elder brothers who see no reason to
     change.
May their vision of mission enthuse us all.
Lord of life and time and eternity,
listen to our prayer.

Lord, we pray for ourselves,
that you will help us to listen to you and our neighbour and
     to each other.
By your Holy Spirit enable us to listen
when we would rather close our ears;
to face the challenge of renewal
when we would prefer to close our minds;
and to receive the courage of your love
when we are ready to close our hearts.

May we have a vision of reaching the lost.
Lord of life and time and eternity,
listen to our prayer. Amen.

234 THINK OF SOMEONE

Think of someone who is frightened;
someone whose whole world has come crashing down;
someone who is concerned for their own health
or the health of someone they love;
someone facing a time of illness
and afraid to share their fears that are bottled inside.

Silence

Think of someone who is hurting inside;
someone whose pain simply won't go away;
someone who feels rejected, unwanted, or unloved;
someone who longs to know compassion, hope and peace
but has no one to offer it to them.

Silence

Think of someone who is challenged;
someone who is increasingly aware that all is not well in their
     lives;
someone whose wrong attitudes, mistaken values or hurtful
     words
are the cause of despair and disillusionment for someone
     they love.

Silence

Think of someone who is broken;
someone who set out with high hopes and great ambitions;
someone who once had important plans for their future
but whose tomorrows are covered with clouds of despair.

Silence

Think of someone who is happy;
someone who is very much aware of all they have received
    from God's gracious hand;
someone who overflows with thankfulness and joy;
someone whose life is daily set alight with the love and the
    presence of Christ.

Silence

Think of someone whose life is being touched by God;
someone whose whole existence is being turned upside down;
someone experiencing for the first time in their life
the presence and the power of the Holy Spirit.

Silence

Think of someone who is discovering what it can mean
to offer and receive forgiveness;
someone whose burden of guilt is being lifted
and whose bitterness and anger are gently being washed
    away.

Silence

Think of someone who is weighed down by their sense of
    responsibility;
someone whose employment has lost the joy and fulfilment
    it once held;
someone overwhelmed by the demands of family and
    friends;
someone who is burdened
by the pain and the suffering they see all around them;
someone who feels helpless to respond to God's suffering
    world.

Silence

Think of yourself, and all that you carry within you;
Think of yourself, and all you must face tomorrow;
Think of yourself, and the promises of God

to hold you, bless you and love you—from now until the
end of all things.
Think of yourself and, in the silence, bring your personal
concerns to the Lord.

Lord, in your mercy, **hear our prayer.** Amen.

235   THINK OF SOMEONE AT CHRISTMAS

Think of someone you know who will be on their own this
Christmas
and ask for God's peace to be upon them.

Think of someone you know who has lost their job
and who will be facing an uncertain Christmas.

Think of someone you know who will be celebrating 'Xmas'
but will give no thought to the King of Kings.

Think of someone you know whose days are filled with
sadness and pain
and who needs the touch of love and kindness.

Think of those around the world whose Christmas will be
filled with hatred and war
and who have yet to know the Prince of Peace.

Think of those who will be sleeping rough this Christmas,
those many people in [*local area*] without a home,
and for whom, like their Saviour, there is still no room.

Think of those we have been asked to remember.

Silence

Think of yourself and all that you must face in the coming
days of this week
in the knowledge that the Christ child has come.

We bring our prayers in the name of the one
who was, is and always will be Immanuel, and Jesus is his
name. Amen.

236   THOSE ON THE OUTSIDE

Lord, we pray for those who feel
that they are on the outside of life just looking in;
those with no home, no food and no future;
those with no hope, no joy and no love;
those with no courage, no strength and no purpose;
those with no laughter, no joy and no tears;
We pray for those who long to be held but have no one to
     hold them;
those who have hopes and dreams but no one to share them;
those who are weary, weighed down with worry and
     responsibility,
but have no one to walk with them;
those who are so busy 'doing' that they have no time just to
     'be';
those who have forgotten to pray
and have yet to discover that you are still listening;
those for whom you are a stranger,
who still need to learn that their names and their days are
     precious to you.
May they yet discover that in Christ
all things hold together and all things can be made new. Amen.

237   BROKEN IMAGES

We pray for those with fragile images;
those whose picture of life has been centred on themselves;
those who have sought to find fulfilment, purpose and
     satisfaction
in the accumulation of material possessions,
the storing up of wealth and their pride of status;
those who have placed great importance on how others think
     about them.
May they find in Christ a picture of renewal and hope
when their images of life have been broken.
Lord of life,
this is our prayer.

We pray for those with damaged images;
those whose journey had been untroubled, peaceful and
    undisturbed;
for whom good health was taken for granted,
success was always assured and life held no fears or
    disappointments;
for those who are now facing times of trial, uncertainty and
    pain;
those for whom each day is a battle to survive;
and for those overwhelmed by the disability
that robs them of their independence;
for those trying to cope with a life-threatening illness
and for those who can find no light at the end of their
    tunnel of darkness.
May they find in Christ a picture of renewal and hope
when their images of life have been broken.
Lord of life,
this is our prayer.

We pray for those with no image,
no picture of life and no goal to which they direct their energies;
for those who live empty, purposeless lives;
and for those who allow each day to drift by—
never thinking it could be their last;
for those whose aimless existence
has been a cause of concern for others;
and for those whose wasted opportunities
are something they are beginning to regret;
for those who now look back to what might have been
and whose 'if onlys' now colour their lives
with a sense of failure and despair
that are beyond the reach of human words of
    encouragement.
May they find in Christ a picture of renewal and hope
when their images of life have been broken.
Lord of life,
this is our prayer.

We pray for those whose image of life is too shallow
and who settle too easily for too little, too soon;
for those whose vision of life is extremely limited
and whose plans, hopes and expectations
are focused on their own wants, needs and dreams;
for those whose image of life is all pleasure
and is centred on the excitement that today can bring;
for those who seek contentment, satisfaction and fulfilment
through the gratification of their earthly lusts and their daily
     desires;
for those who through lotteries seek instant riches
and those who through their addiction
to drugs, alcohol, overeating and over-spending
are escaping into their world of dreams.
May they find in Christ a picture of renewal and hope
when their images of life have been broken.
Lord of life,
this is our prayer.

We pray for those whose image of the world needs re-
     shaping;
for those who give little or no thought to the beauty of God's
     creation
and rarely, if ever, offer any word of gratitude for all they
     have received;
for those whose litter spoils our streets
and whose mindless graffiti and meaningless vandalism
remain a blot on the landscape for others;
for a renewed sense of responsibility by multinational
     companies
and a greater respect by us all for the fragile balance of our
     environment;
for those who treat the whole of creation as if it were their
     own property
and for those who fail to remember that
their ultimate accountability is to their Creator.
May they find in Christ a picture of renewal and hope

when their images of life have been broken.
Lord of life,
this is our prayer.

We pray for those whose image of life stops short of their
  neighbour's door;
for those whose short-sightedness enables them to ignore the
  suffering of others,
and whose deafness prevents them hearing the cries of the
  poor;
for those who turn a blind eye to the deprivation of others
and for those who pretend they are unaware
of the injustice their brothers and sisters are facing;
for leaders of nations whose failure to act
condemns millions to hunger and starvation;
and for those who have crippled whole nations
with debts that are paid with the blood of the poor;
for those who can't face hearing
of the inhuman working conditions and cheap labour
that result from the low prices we demand
for what we buy in our supermarkets;
and for those who once a year put a coin in an envelope
and feel they have done their bit for the poor.
May they find in Christ a picture of renewal and hope
when their images of life have been broken.
Lord of life,
this is our prayer.

We pray for those whose image of God needs remaking
and for those whose immature knowledge of him and his
  purposes
means their faith is inadequate and vulnerable;
for those who see God like a divine Father Christmas
who always rewards them for being good
and for those whose lists of requests
are presented as prayers to their Maker;
for those for whom God is like a cosmic genie
who will always do as they ask;

and for those who see him as the one who does what he's
    told
and never demands obedience and trust;
for those for whom God is like the fairy godmother of their
    dreams;
and for those who require him never to allow
anything bad, painful or evil to cross their path;
for those who have yet to see him as
the eternal, sovereign God who is almighty
and who in Christ has promised to enter the pain of us all.
May they find in Christ a picture of renewal and hope
when their images of life have been broken.
Lord of life,
this is our prayer.

We bring all our prayers in the name of him
who offered bread and wine as the image of his love for us
    all. Amen.

238   THOSE WHO ARE ANXIOUS

Lord, we pray for those who are anxious about the past;
for those who are troubled today
by memories of their yesterdays that won't go away;
for those whose memories still cause them to grieve
and remain a barrier to freedom, peace and contentment.
The Lord is our strength and our song,
and he will hold us for ever.

Lord, we pray for those who are anxious about tomorrow;
for those whose whole lives are crippled by the fear
of what the future might hold;
for those who can find no peace, no comfort and no joy
because they are overwhelmed by a sense of doubt and
    uncertainty;
for those whose fear of failure limits their horizons
and for those whose dread robs each new day
of the sense of fulfilment that could have been theirs.

The Lord is our strength and our song,
and he will hold us for ever.

Lord, we pray for those who are anxious about today;
for those who know what today will bring;
for those who are sinking under the weight
of the responsibilities heaped upon them
and who see no way to lighten their load;
for those for whom each day is filled with a sense of
    foreboding
and for those who are slowly being wrung dry by their
    concerns
for their family, their neighbour and the world of pain and
    despair.
The Lord is our strength and our song,
and he will hold us for ever.

Lord, we pray for those who are simply anxious
and can give no reason for their anxiety within;
for those whose anxiety robs them of sleep
and daily leaves them seeking in vain for an experience of
    rest and renewal;
for those who feel foolish for being so anxious
and count themselves failures when they are not to blame;
for those who live out their lives under a cloud of defeat and
    depression;
for those driven to the limits of coping
and for those whose greatest need is just to be loved.
The Lord is our strength and our song,
and he will hold us for ever.

Lord, we pray for those who are anxious for others
and for those whose concern for family, friends and
    neighbours
outstrips their capacity to respond;
for those who carry the burdens of the world on their
    shoulders
and for those whose joy, hope and peace are destroyed

by anguish for the plight of the hungry and starving
and the endless stream of refugees implanted in their minds
    by the work of the media.
The Lord is our strength and our song,
and he will hold us for ever.

Lord, we pray for those who are anxious—and with real
    justification;
for those whose livelihoods are affected by the vagaries of the
    weather
or through the affects of company takeovers
and the threat of redundancies they know will follow;
for those who are anxious as they await their doctor's
    diagnosis
and the implications it will hold for life and for death;
for those who feel desperately alone and isolated
and long to experience anew the love and the presence of
    God.
The Lord is our strength and our song,
and he will hold us for ever.

Lord, we pray for those with no sense of anxiety
and no feelings of concern in their lives;
for those who are content to drift through life
and never consider the needs and the fears of their
    neighbour,
and for those indifferent to the sadness and suffering of
    others;
for those whose lives are lived in the shallows
and who, in their determination to live for themselves,
refuse to venture into the depths of others' pain and anguish.
The Lord is our strength and our song,
and he will hold us for ever.

In the name of Christ, who holds us all, for ever. Amen.

I am a person in prison. How I got here is hardly the point.
I have spent the greater proportion of my life behind bars.
No, I didn't have the best of role models—
my mother and I visited my father in jail.
Whether I was deprived or brought up in riches
the responsibility for where I am is mine alone.
I am a person in prison
and for the first time in my life I long to be free;
I want to start all over again—
while I still have some life left with which to make a new
    beginning.
Pray for me.

Silence

I am a person in the media.
Whether I work as a journalist for a newspaper,
or as a news reporter for television, doesn't really matter.
I know that what I write isn't always the truth
and that many people are hurt and careers are wrecked
because of what I've reported.
It isn't easy working in the media,
as you know only bad news sells newspapers.
But lately I have been getting very uneasy.
I'm beginning to understand that love, truth and goodness
are more important than I ever realised.
Pray for me.

Silence

I am just a child—well, I am inside.
What happened to me all those years ago has left its scars.
Today it's called abuse—then it was just 'our little secret'.
And so I bottled everything up inside—
all the hurt, the pain and the shame.

I know, deep down, it wasn't my fault
but it has still made it very hard for me to trust anyone, ever
    again.
It is as if I am a coiled spring—I'm all screwed up
and I hide myself away from your gaze.
You have no idea just how much I long to be free
to be the 'me' I know God intended.
Pray for me.

Silence

I am a person who is ill.
The problem for me is that I don't really know what's the
    matter with me.
Nobody tells me, and that makes me very upset.
They stand at the end of my bed and they speak in hushed
    tones.
They think I can't hear
but every word they speak hammers fear and doubt into my
    brain.
I lie there and think about life—my life.
Could I have done things differently?
Could I have cared more? Could I have been more
    understanding?
Could I have made more time for God?
I don't know what time I have left—but I just want to live.
Pray for me.

Silence

I am a social worker.
I hate to admit it because to many people it's like a rude
    word.
But to me it was a calling—
I believed God wanted me to serve him in this way—I still
    do.
Whether my clients are old or young, I always try to do my
    best for them.
Yes, I do get it wrong sometimes.

It's because I'm human that I make mistakes.
When something goes wrong I give myself a hard time
and I can do without the media hitting me when I'm down.
You have no idea how much it would help
if someone, somewhere, stopped and said thank you.
Pray for me.

Silence

I am a church member.
I have attended church all my life;
I can't remember a day or a time when I didn't believe in
    God.
I have held every office in the church
and I have said my prayers and read my Bible
for as long as I can remember.
I envy those who speak of their personal relationship with
    Jesus
and who can worship with such a sense of the presence of
    God.
Deep down, I know, I only wish it could happen to me.
Pray for me.

Silence

Lord, I am myself—we are ourselves, and we are in need of
    prayer.
So we pray for those around us
and ask that your peace, love and joy will fill our hearts with
    hope.

Lord, in your mercy, **hear our prayer.** Amen.

240   BREAK INTO LIFE

Think of someone you know—a neighbour, a colleague at
        work, a friend, someone for whom you are concerned;
and ask that God will break into their lives in a whole new
        way.

Trust him
Think of someone you know—a member of your family,
someone who is ill or in hospital and those who are
    concerned for them;
and ask that they will discover what it means to trust God.

The peace
Think of someone whose life is in chaos,
whose relationships are falling apart,
and they don't know which way to turn or what to do;
and ask that they may experience the peace that passes all
    understanding.

Christ has died
Think of someone who knows all is not well in their lives
and who's found that escapism, materialism and every other
    -ism hasn't worked;
and ask that they may know that Christ has died for them.

Being loved
Think of someone who is lonely or alone,
for whom each day is the same and their home has become a
    prison;
and ask that they will come to know the love of God
    through the love of his people.

Met in prayer
Think of someone for whom God is just a name,
or perhaps someone you once knew a long, long time ago;
and ask that God will touch them, change them and heal them,
and that they will know they have met the living God.

Empty tomb
Think of someone who appears to be successful,
who possesses so much of this world's good things
but who in reality is a living shell and has an emptiness
    inside too deep for words;
and ask that they will meet the risen Christ
who will hold them, love them and fill them with his grace.

Worship
Think of someone for whom worship has become a ritual,
something they always do—they know they are going
    through the motions
but the praises have lost any real meaning;
and ask that the Holy Spirit will transform their whole life
    into a song of glory.

With us
Think of a world leader, your local member of Parliament,
your doctor, or a teacher, or a social worker,
who feels weighed down by the burden of their responsibilities;
and ask that they will experience the strength and the hope
    of knowing God is with them.

Gave everything
Think of someone whose whole life has been changed by
    their experience of war,
those who have lost their loved ones in the futility of war;
and ask that our remembering today may enable us to act
    tomorrow
and bring us closer to an end to all war.

Forgiveness
Think of someone who has a burden of guilt,
who feels or knows that by what they have said or done
they have let others down, spoilt their own lives and the lives
    of others;
and ask that they may know the joy of sins forgiven.

Light for the way
Think of someone whose life is filled with darkness and pain,
with sorrow and loss, with anxiety or despair;
think of yourself and your need for light for the journey of
    life;
and ask that in the darkness you may know the light of Christ.

The Lord hears our prayer.
Thanks be to God. Amen.

Lord, we pray for a church that is honest,
that is ready to confess when it makes mistakes
and all the wrongs that have been done in its name
and the shame it has brought on yours.
May the church of Jesus
always live to honour him.

Lord, we pray for a church that is open,
where everyone who enters its doors
is always aware of the warmth of its welcome;
for a church more concerned for the hurting than for its
     rituals,
more for the broken than for its own image.
May the church of Jesus
always live to honour him.

Lord, we pray for a church that is committed to worship;
that is never content just to sing hymns or say prayers;
for a church where worship, praise and adoration
spring from hearts that know and love their Lord.
May the church of Jesus
always live to honour him.

Lord, we pray for a church that is ready to serve in your
     name;
for a church that cares for the homeless, the lost and the
     broken,
and seeks to reach out to those with no hope and no
     purpose;
for a church that is at the heart of the community
and refuses to be sidelined or ignored;
for a church that is the conscience of the nation
and speaks prophetically the word that must be heard.
May the church of Jesus
always live to honour him.

Lord, we pray for a church that is focused on mission
and whose purpose is that all may believe;
for a church that preaches the gospel and demonstrates its
    truth
through the lives of its people at home, at work and in the
    world;
for a church committed to evangelism
and whose every meeting and every committee is centred on
    Christ
and bringing others to know him as Lord.
May the church of Jesus
always live to honour him.

Lord, we pray for a church that is united in Christ,
    for a church that looks only to Jesus
and has less time for pride and self-concern;
for a church where its people are united, not just in word but
    in deed;
for a church where there is love for each other
because first they have fallen in love with their Lord.
May the church of Jesus
always live to honour him.

We bring our prayers in the name of Jesus
for the unity of Christ's church. Amen.

242   DELIVERANCE

Lord, we pray for those enslaved by their love of money
and ensnared by their grasping after material possessions;
for those who worship wealth and status
and are for ever searching for fulfilment
in their false hope in the pot of gold at the end of their
    rainbow.
Lord, do not bring us to the time of trial,
but deliver us from evil.

Lord, we pray for those whose lives are trapped in their
    commitment to

the false gods of self-aggrandisement, self-centredness and
    self-satisfaction;
for those who have lost their way in the labyrinth of new age
    worship
and the idolisation of mother earth
with no awareness of their dependence on their Creator
    God.
Lord, do not bring us to the time of trial,
but deliver us from evil.

Lord, we pray for those trapped by their web of lies
and whose whole way of life is stained by their greed, pride
    and self-interest;
for those whose lifestyle is built on the sandy foundations of
    corruption and falsehood
and for those whose attitudes and values are a danger to the
    weak and the vulnerable.
Lord, do not bring us to the time of trial,
but deliver us from evil.

Lord, we pray for those caught by the lure of illegal drugs
and the instant solution they seem to offer to their problems;
for those too afraid to say no, to stand out or to be different;
for those who are finding that their bodies are still being
    damaged
even by drugs labelled 'recreational';
for those who turn to crime to fund their habit
and for those who are craving deliverance.
Lord, do not bring us to the time of trial,
but deliver us from evil.

Lord, we pray for those whose hearts and minds are filled
    with evil thoughts
and whose actions bring torment to others;
for those whose sickness of body, mind or spirit
is the harvest of hearts, minds and lives
focused on things far from the heart of God;
for those who, for the first time in their lives,

are longing to be delivered from the torment without and
    within.
Lord, do not bring us to the time of trial,
but deliver us from evil.

Lord, we pray for those who are struggling with temptations
that all but overwhelm them;
for those who each day are in a state of anguish and despair
and those for whom the bottom has dropped out of their
    world;
for those whose life of crime and violence
is wrecking the lives of their victims
as well as those who love them most.
Lord, do not bring us to the time of trial,
but deliver us from evil.

Lord, we pray for those who long for deliverance
from their prison of apathy and indifference
and for those seeking the way out of their never-ending circle
of hunger, injustice and poverty;
for those sleeping rough on the streets of our towns and
    cities
and for those who see no way to be set free
from the daily scavenging for food;
for those locked up without trial
and for those imprisoned simply because of their faith in
    Christ.
Lord, do not bring us to the time of trial,
but deliver us from evil.

Lord, we pray for those who plant bombs
and who give no thought to the suffering and death they
    create;
for terrorists who see only the cause to which they are
    committed
and refuse to see the cost that others bear
through no fault of their own;
for those whose unsocial behaviour destroys communities

and robs their neighbours of the peace they long for.
Lord, do not bring us to the time of trial,
but deliver us from evil.

Lord, we pray for those who are trying to set themselves free
and for those whose self-reliance is a hindrance to hope and
    renewal;
for ourselves and our need to be holy and to be whole;
for our search for peace, forgiveness and joy;
for a new trust in the one whose empty cross and whose
    empty tomb
offer a deliverance already paid for.
Lord, do not bring us to the time of trial,
but deliver us from evil.

Lord, we bring our prayers for freedom from all that spoils
    our lives
in the name of Christ the deliverer. Amen.

243   THE HUNGRY

Lord, we pray for those who are hungry for food
for those who today will have nothing to eat
and for those who will go to sleep not knowing if they will
    eat tomorrow;
for those whose gaunt empty faces rebuke our greed, our
    self-satisfaction,
and challenge our easy acceptance of injustice for others
and our wealth that comes to us at expense of their hope.
Lord of the poor,
hear our prayer.

Lord, we pray for those who are hungry for hope;
for those who, because of their own misdeeds,
are locked up for years without the hope of parole;
for those who are victims of crime
and whose homes and bodies have been violated by others
and now have no hope of feeling safe even in their own
    homes;

for those left behind by their success-oriented society
and for those who sit and watch as life moves on without
    them;
for those who are refugees and have lost all hope of their
    return home.
Lord of the poor,
hear our prayer.

Lord, we pray for those who are hungry for love;
for those who have never known what it means to be loved
    unconditionally
and for those who have felt unwanted, unnecessary and
    unloved
for as long as they can remember;
for those who have lost people they loved and people who
    loved them;
for those whose lives are crippled by their sense of rejection
    and desertion
and for those whose vision of life is coloured by memories
    that hurt
and a future that is now seen through a veil of tears.
Lord of the poor,
hear our prayer.

Lord, we pray for those who are hungry for justice;
for those who work long hours for pay that is little more
    then a pittance
and for those with no voice of their own to rescue them
from life-destroying and dangerous work;
for those forced to live in squalor
and whose bodies and skills are exploited by others;
for those who sit and stare
because they have no way to satisfy their hunger for freedom
    and justice.
Lord of the poor,
hear our prayer.

Lord, we pray for those who are hungry for reconciliation;
for those who work tirelessly to find the roadway to peace
    between nations
and for those who labour to heal damaged relationships
and to build bridges where trust has been broken;
for those who have worshipped and served in the church for
    as long as they can remember
and yet hunger for a deeper sense of oneness with God
and for a life-changing experience of reconciliation
with the Lord of life and the Sovereign of eternity.
Lord of the poor,
hear our prayer.

Lord, we pray for those who are hungry for peace;
for those who have witnessed the appalling impact of war
and for those scarred by the horrors of violence and civil
    unrest;
for those whose lives are in turmoil and whose aching and
    loneliness
is hidden from the eyes of the world but is seen by the heart
    of the Father;
for those whose every waking moment is touched by
    memories
of the wrong choices and the foolish decisions they have
    made;
for those who are only too well aware of the pain, sorrow
    and shame
that their words and deeds have brought to themselves
and to those who care about them,
and which robs them of the peace they long to know.
Lord of the poor,
hear our prayer.

We pray for ourselves and all the things we hunger to know
    and to be;
for those memories we long to forget
and the forgiveness we know we must give;

for the hunger inside that nothing in this world can ever
    satisfy
and for the promise of cleansing, renewal and fulfilment
as we receive the Spirit of Christ.
Lord of the poor,
hear our prayer.

All this we pray for Jesus Christ's sake. Amen.

244 POWER

We pray for those involved with power, for politicians and
    those seeking election;
for those in government or in opposition;
for those who sought power and who entered politics
because they longed to see things change and to bring people
    hope;
for those who have now lost their way
and for whom power itself has become everything;
and for those for whom the vision of service still burns
    brightly.
God of all power,
we place ourselves in your hands.

We pray for those without power;
for those who live on the street and have nowhere to live;
for those in poor housing, or crowded together in temporary
    accommodation;
for those with no voice to be heard, no power to wield, no
    place to go;
for those on the margins of life
and for those who are made to feel poor
in our materialistic, fashion-conscious, status-aware
    generation.
God of all power,
we place ourselves in your hands.

We pray for those who feel as if they have lost power;
for those who were once respected

and had a recognised place in the daily scheme of life;
for those who have lost any sense of their own worth
and for whom each day is a trial;
for those whose enforced retirement or redundancy
was a painful, degrading experience;
for parents whose children have left home
and now feel utterly purposeless and alone.
God of all power,
we place ourselves in your hands.

We pray for those whose powers are a burden
and for whom power carries an overwhelming sense of
    personal responsibility;
for those who work in the health service
and each day are faced with decisions of death and life;
for those in the armed forces
who signed up on a wave of enthusiasm, or despair,
and are now discovering the responsibility laid upon them
to use their powers wisely, with compassion and for peace.
God of all power,
we place ourselves in your hands.

We pray for those whose powers are on the wane;
those who are facing a time of illness
and are too afraid even to think of what the future may bring;
for those whose minds are confused
and who sit all day in their chair, seemingly unaware
of the staff, the other residents, or family and friends;
for those whose memories are all locked up inside them,
having lost the power to recall them or share them with
    others.
God of all power,
we place ourselves in your hands.

We pray for those whose lives overflow
with the power of achievement and the will to succeed;
for those whose lives are in turmoil
because of the misuse and abuse of power by others;

for those whose lives are still being wrecked
by the abuse of power, by dictators and parents;
for those still trying to put their lives back together
as every situation they face seems to trigger memories they
    would rather forget
and experiences they should never have gone through.
God of all power,
we place ourselves in your hands.

We pray for ourselves, and all those things we must face
    together,
or alone, on our journey through each day.
Lord, help us to remember that no matter who we are,
where we are, or what we are facing,
we need never face it on our own or in our own strength.
Lord, you have promised that the power that raised Jesus
    from the dead
will always be available to us, and you will walk with us now,
and wherever we go you will be there before us.
God of all power,
we place ourselves in your hands.

In the name of Christ, the power of God for us. Amen.

245   FRUIT OF THE SPIRIT—LOVE

Father, we pray for those in need of love;
for those left empty and afraid to reach out to others;
for those who have faced painful rejection at every turn;
for those who have never known what it means to be loved
    unconditionally
and find it hard to offer love to others, or to receive it
    themselves.
May the love of Christ
bring them healing and hope.

Father, we pray for those who love the wrong things;
for those who so love the things of this world
they are unable to give a thought for the world to come;

for those who treasure their assumed riches of wealth and
     possessions,
of status and influence with others, of passing pleasure and
     addiction,
yet are as paupers in the sight of God;
for those who have everything that ultimately means nothing
and nothing that counts for eternity.
May the love of Christ
bring them healing and hope.

Father, we pray for those whose love for their neighbour
     takes our breath away;
for those who are prepared to risk everything to care for
the sick and the dying, the lost and the broken, the hungry
     and the starving;
for those whose love for others is a reflection of their love for
     you;
for those whose love for others makes them blind to the
     price they must pay.
May the love of Christ
bring them healing and hope.

Father, we pray for those who have yet to discover
the depth and the wonder of your love for us all;
those for whom you are just a word, or a term of abuse;
for those who pass their days in the darkness of fear and
     dread,
and for those who daily are crushed by their sense of
     aloneness;
for those who are beginning to hear the whisper of your voice
and the sound of your love in their lives.
May the love of Christ
bring them healing and hope.

Father, we pray for those who have lost everything
and from whom the storms and disasters of life
have robbed someone to love and someone to love them;
for those filled with anger and bitterness

and for whom hope and love, peace and joy, are now things
　　　of the past;
for those overwhelmed with regret and remorse for what has
　　　happened,
a disabling uncertainty as they face what is to come
and a deep sense of being unloved and unwanted today.
May the love of Christ
bring them healing and hope.

Father, we pray for those who have been so wrapped up in
　　　their own needs
that they have been blind to the concerns of others;
for those whose attitudes and behaviour
have destroyed the love that once was there;
for those who have abused the love they were offered
and for those who abused others and, as their excuse, called
　　　it love;
for those who want to know the joy of a loving Christian
　　　relationship
but their longing remains unfulfilled.
May the love of Christ
bring them healing and hope.

Father, we pray for those who long to feel the healing touch
　　　of love,
to know the reality of your hand upon their lives
and to experience a joy deep within
that is untouched and untarnished by the pressures of life or
　　　the sin of the world.
We pray for ourselves and for those we name in the silence of
　　　our hearts …

Silence

We pray that we may enter into a deep knowledge of that
　　　love
that will never let us go, never let us off and never let us down.
May the love of Christ
bring them healing and hope.

Father, this love is the fruit of the Spirit,
not something to be won, achieved or deserved.
Your love conquers all things
and brings healing and wholeness to those who are touched
    by your grace.
May the love of Christ
bring them healing and hope.

In the name of Christ
who is the perfect reflection of the love in our Father's heart.
    Amen.

246   FRUIT OF THE SPIRIT—JOY

I am a patient.
I sit here, waiting my turn to see the doctor.
I am torn apart—I don't want to see him, but I know I must.
How can you speak of joy when I know the news that he will
    give me
will change my whole life—for ever.
Yet it would mean so much to have joy
and would help me to face whatever the future brings.
Pray for me.

Silence

I am a world leader.
I don't have the time for joy—it is a luxury that is denied
    me.
You have no idea of the responsibilities laid upon my
    shoulders,
the pitfalls I must try to avoid.
No matter what I say or do, someone will see some evil
    intent
and others will reject everything out of hand.
Joy? My heart says, if only!
When was it that the burden I carry crushed the joy out of
    my life?
Pray for me.

Silence

I am a journalist.
Whether I write for a newspaper
or you see my face on your television screen,
my mind is still so focused on bringing you bad news
I have lost my ability to see the good.
My journalistic antennae twitch uncontrollably
when there is a disaster, a vicious crime or some sordid
     encounter to report.
But joy—you must be joking!
Yet it would make life so much more bearable if I had some
    joy.
Pray for me.

Silence

I work in the health service.
I entered what I considered a caring profession—
to me it was a kind of a calling.
I wanted to care for patients, to help those in need.
It should have been a great joy,
but we have become a political football
to be kicked about by both politicians and patients.
You all forget we are also just human
and are bound to make some mistakes.
But the hassle, the aggression and the litigations
are taking their toll—and rob me of joy.
If only someone would simply say thank you—
what a joy that would be!
Pray for me.

Silence

I am a leader of worship.
Whether I'm a worship leader, a lay preacher or ordained
    minister
the result is the same:
I was told that leading God's people in worship

was the greatest calling and joy there could be.
But all the complaints and the lack of appreciation ...
it's all I ever seem to face.
They don't like the hymns—too old or too new.
Some want constant experiment in worship
while others want to keep it the way it has always been.
The sermon is too honest, too long, too challenging.
No, I haven't lost my faith or my calling,
nor have I lost my joy in serving God—
but others are stealing the joy.
Pray for me.

Silence

I am a married person.
Whether husband or wife—I speak for both.
Our life together has been joyful—especially when we first
    met.
Life was like one long honeymoon, and we thought it would
    never end.
When the children came they simply added to our joy
as we watched them grow and learn.
But somewhere along the way we became just too busy
    transporting them—everywhere!
Then there were the demands of work, church and the things
    we wanted to do.
Each took its toll, as we saw less and less of each other.
Now the children have gone, and so has the joy.
Pray for me.

Silence

I am a teenager.
I guess joy isn't a word I would normally use.
I am looking to experience the moment,
the fury and the fun, pleasure and excitement—now!
Yes, I know I'm a worry to my parents —
they don't approve of me, or my friends, or my lifestyle.
I know they try to listen, to care, to understand.

But I feel as if I'm on a different planet—we just can't
    communicate any more.
I remember the days when I was little
and deep down I wish it could all be as it was.
Joy, you say?
Perhaps that's what I really need, what I am looking,
    searching for.
Pray for me.

Silence

I am a confused person.
I have forgotten what life is all about.
I am surrounded by lotteries and football pools,
by gambling and games of chance.
Is all life like that—just the luck of the draw?
Is it all down to the fall of the dice, or the turn of a card?
Surely there is more to life than is offered
by those whose lives are ruled by superstition
or by what they think they read in the stars?
Yes, I need a new experience of joy,
of knowing God loves me and that I matter to him.
Yes, I want a deep joy of walking with Christ
and knowing I can smile—no matter the storms in my life.
Pray for me.

Silence

Lord, in your mercy,
hear our prayer. Amen.

247   FRUIT OF THE SPIRIT—PEACE

We pray for those who long for peace;
for those whose lives are a picture of chaos;
for those whose life and lifestyle rob them of inner
    tranquillity;
for those whose every wrong choice and selfish decision

closes the door more firmly on the peace that could have
    been theirs.
May the grace of God touch them with his peace.
Our God answers prayer,
and we call on his name.

We pray for those who look everywhere to find peace;
for those who fill their lives with the things of this world
but will arrive empty-handed at the door of eternity;
for those who have lived for today and have given no
    thought for tomorrow;
and for those whose days revolve around themselves
and in satisfying their lust for pleasures of the moment.
May the grace of God touch them with his peace.
Our God answers prayer,
and we call on his name.

We pray for those whose whole life has been a journey
seeking comfort, hope and peace;
for those who long to fill the aching void deep inside;
for those whose ability to find peace was damaged by those
who robbed them of its joy in their youth;
for those too afraid to reach out,
and for those who find it so hard to trust again
now that this fragile gift has been broken.
May the grace of God touch them with his peace.
Our God answers prayer,
and we call on his name.

We pray for those who work for peace between nations;
for diplomats, politicians and delegations
seeking justice, hope and peace for all;
for those who work to bring peace in human relationships;
for counsellors, social workers and those ready to listen and
    care;
for those whose concern for the well-being of others
brings a pain and a sorrow, an anguish and a despair,
almost too great to bear.

May the grace of God touch them with his peace.
Our God answers prayer,
and we call on his name.

We pray for those who have lost peace;
for those whose homes have been wrecked by the storms of
    life
and their lives by the lies of others;
for those who have lost everything in [*current disaster*];
for those who have no one left of those who really mattered
    to them;
for those whose home, family and friends are all gone
and for those who have a loneliness that is all too painfully
    real
and an aloneness that cannot be put into words.
May the grace of God touch them with his peace.
Our God answers prayer,
and we call on his name.

We pray for those who destroy peace;
for those who see only 'the cause' and give no thought
to the pain, suffering and despair their self-centred blindness
    brings;
for those whose claims to be fighting for justice
are drowned out by the screams of their victims;
for those who plant bombs to terrorise and intimidate others
and for those whose cruel indifference
destroys all hope of the peace they claim they are fighting to
    bring.
May the grace of God touch them with his peace.
Our God answers prayer,
and we call on his name.

We pray for those who are being robbed of peace;
for those facing times of illness and uncertainty;
for those who have taken their health and fitness for granted
and for those with endless visits to hospital for treatment still
        to come;

for those robbed of peaceful sleep
as their minds are a sea of turmoil, restlessness and despair;
for those who carry a burden of worry for others
and for those who feel helpless except to listen, understand
    and care.
May the grace of God touch them with his peace.
Our God answers prayer,
and we call on his name.

We pray for those who long to be filled with the peace of
    God;
for those for whom church, faith and prayer
have been their touchstone for much of their lives;
for those who deep down within themselves know they need
    something more;
for those who long to be filled with the Spirit
but are fearful as to what this might mean;
for those who are daily discovering that peace is God's gift—
the fruit that comes from his presence within;
for those for whom this is the moment
to open their lives and to welcome him in.
May the grace of God touch them with his peace.
Our God answers prayer,
and we call on his name.

We bring all our prayers in the name of the Prince of Peace,
Christ the Lord. Amen.

248   FRUIT OF THE SPIRIT—PATIENCE

Think of someone in need of patience;
someone whose eyes are so fixed on the goals they have set
they leave themselves no room to grow, to live or to learn.
Lord, may your patient grace transform all our lives.

Silence

The Lord hears our prayer;
thanks be to God.

Think of someone in need of patience;
someone who set high standards of expectation for others
that guarantee them the chance to criticise and to deplore.
Lord, may your patient grace transform all our lives.

Silence

The Lord hears our prayer;
thanks be to God.

Think of someone in need of patience;
someone for whom others have set impossible mountains to
    climb,
that doom them to failure, weakness and a deep sense of
    being inferior.
Lord, may your patient grace transform all our lives.

Silence

The Lord hears our prayer;
thanks be to God.

Think of someone in need of patience;
someone who finds it hard to be patient with themselves;
whose failure to be loved unconditionally
makes it hard for them to know and accept that they are
    accepted.
Lord, may your patient grace transform all our lives.

Silence

The Lord hears our prayer;
thanks be to God.

Think of someone in need of patience;
someone who finds it hard to cope when things go wrong;
whose immediate response is to blame others
and to avert all responsibility being laid at their door.
Lord, may your patient grace transform all our lives.

Silence

The Lord hears our prayer;
thanks be to God.

Think of someone in need of patience;
someone who makes no allowances for the concerns of
    others
and who passes each day oblivious to their impact on others
and the distress that their attitudes and behaviour create.
Lord, may your patient grace transform all our lives.

Silence

The Lord hears our prayer;
thanks be to God.

Think of someone in need of patience;
someone who needs to begin to take the long view;
who today still sees no answer to their prayer of yesterday
and must yet discover the timetable of God.
Lord, may your patient grace transform all our lives.

Silence

The Lord hears our prayer;
thanks be to God.

Think of someone in need of patience;
someone who is impatient to grow in Christ,
to be filled with the Spirit and to know the love of God
and to serve him in the world
as they learn to open their hearts, minds and wills to him.
Lord, may your patient grace transform all our lives.

Silence

The Lord hears our prayer;
thanks be to God.

We ask our prayers, knowing God will patiently hear and
    answer them. Amen.

Lord, we pray for those who show kindness;
for those who go the extra mile and turn the other cheek;
for those whose kindness has changed lives
and helped others to value themselves and renew their hope
      in you;
for those whose lives will never be the same
because of the kindness they have received.
Lord, the source of all kindness,
fill the earth with your love.

Lord, we pray for those who have received kindness;
for those who have been blessed beyond their expectations
and those whose riches have outstripped their deserving;
for those who have accumulated so many of this world's
      good things
but have no sense of gratitude,
no desire to show something of the kindness and generosity
that has been shown to them.
Lord, the source of all kindness,
fill the earth with your love.

Lord, we pray for those whose kindness is being tested to the
      limit;
for those who are responsible for the care of others;
for those who have spent themselves in the service of others;
for those involved in counselling others,
in bringing healing and hope to broken bodies and damaged
      lives;
for those whose kindness has been the very hallmark of their
      lives,
but who are now themselves at the point of being broken.
The lack of thanks, appreciation and understanding has
      taken its toll.
Lord, the source of all kindness,
fill the earth with your love.

Lord, we pray for those for whom kindness is a thing of the
    past;
for those who have been hurt by their experiences,
damaged by what they witnessed
and broken by what they have been through;
for those who number among the world's forgotten refugees,
and for those whose whole lives have been wrecked by war
    and ethnic cleansing.
Lord, the source of all kindness,
fill the earth with your love.

Lord, we pray for those whose consciences have been dulled
and who have no sense of right and wrong;
those for whom kindness, love and compassion are signs of
    weakness
in a world where only the strong are allowed to succeed;
for those involved in criminal activity, antisocial behaviour
    and violence to others
and give no thought to the pain and distress that they cause.
Lord, the source of all kindness,
fill the earth with your love.

Lord, we pray for those whose kindness changed our lives;
for those who were there when we needed them
and for those who stood by us when others let us down;
for those whose kindness brought us to Jesus
and whose whole lifestyle has been a reflection of his grace;
for those whose kindness and words of witness and truth
pointed us to the source of all kindness and love.
Lord, the source of all kindness,
fill the earth with your love.

Lord, we pray for ourselves, that we may show kindness to
    others,
and that all we say and do
may be shot through with the grace and the kindness of
    Jesus.

We pray that the kindness we show to each other
will not be restricted to those who offer kindness to us.
We pray that our kindness will never be rationed, or even
controlled,
but the indisputable evidence of being filled with the Spirit
and this, his fruit.
Lord, the source of all kindness,
fill the earth with your love.

We bring our prayer in the name of Christ,
in the love of God and through the power of the Holy Spirit.
Amen.

250   FRUIT OF THE SPIRIT—GOODNESS

Lord, you are the source of all goodness.
We pray for those through whom your goodness flows;
those in whom we most clearly experience
a sense of your presence and an awareness of your beauty.
May your goodness touch and change your world and our
lives.

Silence

Lord, you are the source of all goodness.
We pray for those whose words and deeds bring us hope;
those who give us courage to stand firm,
to speak your name and to keep our eyes focused on the
kingdom of God.
May your goodness touch and change your world and our
lives.

Silence

Lord, you are the source of all goodness.
We pray for those whose attitudes and values
so reflect those of your kingdom
that they find themselves in direct conflict
with the assumptions and expectations of their neighbours;

those whose goodness is not something for show, or carefully
    rehearsed,
but the fruit of your Spirit within.
May your goodness touch and change your world and our
    lives.

Silence

Lord, you are the source of all goodness.
We pray for those who are like salt to the earth
and whose lives bring new light in the darkness around
    them;
those whose way of life is designed to care for your creation,
    not damage it.
May your goodness touch and change your world and our
    lives.

Silence

Lord, you are the source of all goodness.
We pray for those whose goodness is never seen,
for those whose words of compassion are heard by few
and yet whose deeds of caring are experienced by many;
those whose lives are so flooded by the grace of Christ
that his goodness overflows through them
to touch friends and family, colleagues and neighbours, old
    and young.
May your goodness touch and change your world and our
    lives.

Silence

Lord, you are the source of all goodness.
We pray for those for whom goodness is an anathema
and whose whole lives are focused on evil and corruption;
those whose minds have become so twisted
that goodness is counted as evil, and evil is the thing they
    desire;
those whose lack of essential goodness has broken homes,

destroyed relationships, brought nations to their knees
and filled hearts and minds with pain and fear.
May your goodness touch and change your world and our
　　lives.

Silence

Lord, you are the source of all goodness.
We pray for those who see goodness as a goal they can never
　　reach;
those who have been repeatedly told they are evil,
so that now they have begun to believe it;
for those for whom goodness is a mountain to climb—
a summit that will always be beyond them;
for those who are discovering that goodness is a fruit of the
　　Spirit
and for those who, as they open their lives to the Spirit's
　　presence,
are learning what Christ can do with and for them.
May your goodness touch and change your world and our
　　lives.

Silence

Lord, you are the source of all goodness.
We pray for ourselves, and for those that we know;
for those whose goodness still touches our lives.
We pray for ourselves, that as Christ touches us,
so we may become channels of his goodness to others.
May your goodness touch and change your world and our
　　lives.

Silence

Lord, you are the source of all goodness.
That is why we bring these prayers in your name. Amen.

251　FRUIT OF THE SPIRIT—FAITHFULNESS
Lord of all faithfulness,

we pray for those whose faithful service brings hope to
others;
for those who are firefighters, social workers or police
officers;
for those who are care workers, probation officers or career
officers.
May their faithfulness open doors to life and freedom for
others.
The Lord hears our prayer.
Thanks be to God.

Lord of all faithfulness,
we pray for those whose faithfulness drives them to care for
your creation;
for those who warn us of the damage we are doing to planet
Earth;
for those who challenge us to change our attitude to the
world around us
and for those who remind us of the responsibilities you have
laid upon us.
The Lord hears our prayer.
Thanks be to God.

Lord of all faithfulness,
we pray for relationships that have been blessed
by a deep sense of trust and faithfulness;
for those who know they can take for granted
each other's love, care and compassion
and who offer nothing but love and faithfulness in return;
for homes where children thrive in an atmosphere of love
without price
and for homes where love and faithfulness are at a premium;
but we also pray for relationships crucified by unfaithful
behaviour
and for homes wrecked by the bitterness and distrust that it
brings.
The Lord hears our prayer.
Thanks be to God.

Lord of all faithfulness,
we pray for those who faithfully seek to use the gifts you
    have given them
to enable others to live fuller lives and reach their own
    potential;
for parents, grandparents and relatives
whose faithful support and encouragement provide
a way through times of stress, self-doubt and fear;
for those who teach in schools, colleges and universities
and who faithfully seek to open minds to the wonders of life
and to a knowledge of each person's true worth.
The Lord hears our prayer.
Thanks be to God.

Lord of all faithfulness,
we pray for those who faithfully respond to the challenges
    laid upon them;
for those who see the pain, hunger and injustice in your
    world
and are driven to turn their words of concern into deeds of
    compassion;
for those who transform their despair at the situations faced
    by others
into actions that change lives and bring hope
to a confused, despairing and divided world.
The Lord hears our prayer.
Thanks be to God.

Lord of all faithfulness,
we pray for those who faithfully proclaim the good news of
    Jesus;
for those whose written and spoken words
touch hearts, change minds and point a new direction
for all who receive them;
for those whose lives are a symbol of hope
and whose words cut through the morass of self-interest
and the barriers of self-sufficiency;
for those who faithfully allow themselves

to be channels of God's grace to others
and for those whose faithful obedience to the call of Christ
comes at great personal cost to themselves and to others.
The Lord hears our prayer.
Thanks be to God.

Lord of all faithfulness,
we pray for ourselves and the challenges and pressures we
    face in our walk with Christ;
for those moments when we are brought face to face with
    our own mortality,
when our faithfulness to you is put to the ultimate test;
for those times when following Christ almost makes the
    journey harder
as we are forced to choose between being faithful to him and
    his will for our lives,
and allowing the world to write our agenda
and so shape who we are and what we shall become.
We pray for ourselves and praise you
for your faithful love that has renewed our lives
and the Holy Spirit who equips us to be faithful disciples
of the Lord of all faithfulness.
The Lord hears our prayer.
Thanks be to God.

We bring our prayer in the name of our faithful God. Amen.

252   FRUIT OF THE SPIRIT—GENTLENESS

Lord, we hold up before you those whose gentleness
    challenges the world;
those whose attitude of self-forgetfulness
stands in sharp contrast to the self-centredness that pervades
    every corner of life
and the self-interest that crucifies love for others.
May your world feel again the challenge of your grace.
Lord of all gentleness,
hold us in your will.

Lord, we hold up before you
those whose gentleness is an avoidance of conflict;
those who would rather pretend that there is no evil in your
     world
and no injustices to fight;
those who hide within themselves
and those whose gentleness masks their fear of taking a
     stand;
those whose gentleness is a deliberate strategy
which covers their insecurity and doubt.
May your people hear again the call to stand in your name.
Lord of all gentleness,
hold us in your will.

Lord, we hold up before you
those whose gentleness comes at enormous cost to
     themselves;
those who, because others see them as different,
persistently face abuse, intolerance and rejection;
those who do not fight back when they face racial abuse
but gently seek to reach out in love,
to change minds filled with hate
and to reflect the love that Christ showed from his cross.
May our society learn once again that God's love is for all.
Lord of all gentleness,
hold us in your will.

Lord, we hold up before you
those whose gentleness brings hope to the hopeless
and courage to those who are broken;
people who stand alongside the lost and those losing their
     way;
servants who welcome strangers and hold those filled with
     sadness and despair;
those who risk everything to lift the fallen
and to heal those who are hurting deep inside;
those who have lost everything the world counts important
because their hearts are set on a treasure more precious.

May riches of God's hope flow out through the sweet
gentleness of love.
Lord of all gentleness,
hold us in your will.

Lord, we hold up before you
those whose gentleness has touched our lives
and given us hope when we most needed it;
those whose names will never hit the headlines
and whose loving concern is known only to those who have
received it;
those whose words of peace and deeds of kindness
make life worth living and each day a new joy;
those who have stood by us even when we least deserved it
and those whose gentle assurance and loving touch
were things we could rely on completely.
May we hear again the call to become unexpected channels
of God's endless love.
Lord of all gentleness,
hold us in your will.

Lord, we hold up before you
those whose gentleness is an example of joy and a witness to
Christ;
those who gently care for the sick and wait with the dying;
those who gently enrich young minds
and open doors of learning and discovery to others;
those who gently care for the poor and bring hope to the
starving;
those who gently but firmly remind us all
of the responsibilities God gave us—
to protect the earth and to remember to whom it belongs.
Lord of all gentleness,
hold us in your will.

Lord, we hold up before you
those whose gentleness enables them to love the unlovable,
to touch the untouchable and to forgive the unforgivable;

those whose gentleness breaks hardened hearts
and heals damaged relationships;
those whose gentle gifts of understanding
have ended conflicts and prevented wars;
those whose gentle skills of diplomacy
enable communities, once deeply embittered,
to reach out across the barriers that divide.
May the love of Christ be the source of all our gentleness.
Lord of all gentleness,
hold us in your will.

Lord, we bring ourselves before you
as those to whom gentleness is not something that comes easily.
We confess that too often we find it more natural to respond
out of selfish ambition and hurt pride.
Lord, we bring ourselves before you
not simply to seek to be more gentle
but that we might be filled with your Spirit
in whom this and all your fruits can find their birth.
May we be filled with the Holy Spirit and bring glory to God.
Lord of all gentleness,
hold us in your will.

In the name of Christ, whose gentle yet powerful love is for
   all. Amen.

253   FRUIT OF THE SPIRIT—SELF-CONTROL

Think of someone whose life is out of control;
someone whose lifestyle is causing pain and anguish to
   others
and whose lack of self-control is a burden to those who care
   about them.

Silence

Think of someone whose life is extremely controlled;
someone whose life is lived on the tramlines of insecurity
and whose lack of self-worth prevents them experiencing

the hope, joy and freedom that life was meant to bring.

Silence

Think of someone whose desire is always to be in control,
who is never content to allow others to express themselves;
someone whose dominant personality and domineering
    attitude
restrict the lives of others and deprive them
of the opportunity to know what their lives could have been.

Silence

Think of someone whose lack of self-control
has led others into addictions that now rule their lives
and into lifestyles that will ultimately darken their days;
someone who knows what their lack of self-control is doing
    to others
but is too weak or too insensitive to care.

Silence

Think of someone whose self-control is a rock for others to
    build on
and a haven where peace can be found;
someone who tirelessly works in the background to resolve
    disputes,
heal relationships and break down barriers that divide.

Silence

Think of someone whose self-control is not of their own
    making,
but comes from their close walk with God;
someone who is filled with the Holy Spirit
and whose self-control is a gift and a fruit from above;
someone whose life is so filled with the love of Christ and
    the power of the Spirit
that each day is lived under his control
and their plans and their dreams spring from his grace.

Silence

Think of someone whose life is still controlled
by the pain they have suffered and the abuse they have
    endured;
someone whose life has been controlled by their poverty
and whose hopes and expectations have been limited by
    ridicule
and by the lack of praise and encouragement from others.

Silence

Sovereign Lord, we acknowledge that nothing is beyond
    your ultimate control,
and we commit our way, and the way of all those for whom
    we pray,
into your loving care. In the name of Christ. Amen.

254   RICHES

Lord, we pray for those who think they are rich;
for those who have filled their lives with the things of this
    world;
for those for whom their material possessions mean
    everything;
for those whose commitment to have more of the wealth of
    the earth
will mean that they will arrive empty-handed at the
    threshold of eternity.
May the Lord open blind eyes,
and help us to see.

Lord, we pray for those whose desire for riches
has brought pain and anguish to others;
for those whose headlong grasping for wealth
and the status they think it will bring
blinds them to the destruction they leave in their wake.
May the Lord open blind eyes,
and help us to see.

Lord, we pray for those whose riches come at great cost to
others;
for those whose wealth comes from illegal trading in arms or
drugs;
for those with no conscience for the lives that are destroyed
just so that they can become richer;
for those whose riches are the result of corruption
and their failure to be worthy of their positions of trust.
May the Lord open blind eyes,
and help us to see.

Lord, we pray for those whose riches cannot be seen
and whose wealth cannot be counted;
for the sick and the dying, whose faith enriches everyone,
and for the disabled, whose courage and hope
add so much each day to the joy of life;
for those who are poor in terms of this world
but whose investments are high in the kingdom of God.
May the Lord open blind eyes,
and help us to see.

Lord, we pray for those on the threshold of riches;
for those who know of you but still haven't met you;
for those who have known your truth and your name all
their lives
but have yet to discover the joy of knowing they belong in
your family;
for those whose knowledge of you is all in their heads
and who long for their hearts to be set ablaze with your
grace.
May the Lord open blind eyes,
and help us to see.

Lord, we pray for those who add to the richness of life;
for writers, poets and painters, whose words and designs
colour each day;
for those whose songs and music multiply the joy in your
world

and for those whose selfless care and service
increase the sum of hope and peace for their neighbour.
May the Lord open blind eyes,
and help us to see.

Lord, we pray for those who are open to the riches of the
    Spirit;
those whose lives daily lie open to his power;
those who are recognising their poverty
and are rejoicing in the riches only Christ can provide;
those whose lives overflow with the power and the presence
    of the Spirit
and whose every word and deed is a demonstration
of the riches which your presence releases.
May the Lord open blind eyes,
and help us to see.

Lord, we pray for ourselves as, like a child learning to walk,
we attempt those first stuttering steps
and open our lives to be enriched by your love.
Lord, hold our hand, steady our feet, help us to trust and
to surrender to you our self-interest, our self-sufficiency and
    our self-centredness.
Though we may be as paupers in terms of this world
you promise untold riches in the kingdom of Christ.
May the Lord open blind eyes,
and help us to see. Amen.

255   MOTHERING SUNDAY

We pray for those with no home;
for those who live on the street and whose home is a
    cardboard box,
their blanket a pile of old newspapers;
for those with a past they have forgotten and a future they
    never consider;
for those for whom today, and the source of their next meal,
is all they ever think of.

May Christ, who had nowhere to lay his head,
help us to care for those with no home.
The Lord is our brother,
and we call on his name.

We pray for those homes with only one parent;
those for whom each day is a struggle to cope,
who are weighed down with responsibilities
and have no one with whom these can be shared;
for those who feel trapped—imprisoned in parenthood,
for whom the doorway to change and hope, fulfilment and
    self-respect
never seems open, but is constantly slammed shut in their
    face;
for those overwhelmed with regret and a deep sense of
    sadness;
and for those whose experience of rejection and betrayal
is a pain too deep to put into words.
May Christ, who brought hope to a woman at a well,
help us to reach out to those who are alone.
The Lord is our brother,
and we call on his name.

We pray for homes under strain,
where every conversation is shot through with feelings of
    bitterness
and fashioned in the mould of their anger;
for relationships that have gone badly wrong
and where separation or divorce are seen as the only way
    ahead;
for those who still long to start again
but are uncertain if their fragile ability to trust has been
    damaged beyond repair;
for those who long to find help
and who still are committed to the promises that they once
    made;
and for those who struggle on out of fear, loss of confidence,
    or concern for the children.

May Christ the healer reach out to them,
that their homes may be filled with the spirit of
    reconciliation.
The Lord is our brother,
and we call on his name.

We pray for those whose home life
is coloured and stained by disappointment and despair;
for those who have longed to be parents, but have found this
    gift is denied;
for those who find it hard to speak of this, their deepest
    need;
those for whom the pain and the hurt, the anguish and the
    anger,
the sense of failure and loss, are simply too deep to share;
for those who are single and are made to feel excluded
by our family-oriented society and churches;
for those with tears in their hearts for the children they have
    lost;
and for those who weep inside for the children they feel they
    are losing
to drink, to drugs or to a life of crime.
May Christ, whose mother watched him die,
grant them peace in his love and joy in the promise of
    resurrection.
The Lord is our brother,
and we call on his name.

We pray for all those for whom Mothering Sunday
is a day of sadness and dread;
those for whom it is a day to avoid, to get through, just to
    cope;
for those around the world who have lost home and family,
especially [*current world needs*];
for those with no happy memories of home
as the place where they felt safe, wanted and unconditionally
    loved;

for those who remember only the abuse, the scorn, or the
   neglect;
for those still grieving for the childhood they have lost, or
   never had;
and for those filled with sadness and loss for the parent who
   has died.
The Lord is our brother,
and we call on his name.

On this Mothering Sunday we give thanks
for our place in God's family, the church,
that with all its faults and mistakes is still meant to be like a
   mother or father
to lead us on the journey of faith.
We pray for those whose lives and words and deeds led us to
   Christ,
and for those whose gentle, clear witness today
still nourishes our faith, and gives us courage to walk in
   hope;
we give thanks for every opportunity to tell our story of faith
and to lead someone else to the empty cross to meet their
   Saviour
risen, ascended and glorified.
May the risen Christ, who through the power of the Holy
   Spirit still changes lives,
be the source of our hope and the promise of glory.
The Lord is our brother,
and we call on his name.

In the name of him who is Lord of the church, the family of
   God,
Jesus Christ the Lord. Amen.

256   EDUCATION SUNDAY

Lord, we pray for all those who are involved in education,
for those who teach, those who are school governors,
those on school councils, parent-teacher associations,

for all involved in the running of schools, colleges and
    universities.
May they demonstrate their commitment to sharing truth
    and knowledge.
Lord, in your mercy,
hear our prayer.

Lord, we pray for those who are being taught,
for children and young people at school, college or
    university.
May learning become a thrilling and exciting adventure.
May they learn to use the power that knowledge brings
for the care and service of their fellow human beings.
May they and we discover Christ as the source of all truth.
Lord, in your mercy,
hear our prayer.

Lord, we pray for an increase in opportunities for education
both in this country and, especially, in less developed nations
    of the world,
for the work of [*name*] and all who seek to bring knowledge
of health, agriculture and Christ to all the world.
Lord, in your mercy,
hear our prayer.

Lord, we thank you for all the ways we can learn about living
    in your world;
for the opportunities to know that you, Lord,
are the source of all that is good and true;
for giving us a lifetime of learning; for opportunities for
    growth and discovery.
Open our hearts, we pray, and our minds and our lives
to the wealth of good things we can learn about living, and
    about life.
Give us a greater sensitivity to each other's needs
and a readiness to learn from one another.
We thank you for all who gave their lives that we may learn
    the way to Christ,

and with him walk the path of peace and joy and love.
Lord, in your mercy,
hear our prayer.

Lord, we pray for the community of the church.
We ask that you will fill your church with the power of the
 Holy Spirit,
that, as your people, we may grow together in love and joy,
and learn from each other more of your love, your
 forgiveness and your peace.
We ask that we may learn what it means to follow Christ.
We thank you that his teaching is a challenge to the world,
that he offers a way through the tangle of life,
and teaches us of the cost of following him.
We pray, as we give ourselves to Jesus, that he may be Lord
 of our lives
and that we may have the power and courage to obey.
Lord, in your mercy,
hear our prayer.

In the name of Christ, the teacher. Amen.

257   PASSION SUNDAY

Father, we pray for those in positions of leadership—
personal, national or international,
for those who hold in their hands
the future of our lives or of the life of the planet itself.
We pray too for those whose lives, and the living of them,
 are out of control.
May your loving will lead them into a new beginning,
that they may acknowledge your sovereignty over all things.
Lord, in your mercy,
hear our prayer.

Father, we pray for those who seek to crush or hurt another
 human being.
May they themselves be conquered by the love that flows
 from the cross.

We pray for those who are mastered by temptation,
for those ruled by an obsession or addiction,
for those governed by anger, hatred, or aggression
and for those ruled by what others think, or expect of them;
for those overwhelmed by the pressures of life upon them.
May they experience the victory of Christ each day.
Lord, in your mercy,
hear our prayer.

Father, we pray for all who seek to build bridges between
      nations and races
of hope, forgiveness, peace and understanding;
for those who seek to overcome the barriers
erected by different sides of industry or sections of the
      community.
We pray for your church, and for Christians everywhere,
that you will enable us to live and speak, to behave and love
in such a way that others may be found by Christ
and, in being found, know that their wholeness of life
is the free gift you purchased on the cross of Calvary.
Lord, in your mercy,
hear our prayer.

Father, we pray for all those who look to build a better
      world,
a more equal society, a more caring community;
for those who long for a more loving attitude, a deeper
      knowledge of you.
But we pray also for those who find the cost of commitment
      too high;
those for whom the cost of following Christ is at the limits
      of what they can bear;
those who know that the world is watching and waiting
to see how they cope with hurt and respond to the sorrow
      and pain,
the disappointment and the suffering that life brings.
May they find in you all the resources they require for every
      need they have.

Lord, in your mercy,
hear our prayer.

Father we pray for those whose lives and living are incomplete,
for those living less fulfilled lives than you planned for them;
for those whose lives are handicapped
by homelessness, fear, loneliness, uncertainty;
for those who are damaged by deep sorrow, or the power of
    sin,
for those who struggle with the hardship of being mentally
    or physically less able,
for those undervalued by unemployment and all the hard-
    heartedness of life.
We pray for ourselves, and we ask that the incompleteness in
    us
may be more than matched by the all-sufficiency of Christ.
May we experience today, and through the rest of this week,
the knowledge that Christ is your final answer to our need of
    a life that is complete.
Lord, in your mercy,
hear our prayer.

In the name of Christ, the Lord of the Passion. Amen.

258   COPING WITH STRESS

I am a worker under stress. I have worked in this industry
    for many years.
I have always enjoyed my job,
and going to work each day was something I looked forward
    to.
But now the job has changed.
When the company downsized the workforce
it meant a huge increase in my workload.
I now do the work that once was done by three of us.
The pressure to succeed is enormous
and I don't think I can cope much longer.
Pray for me.

Silence

I am a mother under stress.
I looked forward to having a family of my own
and my children are a great joy to me.
But they also are the cause of much of the stress I face each
    day.
They are both under school age, and very lively,
and are always demanding more time and energy than I feel
    I have left to give.
My family lives miles away, and I don't know many people
    where we live.
I am very lonely, and beginning to forget who I really am.
Pray for me.

Silence

I am a person in the health service.
Whether I am a consultant or a cleaner, or someone in
    between,
we all feel the pressure when something goes wrong.
We regret every mistake.
But we are all human, and that means every one of us makes
    mistakes.
Unfortunately for us and our patients
ours can make the difference between life and death.
Perhaps if we felt more appreciated and under less pressure
the criticisms might be easier to bear.
Pray for me.

Silence

I am a person who works away from home.
It sounded exciting at first.
It made me feel important to be sent to work in different
    parts of the country.
They assured me that it would be for only a few weeks.
But that was over two years ago.

I see my wife and family only at weekends
when I am too stressed and exhausted to enjoy our few short
    hours together.
I know we are drifting apart, but what can I do?
There is the mortgage and the credit repayments to meet,
and I can see no way out of this mess.
Pray for me.

Silence

I am a young person.
Perhaps you think I am too young to have problems with
    stress!
But the pressure from my peer group is unrelenting.
I am ridiculed because I don't want to get involved with
    drink, drugs or sex.
In a strange way my parents' pride
and desire to give me encouragement and support
sometimes puts me under even greater pressure to please
    them!
I feel so alone, and I have no one to talk to.
Pray for me.

Silence

I am an old person.
Perhaps you think that people of my age don't experience
    times of stress—but we do!
Will I be able to cope on my own? How long can I keep my
    independence?
What if I am ill—how will I manage?
I once longed for time for myself—now I have too much
    time on my own!
I was so used to having family and friends around me.
Now I find the silence and the emptiness almost unbearable.
Pray for me.

Silence

I am a person of faith. I feel ashamed to admit that
serving God and seeking to trust him can be so stressful!
But, at times, it seems as if the whole world is watching and
waiting
to see how I will cope, what answer I will give to each new
world disaster.
They see me as God's spokesperson, and I don't find it an
easy role to fulfil.
The stress comes from not knowing the answers to my own
questions
and realising I will just have to trust that he does.
Pray for me.

Silence

We bring all our prayers in the name of him who is our
peace. Amen.

259   ROOTS

Father, we pray for those who have no roots to their lives or
their living,
for refugees and victims of war,
for the homeless and those who feel rejected and unwanted,
for those who have lost the roots of family and friends
in the turmoil of their lives.
We pray: Give them hope in the strength of your love.
The Lord hears our prayer.
Thanks be to God.

Father, we pray for those who are uprooted,
for those traumatised by all they have faced and are facing
in this troubled world;
for those deeply hurt by violence, injustice and self-interest;
for those facing misery and despair,
and for those crushed by the pain and sorrow that breaks
many hearts.
We pray for those who feel uprooted from all they have
cherished.

Give them a new sense of belonging in the love of Christ.
The Lord hears our prayer.
Thanks be to God.

Father, we pray for those whose whole way of life is rooted in
the wrong things,
for those whose whole way of life springs from violence,
bitterness and greed;
for those caught up in the effects of wrong decisions;
for those whose words and deeds spoil life
not only for themselves but also for others;
for those who traffic in drugs;
and for those who even now are being tempted to abuse a
child.
May the strength of Christ transform their lives.
The Lord hears our prayer.
Thanks be to God.

Father, we pray for those whose lives are rooted in pain,
for those who face the pain of loneliness, of fear and
separation,
for those who face the pain of body, mind or spirit.
We pray for anyone we know to be facing the pain
of anxiety, depression, or bereavement.
We pray especially for those whose pain is caused by sin—
their own or someone else's.
May the love and the joy of Christ be their source of peace.
The Lord hears our prayer.
Thanks be to God.

Father, we pray for ourselves and our own roots.
We pray that you will keep the message of John the Baptist
clearly in our minds
as we seek to prepare and be prepared for the coming of your
Son.
We ask: Teach us and enable us to remember
that our faith is rooted in what you did and what you are
doing in history.

Help us so to be rooted in the power of the Holy Spirit
that we may be ready to face opposition in our obedience to
   you.
Keep our hearts so fixed upon Christ that, being rooted in
   him,
we may be rooted in those things that count for all eternity.
The Lord hears our prayer.
Thanks be to God.

In the name of Christ, who came that we might be rooted in
   his love. Amen.

260   WORDS (BIBLE SUNDAY)

Father, we pray for the world—
the world of politics, of diplomacy and peace negotiations;
for those whose words can bring peace, resolve animosity
and rebuild bridges of hope;
for the right words to be used—words of hope and peace
   and reconciliation.
We pray that the words used by leaders of nations
may be honest, open and compassionate.
Lord, in your mercy,
hear our prayer.

Father, we pray for our own nation.
We think sadly of the divisions among us—
black and white, rich and poor, old and young,
employed and unemployed, haves and have nots.
We pray: Give us the right words to use
that will break down the barriers we erect or allow to remain
   between us.
Lord, in your mercy,
hear our prayer.

Father, we pray for young people at school or college.
We know that they are places of many words,
words that are new and words that are familiar,
words that challenge and words that confuse,

words that lead young minds forward
and words that might lead them astray.
Help young people everywhere to value every opportunity to
learn new things,
discover deeper truth and stand firm against all that is
wrong.
May the words we use teach others the real value of life.
Lord, in your mercy,
hear our prayer.

Father, we pray for our homes.
Forgive us that so often they are the places where we use
angry, bitter or impatient words.
They are the places where we show the least care
about the things we say and how we say them.
Forgive us if today we have said something unkind, unloving
or unhelpful.
We pray: Help us to use words of comfort, love and
understanding.
Lord, in your mercy,
hear our prayer.

Father, on this Bible Sunday, we thank you for those who
down the centuries
have made it possible for us to have a Bible of our own, and
in our own language.
We thank you for the light that your Word brings to our
lives
and for the way that you speak the word we need to hear.
Help us to read the Bible, that we may know more
about ourselves, about you, about your world
and the way you would have us live in it.
Help us by your Holy Spirit not simply to read your Word,
but that in reading it we may know Jesus, the way, the truth
and the life,
and that, in knowing him, we may enter into life that is real.
Lord, in your mercy,
hear our prayer.

We ask our prayers in the name of him who is the Word of
life. Amen.

261   THE HARVEST

Confession

Father, we thank you that everywhere we look
we see the evidence of your existence, the proof that you are
there.
We thank you too that we can see signs of your presence
in the acts of kindness and love in the lives of the people we
meet.
We pray that the way we live—how we speak,
the things we say and the things we don't say,
the things we value, and how we trust you—
will make us a confession, a declaration,
of your presence and love for all the world.
Lord, in your mercy,
hear our prayer.

Celebration

Father, we ask you to forgive us if our attempts to live the
Christian life
have given other people the idea that to follow Jesus is a
negative way of life.
We ask you to help us to begin to live in the knowledge that
trusting him is the most exciting thing in life.
May we be a people who, not only each Sunday,
but every day of our lives, live the life of celebration.
May the joy of harvest, with its celebration of your loving
care,
be the source of hope and challenge to the world.
Lord, in your mercy,
hear our prayer.

Corporate

Father, at this time of Harvest Festival,

we ask that you will teach us and all people the message of
    sharing.
We confess with shame that governments around the world,
    including our own,
have not shared your harvest with any real sense of fairness
    and love.
Forgive us and all nations for thinking that the harvest
    belonged to us,
and was ours to keep, or even ours to give as we thought fit.
Teach us again the painful lesson that
there is only one harvest as there is only one world.
Help us, we pray, to want to share these signs of your love
    that we hold in trust.
Lord, in your mercy,
hear our prayer.

Commitment
Father, we pray that this Harvest Festival may be a special
    one for us.
May this be a time of commitment and recommitment.
We pray that as we have brought our harvest gifts and
    presented them to you,
may we also offer our hearts and lives in your service.
We come now and offer back to you, not only our fruits and
    flowers,
but also the work of our hands and minds:
our skills and our talents, our experiences and our hopes,
our hours and our days, our months and our years.
Lord, we come and commit into your hands our past, future
    and our present.
Lord, in your mercy,
hear our prayer.

We pray in the name of the Lord of the harvest. Amen.

262   HARVEST

At harvest we remember the joy of living in God's world,

and that we are surrounded by so many beautiful things.
We thank God for streams and for rivers, for hills and for
valleys;
for trees and for flowers, for seas and for oceans;
and for all the beauty of his creation.
We thank him too for all the joy and wonder that comes to us
through the appreciation of beauty and colour.
We pray for those who are blind, or whose sight is fading:
may they still marvel at God's gracious gifts;
and for those with eyes but who fail to recognise the gift of
God.
The Lord hears our prayer.
Thanks be to God.

When we think of the flowers, fruit and vegetables
that we thank God for at harvest time,
we remember that many live in places where there are no
fields or gardens
and few open spaces where children can play.
We pray for children who have never picked a flower,
for young people who have never walked in the countryside
and for parents facing the daily frustration
of living in a high-rise flat or filthy slum.
The Lord hears our prayer.
Thanks be to God.

At harvest we are reminded that millions around the world
never have enough to eat.
Let us ask God's forgiveness for forgetting that
much of the wealth of this country was gained by the
exploitation of others.
We pray that our leaders, our nation and we ourselves
may begin to take seriously our responsibility for
those who are starving and those who are hungry for hope,
and for those who are thirsting for the chance to live before
they die.
The Lord hears our prayer.
Thanks be to God.

We remember that we live in a world that rewards success
and despises failure.
We remember too that there are many people, young and
old,
who do not feel that they matter or have anything to offer.
We pray for those who feel rejected, unworthy or
unwanted.
We ask that they might learn that they and their gifts
are already accepted and included in God's harvest.
The Lord hears our prayer.
Thanks be to God.

Today we thank God for the provision of our needs as
individuals,
remembering that he is concerned for the whole world.
We pray for our community,
and those in positions of leadership and authority.
We also pray for those who have recently moved here
and are finding it hard to cope with the changes involved
and are still seeking a harvest of friendship.
The Lord hears our prayer.
Thanks be to God

We ask our prayers in Jesus' name. Amen.

263   ONE WORLD WEEK

Lord, we pray for your world,
your beautiful world that you have entrusted to our care.
In One World Week remind people everywhere
that creation belongs, not to us, but to you,
and you are calling us to respect the world in which we live.
Lord, this is your world,
and we will care for it.

Lord, we pray for a new sense of belonging to the family of
nations,
for an ending of wars over meaningless boundaries,
for a new respect for people of all nations, races and abilities,

for a new determination that everyone should receive an
    equal opportunity
to become the person you meant them to be.
Lord, this is your world,
and we will care for it.

Lord, we pray for leaders of nations and for those in
    positions of authority,
people with the power to make decisions
that can really make a difference for the good for millions on
    planet Earth;
for those more concerned to respond to popular opinion,
and for those who are prepared simply to do what they know
    is right.
Lord, this is your world,
and we will care for it.

Lord, we pray for those who feel left out by our power-
    hungry world,
for those left behind by those forging ahead,
for those who are left empty-handed
by those whose hands are overflowing with this world's good
    things;
for those with no hope, no joy, no purpose and no future,
who are daily forgotten by those who have more than they
    need or can use.

Lord, this is your world,
and we will care for it.

Lord, we pray for those whose harvests have failed,
for those who are not simply hungry, but are starving to death,
for those afraid for their children
whose swollen bellies fill them with nothing but despair,
for those whose only concern is their next meal—
where it will come from, and if it will come in time.
Lord, this is your world,
and we will care for it.

Lord, we pray for your world which you designed to be
    one;
for your world which we have divided and destroyed;
for your world which aches and despairs;
for your world which daily nails you to the cross.
We pray for your world that, again, it may be one.
Lord, this is your world,
and we will care for it.

Lord, we pray for ourselves and our part in your world,
for the choices and decisions we make
with little or no thought for the impact they make on
    others;
for our words and our actions which contribute to the pain
    and the sorrow,
the anguish and fear, the inequality and unfairness,
that are now squeezing your world dry.
Lord, help us not only to pray,
but to act justly, love mercy and walk with you, our God.
Lord, this is your world,
and we will care for it.

In the name of the one God, who is Lord of all the earth.
    Amen.

264   DISASTERS

We pray for those for whom today is a day of darkness and
    pain,
for those who have received bad news
and those for whom the bottom has dropped out of their
    world.
May Christ hold them gently in his hands.
The Lord hears our prayer.
Thanks be to God.

We pray for those involved in *[the incident]*,
for those injured and maimed, for those seriously ill in
    hospital,

and those for whom life will never be the same again.
May Christ hold them gently in his hands.
The Lord hears our prayer.
Thanks be to God.

We pray for those who will be affected by *[the incident]*
long after it ceases to be an item of news for others,
for families and friends of those killed or injured,
for the members of the rescue services and hospital staff
affected by all they have seen and heard.
May Christ hold them gently in his hands.
The Lord hears our prayer.
Thanks be to God.

We pray for those facing years of hardship and anxiety,
for those who have lost everything in flood, earthquake or
storm,
for those who have nothing left and nowhere to go,
for those who are afraid and filled with despair.
May Christ hold them gently in his hands.
The Lord hears our prayer.
Thanks be to God.

We pray for those involved in serious accidents
on the roads, in the air or at sea,
for those awaiting news of loved ones who are missing
and for those who will never know what really happened.
May Christ hold them gently in his hands.
The Lord hears our prayer.
Thanks be to God.

We pray for those who have lost everything because of civil
war or terrorist attack,
for those who are without home and family,
for those left as wandering, unwanted refugees.
May Christ hold them gently in his hands.
The Lord hears our prayer.
Thanks be to God.

We pray for those whose peaceful lives and untroubled existence
have been shaken by knowledge of serious illness;
for those who have received bad news
about their own or their family's health and future.
May Christ hold them gently in his hands.
The Lord hears our prayer.
Thanks be to God.

We pray for ourselves
and the concerns that trouble our own hearts and minds and lives,
for all we know we must face in the coming weeks and months,
and for wisdom to know what to say and what to do,
for strength to stand firm and for faith to trust the one who alone is trustworthy.
May Christ hold us gently in his hands.
The Lord hears our prayer.
Thanks be to God.

We leave our prayers in the gentle hands of Christ
and trust him to reach out in love. Amen.

265   IN TIME OF WAR

We pray for a world at war,
for those for whom today is a day of darkness and pain,
for those who have received bad news
and those for whom the bottom has dropped out of their world;
for those facing illness, stress, or despair,
and for those whose days are empty of hope
but filled with fear and with loneliness.
May Christ hold them gently in his hands.
The Lord hears our prayer.
Thanks be to God.

We pray for those who wage war,
for those involved in attacks by terrorists,
for those injured and maimed, for those seriously ill in
    hospital
and those for whom life will never be the same again;
for those who plant bombs,
and for those whose dogma blinds them to the needs of
    others.
May Christ touch them with his grace.
The Lord hears our prayer.
Thanks be to God.

We pray for a world at war,
for those who will fight and for those who wait for their return;
for those who will be injured
and for the families of those who will never return;
for those who must make the decisions
and for those whose lives will be changed by the decisions
    that are made.
May the peace of God hold us and lead us.
The Lord hears our prayer.
Thanks be to God.

We pray for those who go to war,
for those on the front line and for those providing support
    and aid;
for those who will witness terrible things
and for those who will lose their homes, their loved ones and
    their way of life.
May Christ hold them gently in his hands.
The Lord hears our prayer.
Thanks be to God.

We pray for those who will feel the impact of war,
for ordinary people in [*place*] who may lose their homes and
    their families;
for medical staff on both sides as they care for the sick and
    the injured;

for the leaders of the nations, and all the members of the
   United Nations
as they witness the results of what they have done—or failed
   to do.
May Christ hold them gently in his hands.
The Lord hears our prayer.
Thanks be to God.

We pray for a world at war,
that the peace of God will move stubborn hearts and minds
   and wills,
that forgiveness may restore human relationships,
that the hand of friendship may reach out in hope,
that healing and trust may replace hatred and bitterness,
that words of anger and resentment may be re-clothed in the
   spirit of love.
May the love of Christ touch all our relationships.
The Lord hears our prayer.
Thanks be to God.

We pray for those who feel their whole way of life is at war,
for those whose peaceful lives and untroubled existence
have been shaken by the knowledge of serious illness;
for those who have received bad news
about their own or their family's health and future;
for those who have prayed and go on praying
and are finding it hard to reconcile their suffering
with a God of love and compassion;
for those who see only the evil in the world
and are blinded to the grace of God.
May Christ hold them gently in his hands.
The Lord hears our prayer.
Thanks be to God.

We pray for ourselves and wars we experience in our own
   lives,
for the concerns that trouble our own hearts and minds and
   lives,

for all we know we must face in the coming weeks and
    months;
for wisdom to know what to say and to do, and for strength
    to stand firm,
and for faith to trust the one who alone is trustworthy.
May Christ hold us gently in his hands.
The Lord hears our prayer.
Thanks be to God.

We leave our prayers in the gentle hands of Christ
and trust him to reach out in love. Amen.

266 RESPONSIBILITY

I am a world leader.
I feel passionately about peace and justice, and it seems that,
in every decision I make, I bear upon my shoulders
the responsibility for the peace of the world.
But the burden is too great for one person.
Pray for me.

Silence

I am just an ordinary person.
I am unaware of having done any great wrongs in my life, or
    any great good.
Yet I know that the way I live, the things I choose, the
    demands I make on others
contribute to the store of the world's hurt and pain.
I long to live justly, and to choose wisely, and to love truly.
Pray for me.

Silence

I am someone's child.
I am an adult now, but my parents still see me as their child.
But they are now in their old age, and I have responsibility
    for them.
I find it hard to cope with the unrelenting demands
and the incessant sense of being responsible.

I can't cope much longer.
Pray for me.

Silence

I work in industry.
Whether I am in management or on the shop floor,
whether I am a company director or a member of a union—
I still feel an acute sense of responsibility.
How do I balance the needs of the company with those of
    the workforce?
How do I keep in tension profitability and the needs of
    people's daily lives?
Pray for me.

Silence

I am someone in the health service.
Each day I face life and death decisions.
I entered a caring profession to heal the sick and meet the
    needs of the broken.
But I have been made responsible for deciding
who receives help and who does not,
who is healed and who is left to wait—and go on waiting.
It isn't a burden of my choosing.
Pray for me.

Silence

I am a parent.
I had no training for the most important and most crucial
    task of all.
I did my best. I did what I could. I did what I thought was
    right.
But looking back, I realise now the mistakes I have made—
and the responsibility weighs heavily on me.
I acted in good faith and in love. I need to know
that the responsibility for what has happened is not all mine.
Pray for me.

Silence

I am a person in need. A person you know.
I may be sick, lonely, afraid, alone or hurting inside.
Speak my name in your heart, hold me in your love,
Pray for me; pray for me.

Silence

Lord, in your mercy,
hear our prayer.

267   HOLOCAUST DAY

We pray for those who lost their family and friends
at the hands of those who saw only numbers and forgot they
were people;
for those who are alone with no one to share the memory of
those who were murdered.
Lord, hear our prayer,
that we may not forget.

We pray for those who lost everything—
home and possessions, and a sense of their own worth;
for those who lost hope, peace and purpose,
and for those whose bodies were tortured and abused
through the ideology of others.
Lord, hear our prayer,
that we may not forget.

We pray that those who suffered will never be forgotten;
that those who were allowed to die of hunger, or were
murdered
through the appalling misuse of the skills of others and their
abuse of power
will always stand as a warning to all the nations of the world,
and every generation yet to be born.
Lord, hear our prayer,
that we may not forget.

We pray for those who survived and feel guilty that they did
    not die;
for those who still bear the marks on their bodies,
in their minds, in their lives, of all that they experienced—
the memories that time does not erase.
Lord, hear our prayer,
that we may not forget.

We pray for those who still face our inhumanity today;
for those who still suffer hate and rejection, exclusion and
    death—
simply for being different and daring to believe that in God's
    eyes
everyone matters to him: we are all equal and his love is for
    all.
Lord, hear our prayer,
that we may not forget.

We pray for world leaders and those to whom we have given
    the power
to rule and to govern with justice and openness,
that all may live in peace and with hope,
no matter their name, their colour, or their race.
Lord, hear our prayer,
that we may not forget.

We pray for our world and for ourselves.
We have nowhere to hide; no excuses will count.
When we face you, Lord, what answer will we give
for when we said nothing, and allowed others to pay the
    price?
Lord, hear our prayer,
that we may not forget.

We remember in silence whose who are dying even as we
    pray.

Silence

Lord, hear our prayer,
that we may not forget.

In the name of Christ, who suffered and died for us all.
    Amen.

268   CHRISTIAN AID

Lord, we cry out for those who can cry no longer,
for those who have sat and watched and waited
as they have seen their children wither and die,
for those who hunger and thirst just to live another day
and for those too weak even to care.
Lord, hear the cry of those who have everything …
for those who have nothing.

Lord, we cry out for those who cannot cry for themselves,
for those with no power, no voices and no hope,
for those whose faces we see but whose names are unknown,
for those who remain simply a statistic—
just another one to add to the list of the world's refugees.
Lord, hear the cry of those who have everything …
for those who have nothing.

Lord, we cry out for those who cry for food,
for those hungry in a world of plenty
and for those who are poor on a planet of great riches,
for those who die of starvation
in the midst of those who are dying because of their obesity.
Lord, hear the cry of those who have everything …
for those who have nothing.

Lord, we cry out for those whose tears are never heard
and for those who face great injustice
because they have no voice in the corridors of power;
for those who have allowed the millstone of debt
to hang around the necks of the poor,
and for those who work to see the rich nations of the world
open their ears to the cry of the poor.

Lord, hear the cry of those who have everything …
for those who have nothing.

Lord, we cry out for those who cry out for others;
for those who refuse to allow us to become complacent
and to close our minds to needs of the poor;
for the work and challenge of [*aid agencies*],
for politicians and governments,
that they may exchange words for deliberate actions
and good intentions for justice and love.
Lord, hear the cry of those who have everything …
for those who have nothing.

Lord, we cry out with anger for those too weak even to care;
for little children with swollen bellies and fly-infested eyes,
and for mothers no longer able to feed their babies;
for parents, whose empty faces and whose Auschwitz-like
    stare
speak of a holocaust still taking place.
Lord, hear the cry of those who have everything …
for those who have nothing.

Lord, we cry out in silence as we remember in our own
    hearts and minds
the forgotten millions who will not eat today
and the thousands who will die because others failed to give;
for the world's growing numbers of refugees and asylum
    seekers
who constantly experience rejections and have nowhere to
    call home.
Lord, hear the cry of those who have everything …
for those who have nothing.

Lord, we cry out for those who want a chance to live before
    they die;
for those who want to live but who would prefer not to rely
    on our charity.
At the beginning of Christian Aid Week

we cry out for those who will go door-to-door, and for those
    who will give;
for those who would find it hard to collect envelopes door to
    door
yet who are willing to give themselves freely for the sake of
    the poor.
Lord, hear the cry of those who have everything …
for those who have nothing.

In the name of Christ, who, like the poor, had nowhere to
    lay his head. Amen.

269   LIFE

Think of someone whose life is full of 'might have beens',
someone who looks back with a sense of disappointment or
    disillusionment,
whose yesterdays are so full of 'if onlys'
that they can give no thought for their tomorrows.
May the presence of Christ hold them today.
Lord, in your mercy,
hear our prayer.

Think of someone whose mind is in turmoil and whose heart
    knows no peace,
someone whose hopes have been crushed and whose whole
    life speaks of defeat.
May the presence of Christ touch them today.
Lord, in your mercy,
hear our prayer.

Think of someone who feels lonely even in a crowded place,
someone who feels unable to love others because they cannot
    love themselves,
someone who sees no beauty or worth in others
because they see none in themselves.
May the presence of Christ be with them today.
Lord, in your mercy,
hear our prayer.

Think of someone who is faced with a difficult decision,
someone whose decisions are causing pain for themselves
    and for others,
someone who hears God calling them to commitment or
    service
but who find the price is too high.
May the presence of Christ lead them in his way.
Lord, in your mercy,
hear our prayer.

Think of someone whose aggressive spirit keeps people at a
    distance;
someone whose quiet ways mean people do not hear what
    they are saying;
someone who is hurting too much to speak;
someone who finds it impossible to let go of the pain deep
    inside.
May the presence of Christ bring healing and hope.
Lord, in your mercy,
hear our prayer.

Think of someone with power over nations,
someone who can affect people's lives for good or for ill,
someone in a position of authority
at home, at school, in industry or in the community.
May the presence of Christ's authority shape all their dealing
    with others today.
Lord, in your mercy,
hear our prayer.

Think of yourself—your memories of yesterday,
your concerns for today and your uncertainties for
    tomorrow.
Think of the worries that keep you awake at night
and the burdens that rob you of peace.
Think of the questions for which you have no answer
and the love that has kept you safe.
May the presence of God hold us still.

Lord, in your mercy,
hear our prayer.

In the name of Christ, who holds our lives in the palm of his
hand. Amen.

270   THE CHURCH IN OUR NATION

We pray for those who demonstrate the love of God in the
    community;
for those who go out each day
in the knowledge that they are joining their energies
with the God who is already at work in the world;
for those who go out in expectation of meeting Christ
in the lives of those who know him and of those who do not.
May the Spirit of Christ strengthen their love.
Lord of all creation,
send us out in your name.

We pray for those who reach out in the name of Christ;
for those who reach out to the homeless
and to those whose addiction is ruining their own lives
and the lives of those who care about them.
May the Spirit of Christ strengthen their love.
Lord of all creation,
send us out in your name.

We pray for those who proclaim the love of God;
for those whose words and deeds faithfully declare
the love of God, the grace of the Lord Jesus Christ
and the power of the Holy Spirit to make lives new;
for those whose words of witness to their neighbours and
    their colleagues
come with the ring of truth and the cutting edge of personal
    experience.
May the Spirit of Christ strengthen their love.
Lord of all creation,
send us out in your name.

We pray for all those who are involved in the work of
    mission and evangelism;
for all who plan, lead or organise the life of the congregation
to reach out to their local community with the love of God;
for all involved in the work of [*organisation*]
and for churches who are treating with the utmost
    seriousness
the call of Christ to make disciples.
May the Spirit of Christ strengthen their love.
Lord of all creation,
send us out in your name.

We pray for those who show the love of God
in their work with the young and the old;
for those whose loving care and genuine concern
for the vulnerable and the innocent, the weak and the frail,
the forgotten and the forgetful
is a reflection of the loving heart of God and the gentleness
    of Christ;
for those who serve God through the work of [*organisation*]
and for all who seek to heal relationships
and share the pain of families who have reached the point of
    breaking.
May the Spirit of Christ strengthen their love.
Lord of all creation,
send us out in your name.

We pray for those who witness to the love of God in the life
    of the church;
for those whose words, deeds and service
are examples of compassion, hope and understanding;
for those whose service is always in the background,
those who are never noticed and who serve without thought
    of reward;
May the Spirit of Christ strengthen their love.
Lord of all creation,
send us out in your name.

We pray for those who hold positions of trust and
    leadership;
for those who offer care and faith to those in despair;
for all pastoral visitors, youth workers and lay workers,
those who serve in Sunday schools and youth groups,
especially [*names*],
and for all who seek to name the name of Christ in word
    and deed.
May the Spirit of Christ strengthen their love.
Lord of all creation,
send us out in your name.

We ask our prayers in the name of Christ, the one who is
    Lord of all. Amen.

271   ASH WEDNESDAY

We pray for those who are ashamed of themselves
and of what they have done,
and for those whose words and deeds have made others
    ashamed of them;
for those whose mistakes are known to everyone
and for those whose failures are known only to you;
for those who are filled with despair and a sense of defeat
because of the mess they have made of their own lives,
or because of the behaviour of those that they love.
May the presence of Christ give them peace.
Lord, in your mercy,
hear our prayer.

We pray for those who are depressed and despairing;
for those who once were filled with hope and great
    expectations
and for those whose plans and dreams have come to nothing;
for those who feel crushed and broken and empty
and for those with no one to help or understand;
for those tormented by doubts and fears and temptations

and for those whose thoughts and moods and feelings are
    filled with darkness.
May the presence of Christ give them joy.
Lord, in your mercy,
hear our prayer.

We pray for those who are filled with regret
and for those feeling lost and alone;
for those whose sadness seems unending
and for those whose brokenness seems beyond repair;
for those whose words hurt themselves and others
and for those whose deeds are designed to spoil what could
    have been good;
for those whose selfishness and self-centredness are a source
    of pain to others
and for those who have no idea of the anguish, worry,
    distress and pain
they are causing those who have loved them most.
May the presence of Christ bring them to their senses.
Lord, in your mercy,
hear our prayer.

We pray for those who are trying to come to terms with a
    serious illness
and for those who are finding it simply too hard to bear;
for those whose illness is terminal and who can find no peace
    and no hope;
for those who, knowing they are dying, are ready to meet
    with God;
for those who are sharing the suffering of others,
who care for the sick and the elderly and give dignity and
    love
to those who are frail in body or in mind.
May the presence of Christ give them hope.
Lord, in your mercy,
hear our prayer.

We pray for those whose joy and hope are being crushed
by the cruelty and aggression of others,
and for those whose lives are wrecked by prejudice and
    intolerance;
for those who are indifferent to their neighbours' suffering
and for those who are apathetic towards those in need;
for those who struggle each day for the kind of freedom we
    take for granted
and for those who face a lifetime in prison
in their struggle for liberty of thought, word and deed.
May the presence of Christ give them strength.
Lord, in your mercy,
hear our prayer.

We pray for those who know they have fallen short of living
    the kind of lives
that bring glory to God, and joy and fulfilment to
    themselves;
for those who are facing up to the kind of people they have
    been
and are truly longing to be made new;
for those whose addictions have robbed them of their best
    years
and of all that they might have been;
for those who have lost everything and everyone that once
    mattered to them
and for those aware of the hurt they have caused;
for those filled with guilt and remorse
and for those who long to know that they are forgiven.
May the presence of Christ bring them renewal.
Lord, in your mercy,
hear our prayer.

We pray for those who once walked with Christ
and who knew God's love in their hearts;
for those who have drifted away
and for those who have allowed other things and people to
    take his place;

for those who are finding a glimmer of God's grace coming
    again to their lives
and for those for whom the spark and the wind of the Spirit
are bringing fresh hope, joy and praise;
for those whose whole lives are being set on fire
with the power of God's love and mercy,
and for those who are discovering his truth all over again;
for those who were lost and are now being found
and for those who are on their way home.
May the presence of Christ keep them safe.
Lord, in your mercy,
hear our prayer.

We pray for ourselves
and for all that is troubling our hearts and our minds,
for all that takes away our peace;
for our need of God's guidance and strength
in the face of the growing demands made upon us
and the stress that we face every day;
for the Holy Spirit to open our eyes, our ears and our minds
to the great things he is longing to do in and through our
    lives;
for every new beginning we are offered
and for every chance to offer worship and witness and service
in the name of him who makes all things new.
May the presence of Christ fill us with power.
Lord, in your mercy,
hear our prayer.

Through Christ our Lord. Amen.

272   MAUNDY THURSDAY

We pray for those who, like Peter, are full of promises but
    low on fulfilment;
for those who find no difficulty in offering commitment,
    service and faithfulness,

but whose words and deeds are a denial of their good
intentions;
for those who promise everything and complete nothing.
May the love of Christ enable them to stand firm.
Lord, in your mercy,
hear our prayer.

We pray for those who, like John the beloved disciple,
are close to Christ and are open to his love in their lives;
for those who have known his presence for many years
and have grown closer to him as time has gone by;
for those whose lives reflect their fellowship with God
and whose words and deeds echo the Spirit's presence.
May the love of Christ radiate through their lives
to touch the emptiness of their neighbours' hearts.
Lord, in your mercy,
hear our prayer.

We pray for those who, like James and John,
whom Jesus called the sons of thunder, are full of aggression;
for those whose words and deeds either create conflict,
increase tension or fan the flames of disagreement;
for those who are never at peace within themselves;
for those who are never content with their lives
and are always feeling hurt, offended or insulted by other
people.
May the love of Christ calm the storm within them.
Lord, in your mercy,
hear our prayer.

We pray for those who, like Thomas, do not find that faith
comes easily to them;
for those who are tortured with worries, doubts and fears;
for those who long to believe in God, and to trust him more
than they do,
but are overwhelmed by the anguish and uncertainties of this
world;
for those who have been so hurt in the past,

so let down by those who should have stood by them,
that they find it almost impossible to trust anyone—even
    God.
May the love of Christ hold them and bring them hope.
Lord, in your mercy,
hear our prayer.

We pray for those who, like Judas Iscariot,
were chosen, called and were once, in their own way, faithful
    to Christ;
for those who always think they know what is best for
    everyone
and who seek to manipulate people and situations for their
    own ends;
for those whose words and deeds betray themselves, other
    people and Jesus;
for those whose discipleship is a sham
and whose devotion is an empty shell of self-centredness and
    self-sufficiency.
May the love of Christ forgive them and draw them back to
    himself.
Lord, in your mercy,
hear our prayer.

We pray for those who are like the disciples
who prepared the upper room for the Passover meal;
for those who are prepared to go when, where and how
    Christ sends them,
who follow Christ with no thought for the cost to themselves
and whose faith in Christ's faithfulness shines like a beacon
    of hope and peace;
for those whose love, service and obedience
enable Christ's love to touch and change the hearts and lives
    of many people.
May the love of Christ bring renewal and joy.
Lord, in your mercy,
hear our prayer.

We pray for those who, like the disciples,
need to hear that they have been made clean by the
     reconciling word of Christ;
for those who need to recognise the loving, caring service of
     Christ through others;
for those who find it hard to receive love and compassion,
and for those who have yet to allow the work of Christ to
     transform their whole lives.
May the love of Christ make all things new.
Lord, in your mercy,
hear our prayer.

We pray for ourselves, and for our need to sit at the feet of
     Christ,
and for the sense of unworthiness we feel in his presence;
for our longing simply to know that we are accepted;
for the assurance that we are part of his body
and that he was broken even for us.
May the love of Christ never let us go.
Lord, in your mercy,
hear our prayer.

In the name of Christ,
who gave himself for us that we might live for him. Amen.

273   GOOD FRIDAY

Father, we cry out to you, in love and for love, because you
     are love.
When life is dark and we are alone, we remember your love.
When we feel isolated or used, we remember your love.
When we use others
and hurt them with our words and our actions, we
     remember your love.
When life has no apparent purpose or meaning,
when all we had planned has gone terribly wrong,
when we are lost, afraid, weak or crushed, we remember your
     love.

Father, if you were not a God of love, there would be no life.
If you were not a God who loved us, there would be no
    reason for living.
Father, we cry out to you.
Teach us to know you and your love while it is still light,
that when the darkness comes
we may still find our way illuminated with the love of Christ.
The Lord hears our prayer.
Thanks be to God.

Father, we thank you that you have shown us in Jesus
that everything is safe in your hands,
that nothing we give back to you will ever be wasted.
When the day is bright and life is good
and all that we hoped for comes to fulfilment,
may we be assured that we are walking in your will.
When days are filled with difficulties, and you seem far away,
may we be assured that we are walking in your will.
When we are tempted and when we fall,
when we say and do those things which are not according to
    your will,
may we be assured that the way back into your will is still
    open.
When we face pain or rejection, sadness or sorrow,
when what we are facing feels like crucifixion,
may we be assured that, having committed ourselves into
    your hands,
we are still secure—though not always in ways this world
    understands,
yet most certainly, through the grace of God, in the world to
    come.
The Lord hears our prayer.
Thanks be to God.

Father, we cry out to you for victory.
We thank you for the obedience of Christ,
that though his obedience meant a cross for him,
he was still faithful to you and your will;

that through his obedient faithfulness
your love has triumphed over all that is evil.
We come to you in the victory of Christ on the cross.
We come knowing that there is no situation, no moment,
no power, no weakness, no tragedy, no darkness, no
    wickedness,
there is nothing that can ever defeat you and your love.
We thank you that you have demonstrated, in Christ's life
    and death,
that as you had the first word
so your Word in Christ will always be your final word.
We thank you that your love is the ultimate answer to
    everything we face
and your final word to all your creation.
May your love triumph over all that spoils your world,
all that damages our lives, our relationship with you and
    with each other.
The Lord hears our prayer.
Thanks be to God.

Father, we cry out to you for those who are lonely and afraid;
for those whose lives are in a mess and whose relationships
    are causing them pain;
for those who are overwhelmed by life
and for those who struggle to cope with the results of their
    foolishness;
for those sinking under the demands of home
and for those slowly finding life squeezed out of them
by the insensitive expectations of others;
for those, who themselves, are crying out for justice,
    forgiveness and hope;
for those who have settled for existence
when all the time you are offering new life in Christ.
May your love hear the cry of your people
and share the pain of those who are losing the fight.
The Lord hears our prayer.
Thanks be to God.

Father, we cry out for those who cry for others;
for those who work to help the poor, the hungry and the
    starving;
for those who bring to our attention
the plight of the world's forgotten refugees;
for those who will not allow us to ignore the suffering of our
    fellow human beings;
for the work of [*aid agency*]
and all those whose work reflects your love and compassion;
for those who are left on the margins of life.
May your love hear the cry of those who are fighting for others
and break hardened hearts with your mercy.
The Lord hears our prayer.
Thanks be to God.

Father, we cry out for those who are in positions of
    influence;
for those who work in the media;
for television producers and newspaper editors;
for those in positions to influence parents and teachers,
for members of Parliament and for the government;
for leaders of nations who have it in their power
to set millions of people free from their debts
and to use their authority to call nations to the peace table.
We cry out for those with the opportunity to work for the
    good of all
and to bring hope, justice and freedom to many.
May your love hear the cry of those who cry out to the
    leaders of the nations.
The Lord hears our prayer.
Thanks be to God.

Father, we cry out for ourselves,
and for your help and comfort for the things that are
    troubling us
and robbing us of the peace you meant us to have;
for our fears for today and tomorrow

and for our family and friends, and those for whom we are
  concerned;
for a new experience of your heart-warming, life-
  transforming grace
and for a new realisation that, because of Christ's life, death
  and resurrection,
nothing will ever separate us from your love;
for a new desire to enthrone Christ at the heart of our lives
and for the life-renewing Spirit to empower us for worship
  and service.
May your love hear the cry of our hearts and touch and
  change our lives
by the good news of Good Friday.
The Lord hears our prayer.
Thanks be to God.

In the name of him who died for all. Amen.

274   HARVEST

I am a hungry person.
Whether I live in [*name of countries needing aid*]
I still need food for myself and my family.
I know that people have given money to help us, and we are
  grateful,
but it is not easy to go on saying thank you for charity
when what we really need is a fairer share of the world's
  resources.
Pray for me.

Silence

I am an industrialist.
I know that when I stand before my Maker I will have to
  confess
that I have misused his world.
I know only too well that I have robbed it of its raw
  materials,
its beauty, and damaged its future.

I know that people have been hurt for the sake of profit.
But you wanted more and more material possessions
and you wanted them as cheaply as possible, and there was
    no other way.
Pray for me.

Silence

I am an unemployed person.
It is not very easy to say thank you when you have no regular
    job
and you are worried about the future.
It is not easy to feel grateful when others can take for granted
the things that would be a luxury to me.
It is not easy to express gratitude when you see others
who are obviously successful
and you feel a failure, rejected and unnecessary.
I have a harvest of skills and experience—I just want a
    chance to use them.
Pray for me.

Silence

I am a lonely person.
It is not easy to thank God when every day seems the same.
Being thankful does not come naturally
when you are all on your own and no one ever visits.
I live in this one, small, dismal room, and it feels like a prison.
I have a harvest of memories, but no one with whom to
    share them.
Pray for me.

Silence

I am a Christian.
I remember when I first put my trust in Jesus
and how thrilled I was to know that he was with me.
I look back to those days when he seemed so real
and everything was challenging and exciting.

I still go to church, but I do not often read the Bible,
and unless I have a problem, I hardly ever pray.
I am only too well aware that my life and my lifestyle
are not very different from those who do not know Christ as
their Saviour.
I need a harvest of spiritual growth and the chance to start
all over again.
Pray for me. Pray for me.

Silence

Lord, in your mercy,
hear our prayer.

In Christ's name. Amen.

275   REMEMBRANCE SUNDAY

Father, we pray for those people all over the world who today
remember
and their remembering is filled with a great sense of loss;
for people of every nation who have lost
home and family and friends in hostilities;
for those whose lives have been wrecked by war and by
terrorist attack.
We pray for those who remember their loss of faith
that has left a hole in their lives that nothing else can fill.
May they remember the love of Christ which can make them
whole.
Lord, in your mercy,
hear our prayer.

Father, we pray for those who remember the bitterness and
anger
that crushes their lives, taints their deeds and colours their
every word;
for those whose sense of resentment
has split families and communities, churches and nations;

for those who remember conflicts that have damaged their
    relationships
and for those whose health has been affected by the grudges
    they bear
and the hatred they harbour still.
May the gentle Spirit of Christ hold and heal them
    completely.
Lord, in your mercy,
hear our prayer.

Father, we pray for those who remember with sadness
those they have loved and who are with them no more;
for those whose sadness is tinged with regret
and for those for whom it is filled with feelings of rejection;
for those who feel a great emptiness within
and for those who remember the happy times they once
    shared;
for those who remember with tears and with pain
and for those who have no one with whom to share their
    hurts and their aches;
for those who are still hurting, though time has gone by,
and for those who are hurting because others no longer
    remember.
May the love of Christ share their tears.
Lord, in your mercy,
hear our prayer.

Father, we pray for those who remember with deep concern
the decisions they must make;
for those who carry a heavy burden of responsibility for
    others
and those who are weighed down by the pressure it brings.
We pray for doctors and nurses
and all with responsibility for the health and the safety of
    others;
for magistrates, judges and probation officers
and all who are helping others to face up to what they have
    done;

for those in positions of leadership in government,
the community or the church;
for those with the responsibility of caring for the hungry and
the starving
and the ones with no hope and no home.
May the presence of Christ give them courage and wisdom.
Lord, in your mercy,
hear our prayer.

Father, we pray for those who remember to work for peace.
On this Remembrance Sunday we pray urgently for the
peace of the world;
for those who are genuinely working for peace
and for those seeking ways to build bridges of hope;
but also for those who resist all attempts to end conflicts
and for those who reject all efforts at reconciliation,
those who are blinded by fear and by prejudice.
On this Remembrance Sunday we pray that the Holy Spirit
may work in all our hearts and minds and wills
and give us a new longing to live at peace with each other
and with you.
May the love of Christ fill us with a desire for peace,
whatever the cost.
Lord, in your mercy,
hear our prayer.

Father, we pray for any we know
for whom today is a day of special remembering,
for those who will be remembering those who fought with
them
and who never returned;
for those who returned with their minds damaged by what
they had witnessed,
their bodies broken by what they had suffered
and their lives wrecked by what they had been through.
May the love of Christ hold them.
Lord, in your mercy,
hear our prayer.

We pray for ourselves
and all our remembrance of our missed opportunities
and the promises we have broken and our failure to love,
those memories which are still too painful
and the experiences we wished we could forget.
We rejoice in the memory of the love we have received,
the care and support and the new beginnings of hope, joy
and forgiveness.
May the love of Christ enable us to offer these gifts
even to those who least deserve them.
Lord, in your mercy,
hear our prayer.

We ask all our prayers in Christ's name. Amen.

276   SOCIAL CONCERN

Father, we pray for the world, your world with all its
opportunities,
all its resources and all its potential for good.
We remember with deep gratitude its beauty, its variety,
and the essential goodness it has because you are its Creator;
for every way that it is a reflection of your grace and love.
Teach us and all people, we pray, to remember the
obligations
that you have laid upon us to be good stewards of your
world.
We pray for the leaders of nations
and for those in industry or in commerce
who are responsible for decisions which affect your creation.
May they be reminded that what we have we hold in trust
and we will always be answerable to you.
The Lord hears our prayer.
Thanks be to God.

Father, we pray for our society and for our life together as
one nation.
At this time when all that is good and right, true and just,

is being challenged and threatened,
we ask for your loving hand to be upon us all.
We pray for those in our society who are responsible
for what we see, hear, or read;
for television producers and programme makers;
for newspaper editors and for all who speak or teach or
    preach;
for all who lead, guide or are personally responsible for
    young people.
May we remember our obligation to the truth of your love.
The Lord hears our prayer.
Thanks be to God.

Father, we pray for those who have special responsibility
for people in particular need.
We pray for those who serve in the hospice movement;
for doctors and nurses and all who work in any way
within the health service;
for those who care for people who ruin their lives and the
    lives of others
by their abuse of alcohol or illegal drugs,
by their addiction to gambling or their involvement in child
    abuse or crime.
Again and again you remind us of our responsibilities for
    others—
those who are unemployed and those who are unemployable.
We remember any we know by name
and ask that they may have dignity, hope and joy.
The Lord hears our prayer.
Thanks be to God.

Father, we pray for the church, your church.
We acknowledge that you have called, chosen and
    commissioned us as your people
and you gave us the task of caring for those in need.
We pray for those who are hungry and for those who are
    starving;
for those who are ill and those who are dying;

for those who are lost and those longing to be found;
for those who are afraid and those who are depressed;
for those who are anxious and for those who feel
as if the bottom has dropped out of their world.
The Lord hears our prayer.
Thanks be to God.

Father, we pray for the courage to challenge injustice
    wherever we find it,
to battle on behalf of those who are oppressed,
to carry the burdens of those who are weighed down.
Help us, we pray, always to remember that it is the gospel of
    Jesus Christ
and the goodness of your love that we proclaim
and that it is by the power of the Holy Spirit
that we are called as your church to witness that Jesus is
    Lord.
The Lord hears our prayer.
Thanks be to God.

Father, we pray for people we know.
We remember particularly those people in need
of your power, your love and our care.
We have been asked to remember the following people
and their situations in our prayers: [*names*].
We pray for ourselves and for all that we must face
in the days of this coming week.
May we know that you are with us always,
and you are longing to bless all we seek to do in your name.
The Lord hears our prayer.
Thanks be to God.

In the name of Christ, who calls and sends us. Amen.

277   THE CHURCH IN THE WORLD

Father, we thank you for the good news of the life-
    transforming work of Jesus,
that in him, we can all begin again,

that in him we can be new people, and there is no
  'godforsaken' person,
no one who is ever beyond the reach of his grace.
We thank you that he is your Word of hope
that makes it possible for us to be sure that we are known by
  you
and your love for us all will never be withdrawn.
Enable Christians all around the world, we pray, so to live
  and so to speak
that this good news may be proclaimed in power and in love.
Lord, in your mercy,
hear our prayer.

Father, we thank you for those whom you have chosen,
  called and sent
to serve you in different parts of your world;
for those who have been prepared to leave home and family
to declare the word of grace in every corner of your creation.
May your Holy Spirit rekindle their hope, their faith
and the certainty of your call to them.
Lord, in your mercy,
hear our prayer.

Father, we rejoice in the work and witness
of those who have served you in the worldwide church of
  Jesus Christ,
for those who have served you through the witness of their
  church.
We remember with gratitude those who were willing to pay
  with their lives
that others might hear of the love that never ends.
Help us, now, to recommit ourselves to this important work
of telling the whole world about Jesus.
Lord, in your mercy,
hear our prayer.

Father, we thank you for churches in countries that have
  become self-governing

and now send mission partners around the world.

We thank you for Christians in places where they are a tiny
minority,

that they may be salt and light to their neighbours of other
faiths.

May the unity of your church, we pray, be the symbol of
hope,

not only for us, but also for the church in every corner of the
globe.

Lord, in your mercy,

hear our prayer.

Father, we pray for those who have gone as mission partners
to other countries

and those who have come to share in mission work with us.

We remember, by name, any we know to be serving you
around the world: [*names*].

May they know the peace, the power and the presence of
Christ.

Lord, in your mercy,

hear our prayer.

Father, we ask you to touch our lives with your grace

and renew our faith by your Holy Spirit.

May your love deepen our trust in you and remove our fear
of tomorrow.

May your mercy hold on to us when we are weak

and your grace sustain us and prevent us from falling.

May your truth fill our minds and give us wisdom.

May your Holy Spirit empower us to serve you

when, where, how and with whom you choose.

Lord, in your mercy,

hear our prayer.

Father, we pray for those areas of your world

that are facing particular pain and suffering;

for those whose lives have been devastated

by earthquake or wind or fire, or by drought;

for those who have lost those they loved
and for those whose hearts still bear the scars of their
    tragedy;
for those who feel utterly helpless
and who feel that they cannot cope any more;
for those working to bring hope and relief to the suffering;
and for those whose task is to encourage people to give that
    others might live.
Lord, in your mercy,
hear our prayer.

Father, we pray for the work of all missionary societies,
especially [*names*], and for all agencies
seeking to bring hope, healing and peace to those in great
    need.
We pray for ourselves, and ask that the Holy Spirit
might enthuse, excite and empower us
to serve the present age and share the grace of Christ,
that all people everywhere might confess him Lord of all.
Lord, in your mercy,
hear our prayer.

We ask our prayer in the name of the King of Kings and the
    Lord of Lords. Amen.

278   CHRISTMAS EVE

Lord, we pray for your world where there is so much
    darkness,
and where so many live in fear for their lives;
for your world where there is hatred, violence and distrust;
for those whose homes have been swept away by flood
or wrecked by earthquake;
for those whose homes and families have been cruelly
    devastated
by the effects of civil war.
We pray for those with no hope, no faith, no love and no
    future.

May the Prince of Peace bring light in their darkness.
The Lord hears our prayer.
Thanks be to God.

Lord, we pray for our nation and the society in which we
  live.
It is always in such a hurry to arrive,
but never appears to know where it is going.
It fills its hopes and its dreams with the things of the
  moment,
but possesses nothing that lasts for eternity.
It claims to be seeking happiness, fulfilment and satisfaction,
but too easily settles for passing pleasures.
It longs for contentment, friendship and love,
but accepts lustful gratification instead.
It speaks of harmony and justice for all,
but many are filled with a racial hatred fuelled by fear and
  prejudice.
May the Christ child enter the pain of our society
and bring light into its darkness.
The Lord hears our prayer.
Thanks be to God.

Lord, we pray for those who are undervalued and feel
  ignored;
for those who are single, or struggling as lone parents,
in a community designed for families;
for the elderly in a world planned with the young in mind;
for those who are mentally ill or mentally handicapped;
for those who are differently abled because they are
  physically disabled.
May the love of the Christ child bring them hope and joy
and a sense of their true value to you.
The Lord hears our prayer.
Thanks be to God.

Lord, we pray for those whose lives are in darkness;
for those who tonight will be told that there is no room;

for those who like Mary and Joseph are excluded and
    homeless;
for children who are constantly left on their own
and for those who are struggling to make sense of their lives;
for those who are going through the personal agony of
    bereavement
and for those who are trying to come to terms
with the reality of their partners being in prison.
May the Christ child bring them light, courage and the
    promise of a new beginning.
The Lord hears our prayer.
Thanks be to God.

Lord, we pray for those in need of love;
for those who feel rejected and for those who know that they
    are;
for those whose lives are damaged by racial hatred
and who long for love and acceptance from their neighbours;
for those who are lonely and those who are alone;
for those who long for someone to share their
    disappointments
and for those who need to be hugged, wanted and needed;
for those who have lost the ability to love and to be loved
and for those who long to be loved and to have someone to
    love.
May the love of the Christ child melt hardened hearts,
heal broken lives and restore hope in the human breast.
The Lord hears our prayer.
Thanks be to God.

Lord, we pray for those whose lives are filled with light and
    joy;
for those who are beginning the journey of marriage
and for those who are discovering the pleasures and pressures
    of parenthood;
for those who are enjoying a recovery of physical and
    spiritual health;

for those for whom the clouds of despair and depression are
    beginning to lift
and for those who know what it means to meet the Christ
    child
and to have their whole lives turned upside down;
for those for whom listening to you
through prayer and through reading your Word
has taken on a whole new importance;
for those who are discovering just how much they matter to
    you
and what it really means to belong to your people.
May the Lord of time and eternity open their hearts and
    minds
to the wonder of your grace in him.
The Lord hears our prayer.
Thanks be to God.

Lord, we pray for ourselves;
for all we have done and all we have faced;
for all that we must face in the days that lie ahead;
for the decisions we must make
and the challenges to which we must find ways of
    responding;
for the pressures and the stresses that are part of our daily
    lives;
for our walk with Jesus in the face of the conflicts within and
    without;
for those for whom we are concerned.
May the Christ child hold us, help us, heal us and empower
    us.
The Lord hears our prayer.
Thanks be to God.

We ask our prayers in the name of the Christ,
who came, who comes, who goes on coming and will come
    again. Amen.

Lord, we pray for people in the world; for leaders of nations,
for those with the power to influence the hearts and minds
of millions;
for the people of [*areas in need*].
May the coming of your Spirit bring the fire of cleansing and
the wind that renews.
Kyrie eleison. (Lord have mercy.)

Lord, we pray for the people of our nation;
for those who influence the minds and the wills of the
young;
for those who are responsible for what we see on television,
or read in newspapers or magazines;
for those who are role models for others
and whose attitudes, values and lifestyles undermine all that
is good, true and of you.
May the coming of your Spirit bring the fire of cleansing and
the wind that renews.
Kyrie eleison. (Lord have mercy.)

Lord, we pray for the life of this church;
for a deeper trust, a wider love and a longer-lasting
commitment,
that our worship, witness and service may reach the heights
of your throne;
for guidance as we seek your will for the life and mission of
the church.
Give us grace and joy and wisdom, that we may discern the
truth.
May the coming of your Spirit bring the fire of cleansing and
the wind that renews.
Kyrie eleison. (Lord have mercy.)

Lord, we pray for the people we know;
for those we know to be in need of you and your love,
for those aching for your peace, who truly desire to know
more of you,

for those longing for your health-giving, life-renewing touch
and life-changing grace;
for those we name before you now: [*names*].
May the coming of your Spirit bring the fire of cleansing and
the wind that renews.
Kyrie eleison. (Lord have mercy.)

We pray for ourselves and for all we must face
in the coming days and months and years of our lives;
for our times of aloneness, doubt and fear;
for our longing to be free—really free as we know you long
for us to be,
for a renewal of our hearts and minds and lives
and for a chance to learn to love ourselves.
May the coming of your Spirit bring the fire of cleansing and
the wind that renews.
Kyrie eleison. (Lord have mercy.)

We pray in the name of Christ, the merciful Lord. Amen.

280   HURTING

Lord, we pray for your world, and all the hurting people in
it.
For those who are hurting because of the wrong things
other people have said and done;
for those who are hurting because of war and fighting
between nations;
for those who are hurting because they are hungry and
starving;
for those who are hurting because of the wrong choices they
have made;
for those who are hurting because they have nowhere to live;
for those who are hurting because they have lost those they
have loved most;
for those who are hurting because they feel they have failed;
and for those who are hurting because they long to be
loved.

We pray that they may they know
that on the cross you shared all their hurt and pain,
and that because you are Lord you share all that hurts us
     today.
Lord, we pray, hold your hurting world in your gentle,
     healing, loving hands.
We ask this in Jesus' name. Amen.

281   APATHY

I am a teacher.
For years I have spent time in preparation,
I have agonised over my class and spent sleepless nights
worrying over their problems and fears.
But the endless paperwork, the onerous instructions and
     guidelines from on high,
and the lack of support and appreciation
have squeezed all the enthusiasm out of me, and now I don't
     care any more.
I am near my breaking point. Pray for me.

Silence

I am a parent.
My family have been my life
and I have given the best years of my life to caring for them.
I never looked for anything in return.
But when I look at my life now, I have nothing left.
Through the years somehow I was wrung dry.
I don't seem to be able to value myself or my gifts any
     more—I don't even try. Pray for me.
Silence

I am a Christian.
I have attended church for years and held every office
and served in every way I could.
I was out every night on some committee,
helping in the youth meeting or sharing in the house group.

But now I hardly pray, and I never read my Bible.
I attend worship less and less and I shall probably stop
    altogether soon.
Pray for me.

Silence

I am a young person.
My name doesn't matter, I'm just a statistic.
I come from what you would call a good home.
But though we were never short of money or possessions
we were very short of love.
I tried to do well at school and then at college
in the hope my parents would notice me and love me.
But they never did.
So I gave up and now I'm sleeping rough in a doorway.
And I just don't care any more—
because no one ever really cared for me. Pray for me.

Silence

I am an addict.
Whether my addiction is to drink or to drugs,
to cigarettes or to receiving praise, I still need my daily fix.
I've seen all the warnings on my packet of twenty
and I've read all the horror stories about HIV/AIDS.
I've become case-hardened to the drink-driving campaigns.
You see, I really just don't care.
I eat and drink to be merry—I see no value in life anyway.
Pray for me—if you must.

Silence

I am a preacher.
I heard the call of God as plain as could be—
like the prophets I knew he meant me!
I have preached with the zeal of a convert and agonised over
    God's Word.

I've prepared sermons and led worship and prayed long and
    hard to the Lord.
But somewhere along the way, it all slipped through my
    fingers.
I suppose I depended more on myself than on him.
But now I just go through the motions—and I know my
    words
are as empty as I am. Pray for me.

Silence

I am an employer.
I built this business by the sweat of my brow!
It was like a child to me, as I worried and fretted over every
    part of it.
I tried to be a good employer to my workforce
and to remember that they were human beings and not
    machines.
But they repaid me with exorbitant wage demands
and threatened strike action,
and the government heaped on the paperwork and
    legislation.
Now I couldn't care less what happens or who gets hurt—
I just want out. Pray for me.

Silence

I am a member of Parliament.
I am amazed when I look back to the high ideals with which
    I set out.
I still remember the thrill of winning my first by-election
and getting my seat in the 'mother of parliaments'.
But the party machine has just ground me to dust.
I was never a yes person—but they say that I must toe the
    party line.
Besides, what have my years in this place achieved—
nothing has changed because of my being here.
I keep my head down, I ask no questions
and am just bored and disillusioned. Pray for me.

Silence

I am an environmentalist.
I really thought we could make a difference.
I thought that, because of our stand, things would change.
I was foolish enough to expect everyone to see the logic of
    our argument
and we could change the world.
But I was wrong, so terribly wrong!
Things today are much worse than when we began.
I feel like giving up and giving in—
but where will God's good earth be then? Pray for me.

Silence

I am me!
Yes, I am still me—though sometimes I do wonder!
I am me, with all my faults and failing.
I am me, and God's Word gives me hope
and tells me that His love will never leave me.
Yes, I am me—even when the world ignores me
and others simply take me for granted.
Yes, I am me—and I need to remember me
a little more each day. Pray for me. Pray for me.

Silence

We ask all our prayers
in the name of him whose love is for ever and for all. Amen.

282   JUDGING OTHERS

Lord, we pray for those we judge by the colour of their skin;
for those who are treated unfairly because of their ethnic origins
and for those denied the opportunities that others enjoy
simply because of racial prejudice.
We pray for those whose racist attitudes are a stain on the
    whole country;
for those whose hostile words and aggressive behaviour

incite others to reject those they see as different from
    themselves.
May the Lord of all creation touch our hearts and change
    our minds.
The Lord hears our prayer.
Thanks be to God.

Lord, we pray for those we judge by their outward
    appearance;
for those we avoid because of the way they dress,
the language they use and the lifestyle they adopt;
for those whose addictions mean we offer no friendly
    welcome,
no hand of friendship and no sense of their being valued and
    important,
to us or to God.
We pray for those we exclude and reject simply because they
    are not like us
and for those who are longing to be accepted
but find we have locked our doors and barred their way.
May the Lord of all creation touch our hearts and change
    our minds.
The Lord hears our prayer.
Thanks be to God.

Lord, we pray for those we judge by virtue of their youth;
for those we consider too inexperienced to serve in the life of
    the church
but old enough to die for their country;
for those we think are too young to have anything useful to
    say—
little of value to offer and just not worth listening to.
We pray for those we assume are too young to be given
    responsibility
but old enough to be criticised for what we see as their lack
    of commitment;
for those we relegate to the church of tomorrow
and deny any real place in the church of today.

May the Lord of all creation touch our hearts and change
   our minds.
The Lord hears our prayer.
Thanks be to God.

Lord, we pray for those we judge to be too old;
for those whose years blind us to all they still have to offer
   today;
for those whose experience of life is ignored
and for those whose need for involvement is constantly
   neglected;
·for those whose age we assume will be a barrier to change
and an obstacle to renewal.
We pray for those who hide behind their age;
for those who feel that they have come to the end of their
   time of service;
for those who are simply content to sit and remember;
for those who resist all change and prevent others from
   experiencing
the joy in the Spirit they once knew.
May the Lord of all creation touch our hearts and change
   our minds.
The Lord hears our prayer.
Thanks be to God.

Lord, we pray for those we judge as inferior to ourselves;
for those whose disabilities make them more vulnerable
in a world designed for and by those who are able-bodied;
for those who are excluded by the physical shape of our
   buildings;
for those whose lack of understanding prevents them
from entering into the joy of our worship;
for those excluded by our close-knit groups
and those for whom our fellowship has become a barrier
   they find impossible to penetrate,
instead of the pathway to the heart of God is was meant to
   be.
We pray for those who feel unloved, unwanted, unnecessary;

for those still struggling with painful memories that
    constantly resist healing;
the broken promises that have destroyed trust
and the despair so deep that there is an experience of
    brokenness
that just will not go away.
May the Lord of all creation touch our hearts and change
    our minds.
The Lord hears our prayer.
Thanks be to God.

In the name of him who is the judge of every heart
and the lover of all his creation. Amen.

Prayers of Commitment

283   ONE WORLD WEEK—THE ENVIRONMENT

Lord, this is your world, we are your people,
we commit ourselves to honour you
by the way we seek justice, peace and hope for all.
In the name of Christ, the Saviour of all the world. Amen.

284   YOU ARE OUR GOD

You are our God, and we will serve you.
You are our Saviour, and we will trust you.
You are our Lord, and we will obey you.

Lord, fill us with the Holy Spirit
so that we may serve, trust and obey you
in all things and in all places, now and for ever. Amen.

285   WE COMMIT OURSELVES

Lord, we commit ourselves to visit the lonely;
to hold those who are hurting; to share the tears of the
    broken;
to reach out to the lost; to comfort the fearful;

to stand with the rejected; to seek justice for the oppressed;
to feed the hungry; to speak in the name of Jesus;
and all for the glory of God. Amen.

286 PETER AND CORNELIUS

Lord, we commit ourselves to listen—
to those we don't like; to those who are different;
to those who are poor; to those who are hurting;
to those who are angry; and to those who don't want to
  listen.
We commit ourselves to listen to you. Amen.

287 OUR RESPONSIBILITY

Lord, in Christ you committed yourself again to all your
  creation.
By your grace, enable us to commit ourselves
to be responsible to you and for each other. Amen.

288 OPEN TO GOD

Lord, we commit ourselves to being open to you, and to
  your word for us today.
We commit ourselves to live faithfully according to the Word
  we have received.
We commit ourselves to share your word of grace and, by
  your Holy Spirit,
to be living witnesses to the one who opened our hearts to
  you.
Through Jesus Christ our Lord. Amen.

289 REACHING THE COMMUNITY

We commit ourselves to go,
not to those who need us but to those who need us most.
We commit ourselves to seek every opportunity
to name the name which is above every name, Christ the
  Lord.
We commit ourselves to be faithful servants

of the one who is always faithful and true.
We commit ourselves to the one who is for ever committed
    to us,
Jesus, our Saviour and Lord. Amen.

290   ASH WEDNESDAY

In the name of Christ, the one who makes us whole,
and in the power of the Spirit who makes us one,
we commit ourselves to lay our lives before the Lord of glory
and, by his grace, to serve him all our days. Amen.

291   TIME TO REMEMBER

Lord of the years that have gone, we give you thanks for our
    memories.
We praise you for those whose words and deeds
led us to the foot of the cross where we met our Saviour
and to the empty tomb where we received him as Lord.

Lord of the years still to come, we seek your guiding hand.
We long for our faith to grow, our trust to deepen
and our knowledge of you and of your greatness
to be the source of our hope for all our tomorrows.

Lord of today, we commit ourselves
to trust you, to serve you, to praise you, to obey you, to love
    you,
now and for all eternity. In Christ's name. Amen.

292   MAUNDY THURSDAY

Lord, we commit ourselves to serve you by serving one
    another.
We commit ourselves to love you by loving one another.
We commit ourselves to bring you glory and to honour your
    name
through the lives we live and through our words of witness
    to your love. Amen.

293 GOOD FRIDAY

Lord, we commit ourselves to stand at the foot of the empty cross
and to declare the truth of the empty tomb.
We commit ourselves to Christ as our Saviour and Lord
and to trust him with our lives and to confess his name with our lips.
In Christ's name and for his glory. Amen.

294 HARVEST

Lord of the harvest, we commit ourselves to work for justice,
for fairness and for equal opportunities and shares for all.
Lord of the harvest, we commit ourselves to trust you
and to depend on you for all things, walking faithfully in the footsteps of Jesus.
Lord of the harvest, we commit ourselves to being open to the work of the Spirit
and to seek his infilling, life-changing presence and power.
Lord of the harvest, sow the seeds of your grace in our lives
that we may reap a rich harvest of eternal life. Amen.

295 REMEMBRANCE SUNDAY

Lord, we commit ourselves to remember your love
and to love our neighbours as ourselves.
We commit ourselves to remember those in need of your love and our help.
We commit ourselves to trust you to deal with the past,
to guide us into tomorrow and to hold today safely in your hands.
We commit ourselves to follow Jesus Christ, who is our Saviour,
and to obey him because he is our Lord. Amen.

296 SOCIAL RESPONSIBILITY

Lord, we will go because we have been sent.
We will serve because we have been served.

We will love because we have been loved.
We will come to you again and again because you came to
    us.
We will commit ourselves to you because
in Christ you demonstrated your commitment to us. Amen.

297 KINDNESS

Lord, we commit ourselves to show kindness to others;
to demonstrate the kindness we have received;
to act kindly even to those who offend us,
and in the face of bitterness, carelessness and lack of concern
to offer the undeserved love of God.
We cannot do this in our own strength
so we commit ourselves to rely on the grace of Christ. Amen.

298 THE WORLD CHURCH

Lord, we commit ourselves to love you
with all our hearts, with all our minds, with all our strength,
and our neighbours as ourselves.
Lord, so fill us with your Holy Spirit
that we may be faithful to the commitment we have made.
Through Christ our Lord. Amen.

299 CHRISTMAS EVE

Lord, so many voices clamour for our attention that we are
    confused,
and sometimes we are not really sure what Christmas means
    any more.
We pray: Help us this Christmas to listen to you.
Teach us again that, through the Christ child,
you are telling us just how much we matter to you.
Show us that, in Immanuel,
you are promising to share all that life means to us.
Assure us that, through the one who came,
we can begin to know you as our Father.
Lord, we commit ourselves to being open to you,

and ask that you will make a Christmas in our hearts.
Through Jesus Christ, who is the true Christmas. Amen.

Prayers of Dismissal

300   ONE WORLD WEEK—THE ENVIRONMENT

There is only one God, and there is only one world.
Go now, as God's people in the world,
to live for his glory and to speak his name. Amen.

301   SET ALL FREE

The Father says, I have loved you from before you were born,
and I will love you when life is no more.

Through the Father's love you can be set free.
Through the Son's sacrifice you can know you are free.
Through the power of the Holy Spirit you can live in the
    freedom that was bought for you.

The Lord says, go now and live, not as slaves but as those set
    free
to live and serve the Lord. Amen.

302   WE BELIEVE

Lord, we believe that you called us here—
to worship the King of Glory, to praise the Saviour of the
    world;
to renew our faith in the living God; and to receive the
    power of the Spirit.

Now send us out into the world to speak in the name of the
    King;
that the world may receive its Saviour
as the Spirit renews faith on the earth. Amen.

303 WE HAVE A SONG TO SING

We have sung our songs and we have given praise to the
    Lord.
We have prayed in faith and we have declared our hope.
We have heard God's Word and we have rejoiced in his
    promises.
We have received his love and we have been renewed by his
    presence.

Lord, now we go to sing our songs; to pray in faith; to
    declare your love;
to demonstrate your presence;
knowing that your love will guide us, hold us and empower
    us
for all things, for ever. Amen.

304 YOU ARE THE ONE

Lord, you are the one who turns our ends into new
    beginnings.
By your Holy Spirit transform the end of this act of worship
into the beginning of daily life lived for you;
change our songs of praise into words and deeds that bring
    honour to your Son;
Renew all our prayers, that they may become channels of
    love, life and hope
not only for ourselves but for everyone we meet. Amen.

305 FOR THE GLORY OF YOUR NAME

Lord, it has been good to be here;
to sing your praises; to give you thanks; to say we are sorry
and to share our concerns for others.
Now, as we commit ourselves to you,
send us out in the power of the Holy Spirit to live for Jesus;
to speak his name; to share his love—all for the glory of your
    name. Amen.

306 THE ONE WE HAVE MET

The one we have met here is the one who goes with us.
The Saviour who gives us freedom is the one who will open
    closed doors.
The Lord who accepted our obedience is the one who equips
    us for service.
The Spirit who transforms our worship is the one who
    empowers us for witness.
The Father who pours his love over us is the one who will
    love us now
and will love us for ever. Amen.

307 LORD, WE HAVE MET WITH YOU

Lord, we have met with you
not by our deserving but by your grace alone.

Lord, we have met with you
not by our wisdom but through the power of the Spirit.

Lord, we have met with you
not because we had planned it but because you called us.

Lord, we have met with you
not for our sakes but simply for your glory.

Lord, we have met with you
not that our needs might be met but that your name might
    be honoured.

Lord, we have met with you
not for this brief time of meeting but, having met with you
    here,
that we might recognise all moments of meeting
and share with others the peace, hope and wholeness
that is found in the presence of our Lord. Amen.

308   JESUS IS LORD

Lord, we greeted you with our adoration and we offered our
      words of praise;
we gave thanks for who you are and for what you have done
      for us;
we have listened to your Word and held up the needs of our
      world before you;
now send us out in the power of the Spirit
that we may be equipped to declare that Jesus is Lord
to the glory of your name. Amen.

309   LORD, WE HAVE WORSHIPPED

The Lord we have worshipped is the Lord of the earth.
The Lord we have praised is the Lord of our homes.
The Lord we have trusted is the Lord of our lives.
The Lord we have celebrated is the Lord of all.
The Lord we have met here is the Lord who goes with us
now and always. Amen.

310   PETER AND CORNELIUS

Lord, we came not realising that we are enslaved—
now send us out in unexpected freedom.

We came entrapped in our own little worlds—
now send us out with the message that Jesus is Lord.

311   BREAD OF HEAVEN

Lord, we came to be fed but we have given you glory;
we came to give you thanks and praise
and we have been nourished by the hand that has made us.

Lord, send us out to share the bread you have given with
      those who are hungry.
Send us out, Lord, renewed by your grace
that you may feed others through our words and our ways.

312 JOY

The God we worship is our strength and our song.
The God we serve is our courage and our reward.
The God we trust is our hope and our joy.
He now sends us out to declare his glory and to serve in his
name. Amen.

313 HEROES OF FAITH

The Lord sends us out, not as those who are good,
not as those who are brave, not as those who are strong,
not as those who know all the answers.

The Lord sends us out as those who have found in Jesus
the answers to our deepest questions
and who by the Holy Spirit can be heroes of faith in word
and deed.

314 A SONG OF PRAISE

Lord, may the song of praise that we have offered in your
presence
be simply the overture to life lived for your glory.
We have lifted up our hearts and voices in praise and
adoration.
Now may what we say and how we say it;
what we do and how we do it;
the lives we live and how we live them;
our words of faith and our witness to Christ
lift the hearts and minds of all we meet
to join in the song of praise to your glory. Amen.

315 WE ARE CALLED

Lord, we are called by your name and we are healed by your
grace.
We have been appointed to be disciples and we have been
enabled by your Spirit.

We are called to be your people and we walk as your
      children.
Now Lord, send us out to discover Christ in our community;
to offer his love to our neighbours and to be Christ to all
      whom we meet. Amen.

316   CHRISTMAS

The Christ child has come, so we can begin again.
The Prince of Peace is within us—we can journey in
      confidence.
The Son of God has become like us, that we may be made
      like him.
Jesus is his name and he now sends us out
to bear his name and to share his love. Amen.

317   BE THERE FOR US

Lord, when we are afraid, be there for us;
when we are sad, be there for us;
when we lose our way, be there for us;
when we are full of joy, be there for us;
when we long to worship you, be there for us;
when we take our final breath, be there for us, always. Amen.

318   KINDNESS

Lord, send us out as agents of your grace
and as those filled with the Holy Spirit.
May our lives overflow with your kindness
and bear fruit for the glory of your name. Amen.

319   HAVE NO FEAR

Have no fear, Christ is with you.
Have no doubt, Christ is in you.
Have no despair, Christ is before you, around you and over
      you—
and will be for ever. Amen.

320 HE IS THE LORD

The Lord is great and holy.
The Lord is loving and merciful.
The Lord is patient and forgiving.
The Lord is here and he goes with us,
and will walk with us to the end, and beyond.
He is the Lord. Amen.

321 HIS PEACE

Grace, mercy and peace are ours through Christ our Lord.
We go to show his peace, knowing his mercy,
as we declare his grace to the world. Amen.

322 THE CHURCH IN OUR NATION

Jesus said, 'You will receive power' and, 'You shall be my
    witnesses.'
We go in the assurance of his promise
that he will be with us to the end, and beyond.
We go now, for the Lord is with us. Amen.

323 THE COMFORTER

Our comforter, helper and guide;
our strength, our hope and our joy;
our peace, our courage and our friend;
our Father, our Lord and our advocate.
These are the names of our Lord,
and he will be with us for ever. Amen.

324 ASH WEDNESDAY

We go from this place in the knowledge of Christ's love
and in the power of the Spirit
and in the assurance that no matter who or what we are, or
    where we go,
we shall always be in the presence of the Father. Amen.

325   MAUNDY THURSDAY

The Lord has made us clean, he has accepted us as we are,
and he sends us out to declare his love and his life-
 transforming power.
We go in the love of the Father, in the grace of the Son
and in the presence of the Holy Spirit. Amen.

326   GOOD FRIDAY

We came with many burdens, we go with one Saviour.
We came with our emptiness, and we have been filled.
We came with our stories of defeat and despair,
and we go with the one who has triumphed for us.
We came alone, frustrated and in fear,
but we go with the one who will always be there. Amen.

327   EASTER

Lord, yours is the victory, ours is the hope;
yours is the triumph, ours is the joy;
yours is the glory, ours is the peace;
yours is the power, ours is the trust.
Lord, may your risen presence hold us, guide us and lead us,
now and for ever. Amen.

328   HARVEST

We go in the love of the Father, the name of his Son
and in the power of the Spirit.
We go to reap a harvest that will bring him all the praise and
 glory.
We go because the Lord of the harvest goes with us. Amen.

329   REMEMBRANCE SUNDAY

Go out into the world, remembering that it belongs to God.
Go out into life, remembering it is his gift to you, and to
 each of us.

Go out into service, remembering that all you do in his
name is never wasted.
Go out in his name, in his presence and for his glory.
Go out in the power of the Spirit. Amen.

330   SOCIAL RESPONSIBILITY

Go, because the world is waiting.
Go, because of your neighbour's need.
Go, because Christ came.
Go, because he goes with you.
Go, and go in the name of Christ. Amen.

331   THE WORLD CHURCH

Go out, go out into the world!
Go out, go out in the name of Christ!
Go out, go out to love and serve your neighbour!
Go out, go out and declare in word and deed that Jesus
Christ is Lord,
to the glory of God the Father. Amen.

332   THE WAY

Lord, in our weakness be our strength;
in our pain be our comfort; in our despair be our hope;
in our joys be our fulfilment;
in our coming and our going be our way, be our guide and
be our Lord. Amen.

333   CHRISTMAS EVE

We can go in peace because Christ the Prince of Peace has
come,
and he goes with us. Amen.

334   THE PATH OF LIFE

When the path is hard he will be with you.
When the road is unclear he will be your guide.

When the journey is difficult he will hold your hand.
When the destination seems far away he will stay by your
    side.
When the way is dark he will be your light.
When you cannot see the way ahead he will protect you.
When all seems lost he will give you victory.
When you feel alone, afraid and uncertain he will hold you
    for ever.
When you go he will always go with you. Amen.

335   SUNDAY SCHOOL

We pray for those who teach and for those who learn.
We thank you for a Saviour to know,
a friend to trust and a Lord to serve. Amen.

Offertory Prayers

336   FOR ALL YOUR GIFTS

For all your gifts we thank you, Lord,
and the gifts we now bring are a sign of how grateful we are.
We bring our gifts in Jesus' name. Amen.

337   HOW CAN WE NOT THANK YOU?

Lord, how can we not thank you; how can we not praise
    you;
how can we not worship you; how can we not give you
these tokens of our thanks and praise and worship?

Lord, bless these gifts, that they may be a blessing
so that the whole world will join in the endless song of praise
that rings from one end of eternity to the other,
and declares that Jesus is Lord. Amen.

338   LORD, YOU GAVE

Lord, you gave us laughter and you shared our tears;
you gave us our songs and you received our praises;

you gave us life and you walked our paths;
you gave us yourself and in Christ we received everything;
you gave us each other that we might not journey alone;
you gave us hope and peace and love—
now receive our offering,
which is a sign of our joy for all you have given. Amen.

339   PEACE AND JOY

Peace and joy; hope and forgiveness; life and contentment;
faith and trust; songs and praises; time and eternity;
Father, Son and Holy Spirit;
Jesus Christ our Saviour and Lord—
these are some of the gifts with which you have blessed us.

We offer our gifts, our lives and ourselves
that you may receive praises, and our neighbours a blessing.
   Amen.

340   EVERYTHING

Lord, everything we have and are is a gift from you.

We have earned nothing for which you did not give us the
   skills;
we achieved nothing for which you did not give us the time
   and the energy;
we possess nothing for which we do not owe you grateful
   thanks and praise.

Lord, the gifts we now bring can only be offered
because you have given and we want to give thanks.

Please use these gifts
that the whole world might turn to you with thankful hearts.
   Amen.

341   WITH THE BLESSINGS

With the blessings we have received we bless the Lord.
With the gifts in our hands we praise his name;

with our hearts and hands and voices we give thanks to the
	Lord,
calling on all his creation to bless and praise his holy name.
	Amen.

342 WE GIVE

We give, because we have received.
We have received, because the Lord is generous.

We give, because you are worthy.
You give, because you are Lord.

We give out of what we hold.
You overwhelm us by your abundance.
We give, because we must.

Lord, receive our offering, and use it for the glory of your
	name
and to bring all people to confess you are Lord. Amen.

343 THESE GIFTS

Lord, these gifts are the overture and not the finale on all our
	giving.

Come, receive our gifts.
Then touch our minds, restore our hearts and renew our lives
so that what we give and what we continue to hold
may be used to draw all people, everywhere,
to the foot of your cross and to confess you are Lord. Amen.

344 YOU ARE THE KING

Lord, you are the King and we are your people;
you are our sovereign and we are your servants;
you are almighty, and we come in our weakness
to bring you our offering of praise, thanks and worship.
Now use our gifts so that the whole world may know that
	Jesus is Lord. Amen.

345 LORD, OURS IS THE JOY

Lord, ours is the joy and ours is the privilege;
ours is the wonder and ours is the celebration;
ours is the thankfulness and ours is the blessing.
We bring our gifts, knowing that it is a privilege, a joy and a
    wonder,
a blessing and a celebration,
to brings our gifts of thankfulness to Jesus, our Lord. Amen.

346 LORD, WHAT CAN WE OFFER?

Lord, what can we offer to the one who holds all things?
What can we bring to the one to whom all things belong?
What can we share with the one who has given so
    generously?
What can we withhold from the one who is so open-handed?
What can we do for the one who is almighty?
What can we offer to the one who gave himself for us?

Lord, what can we offer, except ourselves, to Jesus as Lord?
    Amen.

347 FOR YOUR GLORY

Lord, we have brought our gifts as part of our worship.
We have brought our offerings as a sign of our praises.
We have brought our money as a symbol of our gratitude.

Lord, accept our gifts and receive our commitment,
of which our gifts are simply the sign. Amen.

348 LORD, YOU HAVE GIVEN

Lord, you have given us everything we have,
everything we are and everything we shall be.
We bring these gifts as a sign of our joy in all you have given.
    Amen.

349   HERE ARE OUR GIFTS

Lord, here are our gifts and here are our praises;
here are our thanks and here is our worship;
here are our hands and here are our voices;
here are the signs of our thankfulness and joy.

Lord, use all that we have brought,
that everyone, everywhere, may be invited to join in this
        prayer
of thanks and praise. Amen.

350   WITH THESE GIFTS

Father, with these gifts we bring our praises;
with our praise we bring our joy;
with our joy we bring our thanksgiving;
with our thanksgiving we bring ourselves.

Father, take what we have brought,
receive even that which we have kept,
and use all we have and are to glorify your name. Amen.

351   THE GIFT OF OUR LIVES

Father, we bring you the gift of our lives,
the offering of our service and our commitment to love.
Take the gifts of our money, our days and our years,
use all we have and are and will be to lead those we know to
        know you.
We pray for ourselves, young and old, that we may be open
to what you want to teach us today,
so that tomorrow we may be better equipped to live for Jesus.
We ask this in his name. Amen.

352   WHAT THEY MEAN

Father, we bring you our gifts of money
which represent our time, our skills and our service.
We bring them with grateful thanks in the name of Jesus,
your greatest gift to us all. Amen.

353 OUR GIFTS

Lord, we are your people, these are our gifts,
use them for your glory in Jesus' name. Amen.

354 WE BRING OUR GIFTS

We bring you our gifts to acknowledge your presence;
we offer them to you as part of our worship;
we lay them before you as a sign of our commitment;
we present them to you as a symbol of our service;
we set our offerings before you
and with them we give ourselves to you, as a sign of our love.
Amen.

355 WHAT YOU HAVE GIVEN

Father, you have given us everything we have and are.
You gave us what we have given and what we have kept.
Use what we have brought to bring others to Christ,
and what we have kept for your glory. Amen.

Prayers for a Healing Service

356 HEALING—PREPARATION

Lord, it is knowing who you are that gives us the confidence
to enter your presence, to acknowledge your glory,
to offer you our adoration, to sing your praises,
to seek healing and wholeness.
Lord, it is knowing that you are here that gives us hope of
renewal and grace
as we come to you in Jesus' name. Amen.

357 HEALING—PRAISE

Sovereign Lord, every time we remember your glory,
we are overwhelmed with a desire to praise you.
Every time we allow ourselves space to think again of your
grace,

we long to offer you everything we have and all that we are
as a sign of our thankfulness.

Sovereign Lord, it is your sovereignty over all creation
that gives meaning and purpose to all our lives.
It is your indescribable grace, which flows from the centre of
your being,
that once gave us life and daily seeks to renew our lives for
your glory.

Sovereign Lord, you are for ever beyond our reach, yet you
choose to hold us;
you are more holy, more powerful, more glorious than our
mere words can describe.

Sovereign Lord, we try to encapsulate you in our words of
faith
and in our prayers and praises,
but again and again we are forced to confess
that even the best we can offer will never be worthy of you.

Sovereign Lord, we come to you as we are—
empty, longing to be filled; alone, yet coming together;
powerless, simply trusting your grace;
imprisoned in our doubts and fear, aching inside as we wait
for you to set us free.

Sovereign Lord of all that was, all that is and all that will be,
we come to praise you
and in praising you we come to be made whole.

In the name of Christ the healer. Amen.

358   HEALING—A CONFESSION

Lord, you have made it clear that we cannot be healed
unless we are honest with you and with ourselves.

Silence

Lord, you have helped us to see that our cleansing and renewal
must always begin at the foot of the cross,
the place where Christ paid the price of our dishonesty and disobedience.

Silence

Lord, you are making us understand that our experience of liberation
from those things that have held us and restricted our lives for so long
depends on our being ready to receive
whatever you, in your wisdom and grace, are longing to give.

Silence

Lord, we confess your glory, we acknowledge our brokenness,
we ask to be filled with the Holy Spirit. In Christ's name. Amen.

359 LIGHT IN THE DARKNESS

Prayers for a service of healing and wholeness.

For these prayers you will need nine candles. One is lit before each prayer. The candles should be clearly visible either in the front or at different points around the church. The response can be a moment of silence or a sung refrain—perhaps a Taizé chant (e.g. O Lord, hear my prayer).

The first candle is lit.

Lord, we light this candle for those whose days are covered with the darkness of pain;
for those whose every movement comes at the cost of the agony it brings;
for those whose pain is hidden from others
and for those who long for the light that the healing touch of Christ can bring.

[Response]

The second candle is lit.

Lord, we light this candle for those whose lives are clouded
    with despair;
for those whose moments are lived out in the fear of the
    unknown
and the anxiety of what might be;
for those who constantly live under a cloud of depression
    and despair
and for those who need to see the light of Christ at the end
    of their long, dark tunnel.

[Response]

The third candle is lit.

Lord, we light this candle for those whose lives display the
    darkness of emptiness
and the deep void that nothing will fill;
for those who have lost hope and have no expectation of
    peace;
for those whose restlessness can never find comfort
and whose desire for contentment can only be met by the
    light of Christ.

[Response]

The fourth candle is lit.

Lord, we light this candle for those
who have everything that is counted important in this life
but who will arrive empty-handed
with nothing of ultimate value at the end of their days;
for those who seek meaning and purpose
in a life overflowing with unending activity
and for those who have yet to discover
the joy of life and the wonder of each new day;

for those for whom the light of Christ is a challenge too
    great
and an offer of healing they think they don't need.

[Response]

The fifth candle is lit.

Lord, we light this candle for those whose days are a torrent
    of responsibility
and an incessant chorus of demands they can't meet;
for those who long to run away and to hide
and for those who are threatened by the apparent self-
    sufficiency of others;
for those who need to discover that they are accepted
and those for whom the light of Christ is the doorway to
    peace and renewal.

[Response]

The sixth candle is lit.

Lord, we light this candle for those who cannot light it
    themselves;
for those too ashamed to reach out for healing
and for those who can never accept that Christ's light is for
    them;
for those who know they are unworthy
and for those whose sense of guilt is unreal;
for those for whom Christ's light challenges all their
    assumptions and dreams.

[Response]

The seventh candle is lit.

Lord, we light this candle for those whose lives are a constant
    battlefield
as they daily take their stand against temptations that are so
    strong;
for those too ashamed to acknowledge

the wrong thoughts, dreams and desires they are failing to
    conquer
and the secrets locked inside they want no one to hear;
for those for whom the light of Christ is the pathway to
    cleansing and renewal.

[Response]

The eighth candle is lit.

Lord, we light this candle for those who have opened their
    lives to Christ
and have walked in his presence all their days;
those for whom the love of God and the grace of Christ
are the rock on which they daily take their stand;
but also for those whose witness and service is all in their
    own strength
and who deep down know their need to be filled with the
    Holy Spirit.

[Response]

The ninth candle is lit.

Lord, we light this candle for ourselves,
as we wait in your presence and seek your power.
We come as we are, seeking to receive
all that you, through the light of Christ, are longing to give.

[Response]

We bring our prayers, that the light of Christ may touch our
    darkness
and bring wholeness and healing for his glory. Amen.

360   HEALING—COMMITMENT

Lord, we believe it is your will that we should be made
    whole;
that our lives be daily touched by your grace;
that our worship and service be energised by the Spirit;

that you desire to be Lord of every part of our lives.
We commit ourselves to be your people
as we commit ourselves to you as Lord. Amen.

361 HEALING—DISMISSAL

Lord, we came seeking healing and wholeness—
send us out as signs of your grace.
We came searching for cleansing and renewal—
we now go as your channels of peace for the world.
We came happy to meet you and to be changed by your
    power.
Now we go in your name and for your glory,
that others may know that your grace is for all. Amen.

Prayers for a Wedding

362 PRAYER FOR BLESSING

Lord, we praise you for life and for love,
for hope and for joy, for giving and for sharing.

We praise you for the way that you have demonstrated
your own great mercy, love and care in and through Jesus
    Christ our Lord.
We have come here today to ask you to bless us with your
    Holy Spirit,
and to fill our lives and our relationships with your unfailing
    love and care.

We praise you for calling us into relationships of love with
    each other,
and for that special relationship of husband and wife.
We ask you to enable us so to live, love and share,
that our promises to each other may be filled with the
    strength of your grace.
We ask this through Jesus Christ our Lord. Amen.

363 THANKSGIVING

God so wonderful, we give you our thanks.
Lord so mighty, we honour your name.
Father so loving, we offer you our praise.

Lord, we praise you for the life you gave us
and for all with whom we share each day.
We thank you for those who make us feel valued and wanted
and for the relationships that fill our lives with hope and
with love.

We praise you for this day of happiness and joy;
for those who have come to declare their love for each other
and to seal it with their promises to you.

May all we say and do be a reflection of your love that never
ends. Amen.

364 YOU HAVE CALLED US TOGETHER

Lord, you have called us together to celebrate this day;
to give thanks for the good memories we are creating;
to place your love at the heart of the promises we are making
today.

Lord, from the beginning you designed us to share each
other's joy;
to walk with one another on our journey;
to support each other wherever the journey leads.

Lord, you have made us for friendship that is pure;
for fellowship that nurtures peace; for compassion that
brings healing;
for love that bears all things.

Lord, we pray for [bride] and [groom], that you will share
their joy,
walk with them on the journey they have begun today
and touch all they experience together with your grace
that knows no beginning and no end. Amen.

365 PRAYER OF PRAISE

Lord, we praise you for the gift of life; the sharing of dreams;
the joy of friendship; the laughter of love; the commitments
we make;
the journey we make together; the comfort we can offer
when tears are shed;
the forgiveness and love when wrong things are said;
the hope and the courage our praises can bring;
the presence of God whose love never ends.
It is there for us now, through the years to the end of all
things.
We will praise you now and we will praise you for ever.
In the name of Christ, your greatest gift of all. Amen.

366 THE CENTRE OF OUR JOY

Praise and honour, glory and majesty to you, almighty God,
King of Kings and Lord of Lords.
On this day of joy and celebration
we come to place you at the heart of life.
You are the source of all that is good and true;
you are the fountain of peace, joy and love.

Lord, come, and be the centre of our joy;
come, and fill us with thanksgiving;
come, and infuse our promises with the love of the Father,
the grace of the Son and the power of the Holy Spirit.
Amen.

367 YOU HAVE PROVIDED THE WAY

Lord, we praise you that you are not remote, unloving or
unfeeling.
From the beginning it was your plan that we should live in
fellowship
with each other and with you.

Lord, we praise you for life,

for the life you have given to us and for the life we can share
 together;
for the days you have given
and for the laughter, love and friendship that make them so
 precious;
for friendship, fellowship and relationships that mean
 everything to us.

Lord, we are aware that the things we say and do
can so easily spoil our friendships and damage relationships.
In Jesus you have provided the way that, through his love,
we can find the strength to forgive and the courage to begin
 again.

Lord, may your almighty presence fill us with hope,
overwhelm us with joy and enable us to worship you.
May everything we say and do open the way for your love
to enter our hearts and to enrich all our relationships.

We ask this in the name of Jesus, the one who is Lord.
 Amen.

368 THE JOURNEY WE ARE TAKING TOGETHER

Lord, we praise you for the gift of life—its beginnings and
 ends;
for the sharing of dreams and for the pleasure of meeting;
for the joy of friendship and for the laughter of love;
for the commitments we make to each other
and for the journey we are taking together;
for the comfort we offer in times of sadness and when tears
 are shed;
for forgiveness and love when wrong things are said;
for the hope and the courage that our promises can bring
and for the presence of God whose love never ends.
It is there for us now, through the years and to the end of all
 things.
We will praise you for ever in Christ's name. Amen.

369   PRAYER OF CONFESSION

Forgive us, Father, that so often our relationships with each
     other and with you
are filled with selfishness, jealousy and pride.
Too easily we seek to put ourselves and our own desires first,
and neglect to listen to each other
and care for each other in the way you intended, or as we
     have promised.
As [bride] and [groom] come to this moment of entering into
     a new relationship,
we ask that they may have the assurance that they can do so
in the knowledge that the past is dealt with,
the future is in your hands and today is your gift to us all.
Through Jesus Christ our Lord. Amen.

370   THE GIFT OF FRIENDSHIP

Lord, we thank you for the gift of friendship
and for the joy we find when we are at one with each other
     and with you.
We praise you that you designed us to find fulfilment and
     encouragement
in the things we share together
and in the times of harmony that love will bring.

Lord, we pray for [bride] and [groom], that the promises they
     have made
will be a source of strength in times of testing
and a secure foundation on which they can stand firm,
     no matter the storm.

Lord, we pray for the home of [bride] and [groom],
that it will be a place where love is known
and where every visitor feels welcome.
May it be built on the foundation of your love,
where nothing that is said or done
will destroy the peace that comes where Jesus is Lord.

Lord, we pray for the family and friends of [*bride*] and
[*groom*]:
May we fulfil our promise to support them with our prayers,
to be there for them when the way ahead is unclear,
and to stand with them when the stress and strain of life
threatens to take its toll.

Lord, we pray for ourselves
and for the friendships that are important to us
and for the relationships to which we have made our
commitment.
May the grace of the Lord Jesus Christ hold us,
the love of God fill us, and the power of the Holy Spirit
enable us.

This we ask in the name of Christ, the friend of sinners. Amen.

Prayers for a Funeral

371   FUNERAL FOR A STILLBORN CHILD

Opening prayer

Father, down the years you have touched broken hearts,
healed damaged lives, comforted the sorrowful,
wiped away the tears of those who are hurting
and gone on loving us no matter what, and no matter who.
We come to you now, seeking your strength, your mercy and
your peace.
We ask that you will be to us now all that we need,
that by your grace we may know the joy of your abiding
presence.
Through Jesus Christ our Lord. Amen.

Introduction

From our earliest days we are trained to judge everyone
by what they achieve, by what they become, and by their
length of days.

Today we remember that [*name*] has enabled us to learn an
　　important lesson,
that our value to God and to each other simply cannot be
　　assessed this way.
[*name's*] life may not have been completed in the way we
　　would have wished.
But s/he is still precious, and will always be remembered as a
　　member of the family.

Prayer of hope

Father in heaven, we come to you as your children:
We come in sorrow that [*name*] has been taken from us so
　　soon;
but we also come for peace,
for your Son has promised that all your little ones
shall look upon your loving face for ever.

We come to you in prayer for [*parents/relatives*],
who have had no time to care for her/him
and to share with her/him as they grew.
We thank you for their love for her/him
and for your love for us all that gives us strength.

We thank you that through the love of Christ
[*name*] is, like ourselves, offered a share in your promises and
　　a place in your kingdom,
and eternal life in the heaven of your love.
Through the love of Jesus. Amen.

*[Suggested Bible readings: Psalm 16 GNB; Matthew 18:1–5
GNB]*

Prayer of thanksgiving

Father, we thank you that your love is greater than our
　　sorrow,
your mercy wider than our confusion and anger,
your comfort deeper than our despair,
your hope richer than our tears.

Father, we thank you that we can turn to you and know that
   you understand,
that we can open our hearts to you and know you will never
   turn us away,
that we can share our feelings of brokenness and know that
   you will hold us for ever.

Father, we thank you for those who have offered us love and
   care,
those who have shared our tears and held us gently.

Father, we thank you for all they have done for us through
   your Son, Jesus Christ our Lord.
Thank you that through his life, death and resurrection
you have shown us that your love simply has no limit,
and that, when we put our trust in him,
we receive the promise of your eternal joy.

Father, we ask you to help us as we place [*name*] in your
   hands.
Give us peace in the knowledge that in your keeping
s/he is safeguarded, contented and whole.
Surround [*name*] and [*parents/relatives*] with your unending
   love.
Do not let grief overwhelm us, or be unending, or turn us
   against you.
May we find peace, love and hope because of today.
May we know what it means to walk with you all the days of
   our lives,
that at the end we may, by your grace, rejoice to be in your
   presence for ever.
This we ask through Jesus Christ our Lord. Amen.

Commendation

Father, we cannot receive your kingdom unless we come as
   little children.
We thank you for the gift of [*name*].

Now, in love, trust and thankfulness we give her/him back to
    you,
knowing that in your keeping s/he will be safe and happy
and her/him life complete and whole. Amen.

Prayers of assurance

Father, we know that all of life is a gift from you,
and that its value cannot be measured by its length.
Today we have come to thank you especially for the life of
    [*name*],
and for how s/he is enabling us to begin to see life in a whole
    new way.

We thank you too, for the joy s/he gave to the wider family
in the anticipation of his/her coming, and the love that she/
    he inspired.
We thank you for giving courage, hope, love and peace
to us all through these last few days,
and we trust that you will continue to touch our lives and
    hold us in your grace.

We thank you for the hope that knowing you gives us,
into which all of us can enter,
and for the assurance that, with [*name*], we shall, by faith,
share in the joy and gladness and peace in the heaven of your
    love.

Through Jesus our Lord. Amen.

Final prayers

Lord, we know that our journey is not over,
that we are at the start of a pathway that we must walk.
But, Lord, we know that we need not walk it alone,
you have promised to be with us, always.
It is in the courage and strength of your word of hope
that we will walk to the end, and beyond.
Through Jesus Christ, the one who always walks with us.
    Amen.

372   WE PRAISE YOU BECAUSE

Lord, we praise you because you are greater than anything
    we can imagine,
more caring than we can ever understand,
and your love is reaching out to hold us in ways that give us
    hope, comfort and peace.

Lord, we praise you that we can turn to you when our faith
    is weak
and when it is strong;
when we are full of questions, doubts and fears,
and when our faith is strong and our trust is in you.

Lord, we know that you will accept us as we are,
that you will meet our needs and share our pain.
We come with our praise in Jesus' name,
the one who opens the way into the presence of the Father.
    Amen.

373   YOU GAVE US LIFE

Lord, it is your love that gave us life,
and it is your love that welcomes us through death.
It is your presence that gives us hope,
your almighty power that gives us assurance
and your endless love that gives us the courage
to continue the journey of life, putting our trust in you.

Lord, we do not always find it easy to make room for you in
    our busy lives,
we do not always find it easy to recognise your presence,
we do not always find it easy to trust, to believe or to have
    faith.

Lord, we need you now,
we need to know that you are here,
that you are sharing our pain, that you do understand,

and that you will love us, hold us and walk with us, no
matter what.

In the name of Jesus Christ, the way, the truth and the life.
Amen.

374   SOVEREIGN LORD

Sovereign Lord, you hold the universe in the palm of your
hand.
We have come to praise you and to ask you to hold us,
to share our tears and our sadness, our brokenness and our
questions,
and the pain deep inside that won't go away.

Sovereign Lord, we need to know that you are
great enough to comprehend our fears,
strong enough to lift us when we fall
and loving enough to accept
our anger, our doubts and our confusion, and to go on
loving us.

Sovereign Lord, in Jesus Christ you have lived our life,
shared our journey,
and, by faith in him, you have changed our death
from the end of everything into the beginning of life lived in
your presence,
just as you meant it to be.
We bring our prayer of praise in his name. Amen.

375   LORD, YOU WERE THERE

Almighty God, our heavenly Father,
we praise you for being there for us when we needed you
most.
We praise you for sharing our pain and our sorrow,
for being there in the midst of our shock and disbelief.

Lord, you understand that at times like this
we feel so small, weak and vulnerable,

but we have come to be held by your power, your grace and
    your love.

Now as we gather to give you thanks and praise,
make us aware of your presence and power,
and may your gentle, loving Spirit
give us the courage we need and the hope we long for.
Through Jesus Christ our Lord. Amen.

376   THE DECLARATION

We come at this important moment
to place [*name*] in the loving hands of almighty God.
It is when we come face to face with death that we can find
the hope, courage and strength we long for
as we place our trust in Jesus Christ as Lord.
Our hope comes from knowing that, through his life, death
    and resurrection,
Christ has opened the way into the heaven of his love.
God has promised that through his Word in the Bible
we will find the comfort and love we need.
Now, as we listen to God's Word,
may we receive all that he longs to give us.

377   PRAYER OF THANKSGIVING

Lord, we thank you for your greatness, your power and your
    glory.
There is nothing you do not know,
there is nothing you do not understand,
there is no limit to the reach of your love and compassion.

Lord, we thank you for your sovereignty,
which holds the universe in the palm of your hand.
We thank you more for your grace, which strengthens us in
    our weakness,
guides us when we are lost and holds us when we are hurting
    deep inside.

Lord, we thank you for Jesus Christ, and for his life, death
and resurrection.
Through him you have given us the assurance
that when we have put our trust in him,
nothing will ever separate us from your love, for all eternity.

Lord, we thank you for every memory we have of [*name*]
and that each of us remember her/him differently.
We thank you for all s/he meant to us
and for those memories that are personal and special to us.

We thank you for everything in her/his life that spoke to us
of you,
and everything s/he said and did that made your love real.
We thank you for her/his willingness to trust you with their
lives,
and her/his commitment to serve you in ways to which you
called her/him.

We thank you that, though her/his journey on earth is now
ended,
by faith in you her/his pain, sorrow and struggle
have been transformed in your presence and by your power.

Help us, Lord, to be content to leave her/him in the safety of
your love,
and in the assurance that with you s/he has a joy, peace and
wholeness
s/he has never known before.

We pray for all those who are sad and hurting, remembering
especially …
and all the family and friends of [*name*].
We ask that your love will so hold us and help us
that we will be filled with hope and faith because of today.
May we by your grace know the joy of your presence
and through your love receive your gift of eternal life.
This we ask through Jesus Christ our Lord. Amen.

378　THE COMMENDATION

Lord, we commend [*name*] into your loving arms,
and we entrust her/him to your loving presence for ever.

379　ADDITIONAL PRAYER BEFORE THE COMMITTAL

at the crematorium, when the service has already taken place elsewhere.

We have thanked God for [*name*], and we have asked for
　　her/his peace.
Let us pause, be quiet and bring to God our own personal
　　memories
and those things in [*name's*] life for which we want to thank
　　God.

Silence

Lord, so great and so understanding; Father, so gentle and so
　　loving;
we turn to you now.
Be our courage, our strength and our hope;
hold us in our sadness, deal gently with us in our brokenness
and assure us now of your peace and love.
In the name of Christ, our Lord. Amen.

380　AT THE GRAVESIDE OR CREMATORIUM (2)

Lord, we are here because [*name*] has died.
We have thanked you for her/his life on earth
and for the way we will always remember her/him.
Either

We place her/his body in the ground …
or

We have brought her/his body to be cremated …
but we entrust her/him to your loving care for all eternity.
Our hope and our confidence are in you, and in your
　　promise of resurrection,

and a place in the heaven of your love.
Through Jesus Christ our Lord. Amen.

Listen to the promise of Jesus:
'God loved the world so much that he gave his only Son,
that whoever puts their trust in him shall not die but have
    everlasting life.'

Lord, we believe; help us where our faith falls short.

Funeral Closing Prayers

381   LORD, GO WITH US

Lord, go with us on the journey of our lives,
help us to find comfort for our sadness,
peace for our fears, courage to walk in faith.
Lord, help us to trust you with the whole of our lives,
that through your grace we may be made whole.
This we ask in Jesus' name. Amen.

382   GOD OF PEACE

God of peace, go with us from this place.
Lord of hope, walk with us into tomorrow.
Father of love, hold us, guide us and heal us.
In Jesus' name. Amen.

Meditations

383   AM I ALONE?

A meditation based on Psalm 139

Am I alone?
I look down on the view below me, and my eyes take in the
    whole vista.
I turn my gaze from one end of the horizon to the other—
nothing moves; no sign of life; no evidence of our passing;
    everything is still.

I am overwhelmed by the silence, the utter and complete
    silence, all around me.
Am I alone?
Am I alone in a way I have never experienced before?
Then, quite suddenly, the peace and quiet I have so
    desperately longed for,
searched for, has become the source of my fear.

Read verses 1–2

Am I alone?
I push my way through the crowded aisles of the busy
    supermarket.
I am bombarded on every side with sounds of screaming
    children,
unwanted music, of cash tills being filled, of trolleys
    lumbering out of control.
Nobody seems to see me—they are cocooned in their own
    private worlds.
They harvest their shopping and simply head for home.
Even those who ring up my purchases talk to each other as if
    I am invisible—
or not even here.
Why am I here—am I really alone?

Read verses 3–4

Am I really alone?
I drive my metal box on wheels and follow the familiar
    route;
I do the same things.
Like thousands who play this strange game,
we stare straight ahead and listen to sounds from the radio or
    player.
I may see other vehicles but rarely their passengers.
I grumble at the nameless, faceless driver who gets in my
    way.
My metal box—designed to give me freedom—has made me
    its prisoner.

It condemns me to isolation from life and from others.
I'm trapped into believing I can't cope without it,
yet as I sit in the queue going nowhere I ask myself—
am I really alone?

Read verses 5–6

Am I really alone?
I have lived in this town as long as I can remember.
This is where I went to school, where I grew up and started
    my first job.
This is where I raised my family and watched with joy and
    pride
as they too grew old enough to leave home and build a life of
    their own.
So now they have all gone and I'm left alone.
New people moved into our road.
I don't even know their names—and they don't know mine.
I miss the chatter of home
and the fun and the laughter of colleagues at work.
Once each day had a purpose that gave meaning to life.
Now each day is the same—am I really alone?

Read verses 7–8

Am I really alone?
For most of my life I have enjoyed really good health.
It was something I had never questioned.
I just thought it was normal and took for granted it would
    always be so.
But that is all in the past and will never return.
Now each day is a battle just to get through.
More medication—that does little good.
Fewer visitors come with whom I can share
a journey more painful and more difficult as the illness gets
    worse.
You see, I'm locked up inside; my memories are fading.
I see your face, but I can't remember your name.
I look in the mirror to guess who I am.

I have no one to talk to because no one wants to talk to me.
Am I really alone?

Read verses 9–10

Am I really alone?
Sometimes I long just to be alone, to step aside, to be me;
to be alone with my thoughts and feelings.
Sometimes I ache to be free of the pressures and the stress,
the anger and the bitterness, the doubts and the fears;
to leave behind the responsibilities that others have laid
        upon me.
But they all still crowd in and I am never allowed
just to live, to walk in your world, to enjoy your presence
as you always intended I should.
Will I never be alone, just to be me?

Read verses 11–12

Am I really alone?
Every day is a day of discovery, a pristine moment
filled with rich opportunities to know who I am and what I
        can be.
But the pressure is on—and there is no escape.
My parent's expectations almost crush my spirit;
The tests and the examinations wring the joy out of learning.
And all the time I am wondering:
Where is it all leading; what does it all mean?
The message is clear—I must study and strive to secure my
        future
and ensure wealth and possessions in the years yet to be.
While my head understands this, my heart is full of doubts
        and questions—
surely there is more to life's story than I have so far been
        told.
The temptations are real—just to escape.
It's so easy to get hooked into habits I will find impossible to
        break.
But no one will listen. Am I really alone?

Read verses 13–14

Am I really alone?

Perhaps I am. Perhaps I always was—or that is how it
seemed.

But even Jesus had times of aloneness, moments when no
one was near.

Some he chose for himself, as he made time to be alone with
his Father.

Some came when those he had chosen let him down, and
just ran away.

But on the cross he cried, 'My God, my God, why …?'

He deliberately entered my emptiness

and bore the cost of healing my aloneness.

Now, deep within me, I know the truth: I am not alone!

I never was and I never will be.

The God whose love gave me life

has walked with me and ahead of me all my days.

His grace has opened my eyes and set me free

to live a life of hope, joy and peace.

Now I can cry, 'My God, my God, you are with me!'

and I will know its truth for all eternity. Amen.

Read verses 17–18

384   BUT MARY SAID YES

Lord, when you ask us to follow you

it would help if you told us where it might lead and what it
would cost us.

We would be ready to trust you if we knew what you
wanted.

If you made it a bit clearer, just what is involved,

then we might be more willing to go with you.

Lord, how can you expect anyone just to say yes;

to be ready to follow without really knowing what it all
means?

We know of the angel who came to Mary.
We have read of the amazing news he gave to her.
She must have been shocked when he spoke of the baby
and probably felt like saying it had nothing to do with her.

But Mary was different—she simply listened and wondered
what it all meant.
Then, when the angel had finished, she simply said—yes.

Lord, Mary has taught us to trust you, even when we don't
understand,
and to walk along with you, trusting that you know the way.
It is only when we accept your invitation, and hold onto
your hand,
that we can set out on the journey with you.

Lord, what matters is that *you* know
just where you are leading us and what it all means;
you know what it costs, and where it all ends.
So help us to trust you with the whole of our lives
and give us the faith just to take the next step. Amen.

385   THE RICH YOUNG MAN

What a choice he was given! Follow Jesus and give
everything away!
Are we really sure what we would have done in his place?

His conversation with Jesus started out so well.
He wanted to know more about God
and how he could be sure that God was happy with the way
he lived.

He was such a serious young man.
At first he seemed to have more interest in the things of
heaven
than the things of earth.

Somehow or other he appears to have got the wrong end of
the stick.

He seems to have got it into his head
that getting his life right with God was something that
    depended on him
and what he could do himself;
he almost left God right out of the picture!

It was as though he thought that he could work his own way
    to heaven
and eventually deserve his place there.
What he had yet to learn was
no one's place in heaven can be won, earned or deserved.
It can only be entered through the victory Jesus has won
by his death and resurrection.

The day had promised so much—not a cloud in the sky.
The problems started when Jesus told it to him straight.
He always seemed to know just who or what people were
    putting first in their lives.

Lord, we praise you for Jesus' confrontation with this young
    man
and the challenge this story has brought into our lives.
We know that you will put your finger on the things in our
    lives
that are getting in the way of your being Lord, if only we will
    let you.

Come, Lord Jesus, come. Amen.

386   WHY LORD?

Lord, why is it that things happen the way they do?

When he picked up his brushes
to create a picture of what he saw all around him,
it was as if he was seeing the true colour and shape of your
    world
for the very first time.

When she held her newborn son,

it was as if she was seeing life and its wonder for the very first
   time.

When he sat with the dying
and shared something of the pain and tears of the bereaved,
it was as if he was experiencing loss for the very first time.

Lord, what does it mean when you tell us that all things are
   made new in Christ?

My child, in my Son you can see my beauty,
experience my grief and enter into the joy of life—
just as I planned it for you. Amen.

387   HE JUST SAID GO!

Genesis 12:1–3

He just said, go!
Of course, I didn't take any notice,
I never thought he could be speaking to me.
I went on doing what I wanted to do,
and hardly gave a thought to what I'd just heard.
So he said it again.
Abraham, I want you to go!
He'd spoken my name now, so I knew he meant me.
But I tried to side-step his challenge, and act as if I didn't
   know.
I beg your pardon, are you speaking to me?
But he just took no notice, and ever so quietly whispered,
I am telling you to go.
I have been telling you to go since the day you were born,
but you chose not to listen; you had made other plans,
and being open to God wasn't high on your list.

He was right, of course.
From my earliest days, somewhere deep inside, there had
   been an awareness
that there was something more—a part to be added to my
   life.

But I didn't know what.
The whole of my life I have been conscious of promptings
    and nudges—
like a hand on my days.
When I told my friends and my family, they thought I'd
    gone mad,
or was just trying to appear holy when they knew the truth!
They jokingly warned me that I had better watch out;
but listening to the Almighty is certainly no joke!
So I thought, if I just keep my head down, and don't say a
    word;
if I pretend he's not there, and that he means nothing to me;
if I keep myself busy, be religious, a good citizen and live for
    today,
he'll simply stop speaking and just go away.

It didn't work.
But then, with him it never does.
He looks deep inside—even deeper than I can comprehend.
He knows things about me I don't know myself.
One thing I've discovered: With him you can't hide.
Even if I tried to run,
I can never escape his all-seeing, all-knowing, all-
    understanding gaze.
Wherever I went, he always arrived first.
He was always there to meet me, round every turn.
He ignored my excuses, and said he would deal with my
    doubts;
he had followed my journey from before my birth, until
    now.
And he promised to journey with me to the end, and
    beyond.

So I made my decision—there was little else I could do …
he wouldn't give up, and I couldn't run!
I turned and said, Yes, Lord, what is it that you want?
He said, I have already told you—I want you to go!
I know that—but you didn't say where.

I'm really quite happy to stay where I am.
It has never crossed my mind to leave home, to leave family
and to leave what I know best.
I'm comfortable here—give me one good reason why I
    should change.

He paused, and he looked into my face;
his eyes filled with tears and yet, offering hope,
he gently held out his hand and drew me to himself—
and then with a voice that shook mountains, though as quiet
    as could be,
he said, Because I have spoken, and this is my word;
because you are my servant, and I am your Lord;
we must journey together; but we'll start from where you are.
You are part of the jigsaw that will transform my world.
The part that I am asking you to play may not seem so
    important,
and many will accuse you of just running away.
But with the faith that I give you, and my grace
    overwhelming,
we must journey together on the route that I have planned.

I have a plan and a purpose for your life—and my world,
but you will only be able to see when we walk hand in hand.
The path may seem narrow, and the journey unending,
but I know where I'm going and I know what lies at the end.
You must look through my eyes if you would know life,
and you must trust me if you want to live.
For you are the seed, but the harvest is mine;
my purpose for you is wider, longer, greater than you ever
    thought possible.
But it all begins here with your willingness to go.

But Lord, you haven't said where.
I'm willing to journey wherever you choose.
But you said you knew me—then you'll know I'm insecure,
and that I need all the answers before I'll take a step of faith.

Be fair, Lord, no one would ask someone else to journey
     without saying where!
If I don't know the destination, how will I know when I've
     arrived;
when will I know that the journey is finished?

But that's the whole point, my son;
I want you to journey, and leave the arriving to me.
Learn to trust me—perhaps not for the whole of the journey,
     just the next step.
At present your faith is something to carry with you; it's all
     in your head.
My challenge is to turn faith into trust;
not a set of beliefs like baggage that will weigh you down
     and hinder your journey—
but a trust in me that weighs nothing at all;
one that's strong and compassionate, and can move
     mountains of doubt.

So when I say go, what will *you* do?
Will you keep your ears closed and pretend you've not heard?
Will you pull up the drawbridge and lock all your doors?
Will you spend your days dreaming of what might have been
if you'd taken the risk and said yes to me?
You see, the choice is all yours, to stay or to go, to die or to
     live.
When I say go, I'm asking, Do you trust just enough to take
     that first step?
Now what will you do?

388   WORDS

Lord, they are everywhere. I can't get away from them.
Everywhere I look I am confronted by them.
They won't leave me alone! They are always there.
I can hear them, see them, feel them.
I can even speak them myself.

Words!
They come as a challenge—to change my ways;
to amend my behaviour; to follow a different path;
to be a new person; to trust, to obey—to love.

Words!
They come as a warning—that my way may be leading to
    danger;
that there is trouble ahead—the ice is thin; the water is hot;
the knife is sharp; that my lifestyle is a danger to me and the
    planet;
that my obsession with work or with leisure
is slowly stealing my days and my time just to be;
that I'm always having to make time and space for God—
that I'm simply existing, when I could be experiencing a
    deep sense of my own worth.
The words come in my face and warn me to consider the
    direction of my days
before there are no days left for me to consider.

Words!
They come with hope—they say I can begin again, that my
    life does matter, there is a purpose to my being here, at
    this moment in time.
They say that there is a God
who does hold me and my time in the palm of his hands;
that I am forgiven, accepted and loved;
they say that Christ has died, Christ is alive and that Christ
    will return.
These are the words of the greatest hope of all.

Words!
Then, Lord, there is your Word that comes as a challenge;
your Word that comes as a warning;
your Word that comes with hope and in love.
Your Word is Christ.
He is the Alpha and the Omega, the beginning and the end.
He is your first Word,

and you have promised that he is your ultimate Word
to me and to all who will listen.
Christ is your Word to us, that comes in human form;
Christ is the Word alive in me.
Here and now and for ever, Christ is the Word. Amen.

389   I WANT TO BE STILL

Lord, why won't they leave me alone?
I just want to be still, to sit here quietly in your presence;
to enjoy a few brief moments in your gentle, healing love.
But I live in a world addicted to making noise,
so my quiet space is under constant attack.
The telephone rings, someone demands my attention;
the passing car pollutes my silence with its unwanted,
      discordant sounds;
in every shop I am assaulted by unwanted music.

Lord, is that why you went away to the lonely places—
to find stillness in the presence of your Father?

Lord, teach me to find space
even in the hubbub and turmoil of my daily life;
to discover moments of tranquillity in the most unlikely of
      places.
Help me to transform the frustration of a traffic queue,
standing at the checkout and waiting for my turn in the
      doctor's surgery
into an oasis of stillness within,
as I allow Christ to be all things in all places to me. Amen.

390   THE LORD IS MY SHEPHERD

A meditation based on Psalm 23.

'The Lord is my shepherd.'

Lord, you call us to follow, and you call us by name;
you know our hopes and our dreams, our doubts and our
      fears;

our strengths and our weaknesses.
You still call us to follow, to be held in your gentle grace—
for you are the Good Shepherd and we are your sheep.

'I shall not want.'

Lord, we come as we are, assuming we are already full;
believing we can do everything; expecting to cope.
We come with our frailty, our foolishness and our plain
    stupidity.
We come fearful and uncertain.
But you still promise to meet our needs, to transform our
    desires
and to be yourself the fulfilment of our hunger for peace and
    hope.

'You make me lie down in green pastures.'

Lord, we live in a world that rushes by in its search for peace
    and meaning.
We have wandered down endless by-ways that promised to
    be the way to life
only to discover that we too have been deceived by the
    world's half-truths.
You call us to rest in you, to trust in your promises
and to seek our renewal in the presence of Christ,
for he is the one who knows where we can be fed.

'You lead me beside still waters.'

Lord, once again we turn to you;
once again we long for peace;
once again we yearn to be set free from the inner turmoil
that not all our searchings and strivings can ever heal.
You are the gracious one;
you are the one who lifts, renews and makes us whole.
Now we know that even in the turmoil of doubt, pain and
    despair

your presence provides a stillness and an oasis
that nothing, but nothing, can ever destroy.

'You restore my soul.'

Lord, we come into your presence,
battered by life and weighed down by the load
of mistakes, weaknesses and sin
that squeeze real life out of us and form a barrier between
     you and ourselves.
Lord, we have made every effort
to overcome the baggage and the clutter of our days.
We rejoice in your free gift of grace,
which is more than sufficient to restore who and what we are
and to help us become all that you meant us to be.

'You guide me in paths of righteousness for your name's sake.'

Lord, you touch my life and you hold my hand;
you surround me with your word of truth.
From your gracious hand you liberally flood my life with
     your good gifts
and you seek the fruit you planned
when you planted the seed of the Spirit within me.
Lord, you have done all these things to guide my life
into a new, whole and right relationship with you.
It is your will that everything I say or do
should bring honour and praise to your name.

'Even though I walk through the valley of death ...'

Lord, you leave us no doubt that walking with you
is no proof against the problems and the pain of life.
You warn us against living in a fool's paradise
of a life untouched by the sadness and sorrows of each day.
This journey is a real one, and the life you call us to live
is not exempt from all the twists and turns that life can
     throw at us.
But you have assured us that we will never journey alone

and that, no matter how deep we feel we are sinking,
underneath for ever are your loving, caring arms.

'I fear no evil.'

Lord, we must confess that often we are afraid
and our lives are all but conquered by despair.
In our humanness we do not always find it easy
to walk the path of faith that you call us to follow.
There are too many whose words and ways
cause us to question your love and to doubt your sovereign
    power.
It is then that you point us to Jesus, and fill us with your
    Holy Spirit.
It is then, as we fall in love with you all over again,
that we discover your love conquers all things.

'For you are with me …'

Lord, our hope and our joy knows no bounds
and our rejoicing has no limits!
For no matter who we are, and no matter where we go,
no matter what we have done, or failed to do,
we simply cannot escape your loving presence.
Your Holy Spirit will embrace us and empower us and enable
    us—always.
Whatever we are facing, just to know you are there changes
    everything.

'Your rod and your staff comfort me.'

Lord, in the world of half-truths and false promises
your Word gives us hope.
You have promised to give us strength to stand, courage to
    walk in faith
and the enabling power that raised Christ from the dead.
The presence of your Holy Spirit around and within
provides all the protection we need to continue our journey
in the knowledge of your grace and favour.

'You prepare a table before me …'

Lord, we seem to fill our lives with so many things
and to find fulfilment in the acquisition of this world's good
  things.
But each day we discover that
even when our days are overflowing with this world's riches,
real life and peace simply slip unnoticed through our fingers
and we turn to you as empty-handed paupers.
You shake your head at our continued foolishness
in the face of the provision of your grace.

'… in the presence of my enemies.'

Lord, you have never promised us a trouble-free existence
where nothing ever goes wrong;
everything we plan succeeds and all we hope for is fulfilled.
You point us to Jesus, who promised us resurrection life—
if we are prepared to carry a cross.
Again and again you remind us of the way that leads to life,
  hope and peace.
It begins at the foot of your empty cross,
it passes through the empty tomb
and is empowered by the 'emptying out' of your Holy Spirit.
Your grace is sufficient for all our needs.
your mercy will overcome all our weaknesses
and your love will enable us to stand in the face of any
  storm.

'You anoint my head with oil and my cup overflows.'

Lord, we have come because you have promised to bless us.
We have come because your blessing cannot be earned.
We have come because your blessing is free.
We have come because your blessing is for all who will come.
We have come because you have more blessings to give
than we have ever dared to ask for.
We have come to you Lord, the fount of all blessing,
that our cup of life might overflow with your love.

'Surely goodness and mercy will follow me.'

Lord, we live in a world that is overflowing with uncertainty.
Wherever we look, and whatever we hear,
we are overwhelmed by the knowledge of our human
    vulnerability.
Our mortality stares us in the face.
But we can face each day with your promise
not of immunity from life's troubles and sorrows,
but that your goodness and mercy will be
the safe foundation on which we can stand secure.

'I shall dwell in the house of the Lord for ever.'

Lord, walking in the knowledge of your presence is the joy
    of life.
Simply to know that wherever we go, and whatever we face,
it is always in full view of your loving gaze,
and our every thought and our every word lies naked before
    your sovereign will.
We rejoice in the promise
that our experience of living in your presence
will not be limited by time or space or by eternity.

Lord, our eternal shepherd,
we come to be led and nurtured at your loving hand
now and for all eternity. Amen.

391   A GLIMPSE OF GOD

I didn't know you were there, Lord.
It seemed from all that I had heard that you were just a
    name;
a heavenly being; a prop for the weak; a figment of the
    human imagination.
When I said my prayers I never really expected you to
    answer;
how could you, if you were not really there?

But now—now it's all different.
Just the other day it was as if I had actually caught a glimpse
    of you!
And now the God I didn't know I meet everywhere.
I see you in the sunrise and in the sunset.
I meet you in the kindness of friends and in the compassion
    of strangers.
I recognise your face in the nameless multitude
who rush to respond to the latest appeal for the hungry and
    starving.

I hear your voice when I read your Word
and find you near when I turn to prayer;
when I am alone and have lost my way
I rediscover your presence, even in the darkness;
when the bottom drops out of my world
and all that mattered seems to slip through my fingers
your peace and your joy hold me in your grace;
when I have more questions than I have answers
and my heart and my mind are in turmoil
I catch a glimpse of you in the face of Jesus, who comes
and promises to hold my hand, now and for all eternity.

For now, I must be satisfied with a glimpse of you—
one day, by grace, I shall see you face to face. Amen.

392   TEACH ME, LORD

Lord, in a world of rushing feet, teach me to be still.
When I am surrounded by greed and materialistic excess,
teach me to be content.
In the midst of those with angry or demanding voices,
teach me to be gentle and wise.
When those around me have eyes and ears for their own
    desires,
teach me to remember the needs of others.
In the crush of self-centredness and self-sufficiency,
teach me to stand aside and trust in you.

When those with whom I share each day at work or in the
   world
see no further than what can be seen or touched or
   understood,
teach me to focus on you, and to walk in faith—always.
   Amen.

393   THE IMAGES WE DESIRE

Lord, you told us to have no graven images,
but we have surrounded ourselves with pictures
of those who are famous as the gods of success.
We fix our eyes on the symbols of wealth and material
   possessions—
they are our images of worthwhile achievement.
We breathe in the atmosphere of indulgence and indifference
as if these were the mark of goals worth pursuing.
We seek to follow in the steps of those we consider our role
   models
and listen attentively to those we have long sought to
   emulate.

Lord, too often these are the gods that we worship;
and, although we are quick to deny it,
we still allow them the place in our devotion
that was always meant to be yours.

Lord, you are the King of creation and sovereign over all
   things—
there is nothing and no one your equal.
Lord, you are the King of creation and sovereign over all
   things—
you are the one before whom nothing existed
Lord, you are the King of creation and sovereign over all
   things—
and when time is no more you are still God. Amen.

Lord, I feel totally overwhelmed by the problems of the
    world.
I don't really need the news reader to remind me of the
    hunger and starvation, the fighting and the wars.
I'm fully aware that all is not well in this world that once was
    good.
You designed it to be a reflection of your beauty and love.
Everything appears to have been just fine until we came
    along.
Then our coming brought havoc and suffering and pain in
    its wake.
From the day we arrived nothing has changed.
We've erected mountains of selfishness, self-centredness and
    greed.
We created deep valleys of loneliness, hatred and fear.
All around us we see lives wrecked by addictions,
which those trapped by them can't break.
Our young people are presented with role models that lead
    them astray
and the old are ignored, no longer part of our plans for
    today.
We live in a world where promises mean very little
and today homes are broken with seemingly little thought
    for the consequences tomorrow.
No wonder we show so little respect for you, for our
    neighbours, or even for ourselves.
We have even forgotten that the planet isn't ours—
as each day our words, deeds and lifestyle pollute it just a
    little bit more.

Lord, in the face of this catalogue of sorrow, pain and
    suffering
the cry from our hearts is, 'But what can I do?'

What I can do is to draw a circle on the ground, then kneel
    in the centre

and, in my prayer for the world and my neighbour,
ask God to make a start in this circle: Lord, begin with me.
   Amen.

395   MEDITATION—HORIZONS

Lord, I've been meaning to speak to you for some time now.
There is something on my mind, or rather, it's staring me in
      the face.
Everywhere I look, whichever way I turn, there it is—
      another horizon!
Each one is different; each one has a different message;
each one seems to look at me expecting some kind of a
      response.

Sometimes the horizon is clear and sharp,
set against the unrelenting and apparently unending skyline.
I try to look the other way
but my eyes are constantly drawn back to this razor edge
      between earth and sky.
It gives me a feeling of finality.
Its clear-cut image seems to say, 'What you see between us
is all that there is, all there ever was and all there ever will
      be.'

Is life just this circle, Lord,
cut out crisply like a pie cutter in the divine baker's hand?
Is there nothing beyond this circumference of days?
Will they write 'finished' at the end of the journey of three
      score years and ten?
Is my end the horizon
that acts like some unseen and unfelt guillotine
as the curtain descends on my one-act play?

If this is all there is—this limited space I see before me,
little wonder some seek to fill it with anything and
      everything
that will take their minds from that horizon
that threatens them with its impending finale.

Just when I am preparing to accept what appears to be our
    fate;
at the very moment when I have determined to live
like some long-forgotten prisoner,
locked up and with no expectation of parole
and all for the crime of being born in this vale of tears;
just as I, overwhelmed by a deep sense of injustice,
have become resigned to what seemed to be my situation—
everything changed!

Now the horizon is no longer a clear, sharp, threatening
    beast—
it is now unclear and indistinct.
Now it seems that at times the earth and the sky merge into
    one.
The horizon, with its blurred edge,
is like a cosmic hand that reaches out, beckons me on
and calls me to come and see what lies beyond.
It speaks of further horizons, as yet unknown and unseen.
The very vagueness of the horizon challenges me to look
    beyond the here and now.
It tells me not to allow my life and my dreams
to be limited by what I think I know, or by what I assume I
    understand.

I feel the beat of my heart as I consider—new journeys to
    take;
new hopes to hold on to; new dreams to explore; new
    meetings with you, Lord.
I am grateful for the horizon, with its hint of a life to come,
a life I cannot see, let alone comprehend.
It seems to say 'trust me'—me who has held your hand.
I who have walked where you walk. I who am faithful—trust
    me.
All that lies beyond the horizon of time
is held in the arms of the one who is eternal.

So peace descends. The emptiness has gone.

The prison doors have been thrown open,
and I am free to journey where he leads.
Yet as I ponder unlimited horizons of praise and adoration;
as I prepare to enter his kingdom which has no horizon;
as I once more look to him who always sees everything there
is to see
and who sees that which is for ever—and therefore cannot be
seen—
it is then I perceive the horizon that stands between.
Its sharpness doesn't divide or threaten.
Its indistinct edge no longer offers its great promise.
For this is a horizon of human construction
and is therefore no true horizon at all!
This horizon blocks my view and empties my thoughts.
It acts like an anaesthetic, as it dulls the senses and fulfils
futile dreams.

We have no one to blame but ourselves.
We have settled, too easily, for a horizon that we have
created.
There it stands, erected on the foundations of our greed.
Each day we have allowed our love of money
and the false sense of security it brings,
brick by brick to build our own personal horizon.

From the raw materials of our prized possessions—
our lust for pleasure of the moment; our desire for power;
our longing for personal satisfaction; and our assumed self-
sufficiency:
we have created our horizon out of our own dreams,
our family's needs and our own self-centredness.

Now our foolishness comes back to haunt us.
Our human horizon, which we have spent our lifetime
creating,
is now seen as the barrier it always was,
which on the cross Christ's outstretched arms pointed to us.

My own grand schemes are now seen in the light of your
    empty tomb.

Lord, before it's too late; before I settle for my own horizon
that is leading precisely nowhere
and is the barrier to my seeing those that reach everywhere;
whatever it takes, Lord, make me listen.
Whatever is needed, help me to see.
Whatever you want, Lord, I am ready to give it to you.

By your grace, may Christ and his glory be my only horizon,
that he may show me horizons of love, peace and heavenly
    joy yet to be. Amen.

396 WHY PETER? (WHY ME?)

Lord, there are many things in this world that I don't
    understand.
There are many things that are beyond my comprehension.
There are many things about which I wished I knew more.
My head is full of questions for which I have no answers;
things that puzzle me as I search for a solution.

Lord, I would love to know: Why Peter?
What was it about him that was so special, so different?
What was it about Peter that made you reject the others
and choose him to be your disciple?
What did you see in him that marked him out from the
    crowd?
Lord, I would love to know: Why Peter?

Lord, I would love to know: Why Peter?
Why was he the one who first voiced the word of faith and
    named you his Lord?
What was it that he saw in you that touched and
    transformed
this uneducated, illiterate, working-class fisherman?
How was he changed into the spokesperson

for all your disciples—then and now, and for all time to
    come?
Why Peter, Lord?
Why was he the one on whom you committed yourself
to build the new people of God?
It wasn't as if his faith was so very deep
or that he really understood who you were or what it all
    meant.
So why Peter, Lord?

Why Peter, Lord—why did he get it all wrong?
How did he manage to miss the signs of Judas planning his
    betrayal,
and how did he fail to protect his Lord?
How could he not understand why you were washing his
    feet?
How could he fall asleep in the garden
at the moment you had asked him to pray?
Why Peter, Lord?
How could he deny all knowledge of you—he who had
    confessed you as Lord?
I know he wept over his failure, all done in the face of a
    hostile crowd.
But why Peter, Lord?

Why Peter, Lord? Why was he the one to run to the tomb
and discover that you had been raised, and the victory over
    death had been won?
Though if the truth be known,
he didn't understand a great deal of all that it really meant.
Why was it Peter who found the grave empty
and that there was no body there?
How was it that it was Peter who was faced with your three-
    fold challenge
to care for your lambs and your sheep?
And why was it possible for this man
who was known to have feet made of clay

to declare on the day of Pentecost the truth that Jesus is
    Lord?
Why, I ask—why Peter, Lord?

What I really mean, and what I really want to ask,
is not why Peter, but why me, Lord?

Why did you choose me and use me and fill me?
Why did you call me and shape me and send me?
Why did you love me and restore me?
Why did you offer yourself as my Saviour and Lord?

For Peter and for me, the answer is grace.
Your undeserved love has made me your own
and by your Spirit Peter and I have received
all the power we needed to declare to all who will hear
that Jesus is Lord, to the glory of God the Father. Amen.

397   I'M HERE AGAIN, LORD!

I'm here again, Lord.
You must get really fed up listening to me listing the same
    old mistakes,
the usual catalogue of sins.
I know I get fed up coming here into your presence,
telling you everything that's wrong in my life.

I don't know why I do it—not the sin, I mean—that's obvious!
I'm human. I'm not perfect. I want my own way.
I don't love enough, and I certainly don't love my neighbour
    as myself!

But then, that's part of me being human—the Bible says
    'fallen'
and I guess, if I'm honest, that's how it feels.
Every time I come into your presence
I want to lie flat on my face before you
and not even dare to try to catch a glimpse of your grace.
You see, I know I'm not worthy—
compared to you I'm worth just about nothing at all!

When I say I don't know why I do it—
I mean I don't know why I keep returning with my lame
    excuses.

Perhaps, the truth is, Lord, it always feels less like me simply
        coming
and more as if you have called me,
that you actually want to hear me give you the update
on my messy life and my broken relationships.

Why, Lord, why? Surely if you are God,
then you already know all there is to know about me.
and everything I'm going to say.
As the psalmist said, 'Before a word is on my tongue, you
    know it completely.'

So I'm back to my question, why do I do it?
Why do we need to go through this charade again and again?
Why don't you just give me a printout from your heavenly
        records?
What difference does it make
to make me speak these miserable words of personal failure?

Is that it, Lord?
That though you do know absolutely everything there is to
    know about me—
now you are waiting, hoping—that just for once, I will be
    totally honest
with you, and with myself?
It's only then that you are able to break down the barrier
    between us
as you come and kneel with me at the foot of the cross
and help me look into the face of your Son.

Deep down within me I know he is dying to make this
    moment—
this new beginning between us—a living reality, for ever.

Thank you, Lord, that you accept me as I am,
and love me enough to want me to accept myself
and to accept that I am accepted
and to accept you all over again as Lord of my life and Lord
    of all. Amen.

398   I NEVER THOUGHT IT WOULD END

I never thought it would end.
It seemed that good health would last for ever.
I suppose I simply took it for granted that being fit and well
    was normal—
at least, it seemed as if it was for me.
I didn't mean to take my health for granted,
yet it's hard to imagine something changing when it's always
    been the same.
The doctor's diagnosis means that nothing will ever be the
    same again.
I am afraid. I find it hard to cope.
These are uncharted waters for me—but not for you, Lord.
Walk with me. Hold my hand, and show me the way.

I never thought it would end.
It felt as if our relationship would last for ever.
I guess that we took each other for granted.
We put all our time and effort into the children and the
    things they wanted to do.
Deep down, we knew that the love that first brought us together
wouldn't last if it wasn't nourished and fed.
If we failed to make time and space for each other—it would
    die,
and trust would be lost.
But we forgot, and we thought we knew better.
We said 'one day' things will be different.
But 'one day' never came, and our love and our friendship
    have died.
Lord, help me to remember to make time and space for you
in the endless rush of activities that I call life.

Hold me. Touch my days, and help me to want to spend
    time with you now,
or we shall meet as strangers at the doorway to your heaven.

I never thought it would end.
Being parents has been the whole of our lives.
At the time, there were moments we longed for peace—and
    patience.
Their demands seemed endless, and their expectations
    beyond all reason.
They were good days, and we have our memories
and the stories we tell of their laughter and fun.
But it's all in the past—they have grown up and gone.
They have their own lives, their own plans
and other relationships in which we have no part.
It's like a bereavement, and the sense of loss is sometimes too
    hard to bear.
Lord, we need you to hold us and help us
to rediscover that your purpose for our lives isn't ended—it's
    just different.
By your grace we can begin again
and learn to be parents and to be ourselves in a whole new
    way.

I never thought it would end.
I had given the firm the best years of my life.
I gave unstintingly of my time and effort
and was delighted to use my skills in the way that I did.
But one day I was told that I and my skills were not needed
    any more.
It was like walking into a brick wall.
Redundancy or retirement are simply alternative words
for the end of employment that was the whole of my life.
It was hard to realise I was just a number, a unit, a statistic.
I gave of myself and lost so much—the colleagues, the
    income
and the sense of shape to my life.
Lord, is it the downhill road for the rest of my days,

or can I make a new start and learn your ways?
Hold me and help me, Lord, to trust you completely,
even though the way is unclear.

I never thought it would end.
Every day was a joy—new things to learn,
new friendships to make, new experiences to discover.
Every moment was like a catalogue of new things to do and
    to be.
I never really gave death a thought.
It was something that happened to others or at the end of a
    long life.
But the years have flashed by,
and more and more I'm aware of my own vulnerability,
and my mortality stares me in the face.
I'm beginning to ask the questions that matter,
to consider what my life really means,
and to wonder what will happen when my end actually
    comes.
Lord, I need you to hold me and help me,
so that I can begin to trust that you are
the one who has promised that in Christ life never ends;
that death is a doorway we can't cheat or avoid.
But knowing you as my Saviour and Lord
means even death becomes the gateway to a life
in heaven with Jesus my Lord.

I never thought it would end.
Life's temptations and fears, its mistakes to avoid,
more pitfalls to catch me, always seemed to be there.
Every day overflowed with more than its fair share of
    disappointments,
its failures and its times of despair.
No matter how hard I tried, whatever I said or I did—
anxiety and insecurity were my companions
and self-centeredness and self-interest guided my way.
I was ashamed of my thoughts, and my attitudes and values.
I simply got used to my experience of failing to climb

to the heights you seem to expect of me
and not even reaching the lowlands of my dreams.
Lord, I need you to hold me and help me,
to reach out and touch me, and to whisper your word of
    forgiveness—even to me. Amen.

399   IS IT YOU, LORD?

Meditation for a service of healing

Is it you, Lord?
Are you looking at me—searching deep inside where others
    cannot see?
Are you looking and seeing what I don't want to know
and what I try to fool myself is just not true?
Lord, you know everything that there is to know,
even the things I hide from myself.
Is it you, Lord?
Are you looking and helping me to see myself as you see
    me—
human, frail and in need of the healing only you can give?

Is it you, Lord?
Are you touching me, are you putting your finger
just where my life hurts most?
Like the divine physician you are,
you always seem to know where to locate all my aches and
    my pains.
You know precisely the pain in my body, in my heart and in
    my mind.
You know just where my relationships are causing me
    distress.
You know where to touch the sadness inside,
and you handle with care the feelings of failure, rejection
and trust that's been broken
with a gentleness that surprises—but still gives me hope.
Is it you, Lord?
Still touching with the healing only Christ can provide?

Is it you, Lord? Are you holding me?
Whenever I enter your presence
I am overwhelmed by your glory and amazed by your grace.
Me, Lord? Do you seriously intend to hold even me?
Do I matter that much—does your love and care reach that
    deep?
All my life I have longed to be held!
Deep inside, I'm still the child that just wanted to feel safe
in the arms of a parent who gave love with no strings.
Just to know, to really know that you are holding me
would be the most wonderful experience in the whole of my
    life!
Just to know, to really know that Christ's arms still reach out
wide enough to hold even me!
Is it you, Lord?
Still holding, caring, loving, as only a crucified Saviour can?

Is it you, Lord?
Are you so determined to deal with me?
Will nothing put you off or drive you away?
Will nothing I say or do ever stop your loving me,
stop your wanting to change my life and make me new?
But where to start, that is the question!
It seems that in every corner of my life there is some work
    for you to do,
some changes to make, a new beginning to offer.
Lord, why can't I try just a little bit harder?
Why can't you simply look the other way?
Is it you, Lord?
Are you dealing with me because you know
I can't change myself—only Christ can do that!

Is it you, Lord? Are you speaking to me?
I have never seen myself in need of healing or wholeness.
I have done my best—what more can I do?
If I'm honest, I need both healing and wholeness.
I have things my body would like to be rid of.
I have aches and pains that long for your healing touch.

I have things in my heart, my mind and my life
that prevent me experiencing the wholeness you promise.
But I'm afraid, Lord.
What if I seek healing and you give me wholeness?
What if I ask for wholeness and it's healing you give?
I'm afraid to commit myself, in case nothing happens.
The real truth is, I'm scared of what it would mean if it does!
Is it you, Lord? Are you speaking to me?
Of course it is! Your insistent voice is never far away.
I may close my ears, but in Jesus you will speak to me for
      ever.

You ask if it is me that is looking, touching, holding, dealing
      and speaking.
You know it is.
So trust me, just this once.
Trust me, with just the next step in your life.
Trust me now, and then trust me for ever.
Yes, it is I, your Lord, who heals and brings wholeness
to all who will simply trust me.

400   THE GOD OF CHANGES

Meditation with gentle music from flute, guitar or organ.

Lord, you are changing everything.
I thought I knew who you were!
I thought you were the one that I could treat like an elderly
      relative
whom I visited faithfully once a week, or when I had time,
when I was in the mood, or when I felt the need.
But you have broken into my life and made your presence
      felt
everywhere, everyday and in every way.
You have shown yourself to be the one, true, living God
and you will not let me rest until I know you more.

You are changing what I know about you.
I thought I knew what you expected!

I thought if I read your Word, if I gave to charity
and tried to live a good honest life,
that would give you what was expected of me.
I thought if I gave you part of my life you would not ask for
more.
But you have broken down my defences
and now I realise that you never ask for a share of my life—
my gifts, my skills, my money, my time or my home—
you insist on having it all!

You are changing my expectations of you.
I thought I knew what you could do!
I thought that you were simply Creator,
that long, long ago you set in motion all your creative power.
I thought that I could thank you for the wonder of your
world
and the beauty of all that you have made, and leave it at that.
I never thought about turning to you to guide me,
to lead me through the many changing phases of my life.
But you have opened my eyes to see you as Lord—
Lord of my body, my mind and the whole of my life.

You are changing what I know you can do in my life and my
world.
I thought I knew what I needed!
I thought that I knew myself very well.
I knew where I was weak and where I was strong.
I thought, too, I knew what I needed to make my life whole
and by filling it with more and more of this world's good
things
it would make my life complete.
I thought, too, I could lift myself out of the mess I got
myself into.
But you have destroyed the illusion!
You have pointed to your Son on the cross
and shown me that only in him can my life be made whole
and only through him can I enter the completeness of your
heaven.

I thought I knew where you were.
I thought that I could trust you in the religious parts of my
    life
and leave you in church when I left.
I thought you did not mind what I said or what I did or
    what I planned.
I thought it was my life to do with as I wanted.
But you have gate-crashed my thoughts, my plans and my
    dreams!
You have entered into every corner of my life
and into every second of every day.
You have shown me that you are the Lord
and I must trust you to touch me and to change me
and to go on changing me into the person you meant me to
    be
when you gave me life.

I am beginning to know, Lord,
I am beginning to know who you are and what you are
    doing.
You change everything—you are changing even me!
I once thought I knew so much,
but now I realise just how little I really understood.
I once thought I knew what life meant, and what I was
    meant to do with it—
but now I recognise my arrogance.
I once thought that everything depended on me—
but now I know and confess that Jesus is Lord
and he is the one who changes everything, even me. Amen.

401   CHRISTMAS—THE WORLD OF SNOW

Lord, we saw the snow, your snow.
It fell to the earth. It was soft and gentle; it was white, pure
    and white.
It covered the whole landscape—trees, bushes, fields,
    hedgerows,
fences, roads, pavements and houses.

Everywhere was covered with a layer of white.
It was pure and white, brilliantly white.
We were blinded, dazzled by its whiteness—it hurt our eyes.
Everywhere was pure and white and clean.

And then; and then we came.
We came with our cars and our buses, our lorries, our
  bicycles and our feet.
We churned up the pure white snow into a filthy black mess.

Your world, Lord, was once pure and clean—just like the
  snow.
Everything that you had made was 'very good'.

And then; and then we came.
We came and we spoilt your world, as we have spoilt our lives.
Your pure white world we have polluted with our greed,
  pride and selfishness.

And then; and then you came.
Immanuel, born in a manger in Bethlehem.
You came to make it possible for the world—for our hearts
  and lives—
to be pure and white and clean again.

Lord, thank you for Christmas,
and that you have declared the love that never ends,
which can fill our lives and make all things new. Amen.

402   IF I HAD TIME

Meditation for two voices.

Lord, if I had time, I would want to share more of it with
  you,
to listen for your voice, be guided by your presence,
to know you are there, to enjoy being in your company,
to rejoice in being your child, to acknowledge you as my
  Father.
If I only had time.

Lord, if I had time, I would use it to bathe myself in your
      love,
to allow you to touch me and change me,
to heal me and enfold me, to correct me and to challenge
      me,
to bless me and to make me a blessing for others.
If I only had time.

Lord, if I had time, I would use it to listen to those who are
      hurting,
to hold the broken, to heal the sick,
to share the tears of those whose pain is deep inside,
to speak of your love to those who are empty,
to those who are crushed, to those whose hopes have been
      dashed
and to those who feel all hope is gone.
If I only had time.

Lord, if I had time, I would use it to care for the poor,
to fight injustice, to speak for those with no voice,
to stand with those in danger of falling,
to reach out to those with no home,
to walk with those who have lost their way,
to listen to those who feel they have no name,
to care for those who couldn't care less
and to speak of him who couldn't care more.
If I only had time.

Lord, if I had time, I would use it to care for your world,
to enjoy its rich beauty, to walk its highways and byways,
to try to live simply, so that others might simply live,
to act responsibly as I journey through your world,
to do what I could to protect your creation,
to challenge those whose activity today
leaves destruction and damage in its wake for tomorrow,
to remember we are stewards not owners of all that we see.
If I only had time.

Lord, if I had time,
I would use it to love my neighbour as myself, to love my
    enemies,
to seek to heal relationships that have been scarred and
    broken,
to love the unlovable, to touch the untouchable,
to forgive the unforgivable, to be all that by your grace I
    know I should be.
If I only had time.

Lord, if I had time, I would use it to read more of your
    Word,
to seek you more deeply in prayer,
to allow the Holy Spirit's presence in my life to bear fruit for
    your glory,
to release the gifts he has given for the renewal of your
    church,
to speak more openly of my faith in Christ,
to trust him completely, to allow him to take me and mould
    me,
to use me and fill me,
to make me a channel to others of all the good things he is
    longing to give.
If I only had time. If I only had time.

The Lord says to me—but I have given you time, enough
    and to spare,
time to do everything I have chosen for you.
I intended you to have the time that you have received,
but you have used it the way that you wanted,
and for priorities of your own choosing.
My child, you will never have time to do all that you
    wanted,
but you do have the time for all that I planned.

Lord, I will listen and I will obey.
I will trust you, and allow you to love me, to hold me, to be
    Lord of my time.

Lord, I have time—your time is now, it is all that I have.
By your grace I will offer each second, each minute, every
    day of my life
back to you, and for your glory. Amen.

403   LIKE A STONE

Lord, I am like a stone, a pebble on the beach.
I have been battered by the waves of stress, frustration and
    responsibility;
caressed by the gentleness of the hand upon my shoulder,
the quiet word of reassurance in my ear,
the deep, deep trust of a friend.

Lord, I am like a stone, like a pebble on the beach of life.
Sometimes I feel so alone, so far from the safety of the shore
of love and understanding and genuine concern.
Yet, strangely, I am always aware of your presence.
Even in the darkest times
I know you are holding even me in the palm of your hand.

Lord, I am like a stone, a pebble on the beach—
just one among so many.
How could anyone—how could you—ever remember me?
All that I have faced has forced me to wear
this smooth, rounded and apparently untroubled surface
that protects me and gives me a false sense of security—
and keeps me alone with just me.
But you know me, Lord;
you know this pebble is fragile, weak and hurting.
This pebble can be broken by an uncaring word,
a thoughtless action, or by unmet needs of touch, holding,
    loving.

Lord, I am like a stone, a pebble on the beach.
But this is your beach, and I am your stone—
though there are times when even you must wonder
at the price Christ paid for me!

Perhaps you were looking for a pearl—
and all you now hold is the stone of my life.
But hold me, Lord, go on holding me.
Treasure me beyond the value given to me by the world.
Only in your hand can I be healed, made whole;
only in your hand can this stone become like soft, supple
    clay,
to be shaped and moulded by nail-printed hands.

Lord, I am like a stone;
make me a pebble on your beach of eternal life.
Then hold me, and go on holding and using me,
for the glory of your name. Amen.

404   THE GOD OF SURPRISES!

Lord, you are the God of surprises!
We know that you inhabit eternity—
but have promised to hold us in the palm of your hand.
We know that you are infinite in wisdom, truth and love—
but you have made yourself known
in the life, death and resurrection of Christ.
We know that you are Lord of all things—
but you are still seeking to be Lord of our lives.
We know that you are love—
but in Christ you have loved us to the uttermost!

Lord, you are the God of surprises!
You come to us when we least expect it,
and you come in ways that leave us totally amazed.
When we are hurting, you come gently to hold us.
When we are alone, you come close to give us peace.
When we are at the point of breaking,
you reach out and touch us and make us whole.
When we go wrong and hurt you, those around us and
    ourselves—
you speak the word of grace that says it's time to begin again.

Lord, you are the God of surprises!

As your Spirit overwhelmed those on whom he fell on that
    day of Pentecost,
come and shake us to the very core of our being!
Come and remould our lives! Come and fill us and renew us!
Lord of surprises—come touch us, hold us, change us and
    empower us,
that we may worship you in spirit and in truth, as you have
    always deserved.
Come, Lord Jesus, come! Amen.

405   LORD, YOU ARE THE ONE

A prayer with soft music.

Lord, you are the God who is worthy.
You are the one to whom we give thanks and praise.
You are the one that we celebrate;
You are the centre of every song and every prayer.

Lord, you are the God who is worthy.
You are the one who is high and holy;
You are the one who is great and powerful;
You are the one who is faithful, the one we can trust.

Lord, you are the God who is worthy.
You are the one who through Christ created all things;
You are the one who through Jesus opens the door to
    beginning again;
You are the one, the only one who died to set us free.

Lord, you are the God who is worthy.
You are the one who has all authority in heaven and on
    earth;
You are the one who is nearer than breathing, closer than
    love;
You are the one who never leaves us and never gives up on
    us.

Lord, you are the God who is worthy.
You are the one, the only one we will worship;

You are the one we will praise for all eternity;
You are the one who holds time and space in the palm of
your hand.

Lord, you are the God who is worthy.
You are the one who gives the Holy Spirit;
You are the one who gives gifts to your church;
You are the one who heals the sick and opens the eyes of the
blind.

Lord, you are the God who is worthy.
You are the one who forgives our sin;
You are the one who makes us whole;
You are the one who is King, Sovereign, Saviour and Lord.

You are the one, the only one who is worthy.
You are the one who is there.
You are the one, and we give you our thanks and praise.

Lord, you are the God who is worthy. Lord, you are the one.
Amen.

406   CHRIST IS NOT JUST FOR CHRISTMAS

In our times of darkness, Christ comes with his light;
In our moments of loneliness, Christ comes to walk with us;
In our experiences of loss, Christ comes to share our pain;
In our times of emptiness, Christ comes to fill us;
In our experiences of brokenness, Christ comes to hold us;
In our times of despair and delight, of joy and sorrow, of
faith and of doubt,
Christ still comes—for me and for you.
No matter who we are or what we have done—Christ comes.

407   LORD, YOU GAVE ME TODAY

Lord, you gave me today. I am glad to receive it.
You gave it to me as a free gift
and not as a reward for how I made use of yesterday.

Lord, you gave me today.
It came from your hand, fresh and new, clean and unspoilt.
Lord, you gave me today. It was just the right shape and size
for all you planned for me to do in and with it.

Lord, you gave me today.
Twenty-four hours to fill with love, joy, peace, hope and
    service.
Lord, you gave me today, only today.
But I forgot and filled it with so many things
that there was no time or space for you.

Lord, you gave me today.
But too often it is spoilt with thoughts and memories of
    yesterday.
Sometimes my mind is filled with the anger, the bitterness,
    the weakness,
the broken promises and mistakes,
of the day you gave me that will never return.

Lord, you gave me today.
But I can't rest, peace is a long forgotten dream
and I am afraid about the tomorrow you have yet to grant me.
Tomorrow may never be mine,
but I still worry about what it will bring and how well I will
    cope.

Lord, you gave me today.
Help me to receive it as the gracious gift that it is.

Lord, you gave me today.
Forgive my misuse of yesterday,
and by your Holy Spirit enable me to live your precious gift
    of today
to the full and for you and your glory.

Lord, you gave me today. I give it back to you now.
It is all I have to give, and it is my sacrifice of praise and
    thanksgiving. Amen.

In all the hurt and the hassle,
in all the confusion, frustration and the pain of life,
it is not always easy to know just what to say
or to find the right words to express how we feel.
Sometimes it seems just the right moment
to use words of hope and joy and thanks,
but at others times we are not so sure.
What I hear you saying, Lord, is that it is always the right
    time to say Immanuel! God is with us.

When firefighters, police officers and members of the rescue
    services
risk their lives to save others;
when the medical team gives their all to help and to heal;
when earthquake, wind and fire have devastated people's lives
and the world reaches out in sacrificial concern—
it's time to say Immanuel!

When the disabled, those who are differently-abled,
struggle to overcome their immense disabilities
and smile at us in hope and joy—
it's time to say Immanuel!

When all we see and hear is bad news;
when everything speaks of humanity's inhumanity to each
    other;
when the terrorist and the murderer appear to have
    everything their own way,
and their victims offer nothing but forgiveness and
    understanding—
it's time to say Immanuel!

When human foolishness, greed and the exploitation of
    God's good earth
are reaping their reward in the damage being done to our
    environment,

and someone says 'Enough!'—
it's time to say Immanuel!

When those who have been beaten and crushed by the evil
    work of others;
when those who know they have been abused, misused and
    misunderstood
find someone they can trust to touch, hold, care and bring
    healing and wholeness—
it's time to say, Immanuel!

When relationships are strained, spoilt, broken and brought
    to an end;
when someone is rejected, made to feel they don't count and
    have no value;
and then someone says they are sorry and reconciliation
    begins;
when healing and hope conquer bitterness and hate—
It's time to say Immanuel!

When all is dark and we have lost our way;
when we are not sure how to find our way home, or if it is
    possible;
when it seems there is no one who cares
and no one who wants to understand;
when we feel alone, isolated, and someone listens—
it's time to say Immanuel!

When we know in our heart of hearts that we have left no
    time or space for God;
when we know that again and again he has knocked at the
    door of our lives
and we have left him standing on the threshold of our
    existence;
when we have long since closed the door in the face of his
    extravagant love,
yet find he is still there, still knocking, still waiting, still
    longing to give us new life—
it's time to say Immanuel!

When we feel self-satisfied, and think we can cope in our
    own strength;
when we feel no need of God's grace, see no purpose in
    walking in faith;
when we know we have made a mess of our lives,
and we are ashamed by what we have said and done;
when we open our eyes to his mercy and our ears to his
    words of love;
when we discover that we, even we, are accepted—
it's time to say Immanuel!

When life is full of joy, laughter and peace, and someone
    shares it all with you;
when all that you planned, dreamt of and longed for
goes terribly wrong and the bottom drops out of your world,
and someone says, 'I will listen, because I care—trust me'—
it's time to say Immanuel!

When you have been so deeply hurt and the pain inside
    won't leave;
when you find it hard, if not almost impossible, to forgive
    and let go;
when you look at the cross
and remember that the way of being made new and clean
    has been opened—
it's time to say Immanuel!

When life is full of questions for which you can find no
    answers;
when there are important choices to be made, difficult
    situations to cope with;
when you feel unwanted, unnecessary and unloved;
when you lose your job, your hope and your faith
and others turn their backs on you;
then someone puts an arm around your shoulder and shows
    that they care—
it's time to say Immanuel!

When the years have rolled on, and strength and health
    begin to decline;
when family and friends are no longer there
to share the journey and to make it worthwhile;
when life nears its end, and death stares you in the face, and
    you are afraid;
and you hear of an empty cross and an empty tomb
and the message of hope and the victory won—
it's time to say Immanuel!

When we sing and when we praise; when we serve and when
    we give;
whoever we are, whatever we are facing, whatever the
    situation, whatever the need—
because two thousand years ago a baby was born,
who was the man who died on the cross,
who was the one that was raised, and is the one with us
    now—
though we may not always recognise it,
though it may be in ways and through those we least expect,
the truth remains—best of all—
it's always time to say: Immanuel, God is with us!

409   SOMETIMES

Lord, sometimes I want to run away, to hide in my small
    corner,
to pretend the world and its troubles have all gone away!
Sometimes I simply want to escape, to be myself,
to shut my eyes, to close my ears to the clamour for my help
and to the challenges to my faith.

The Lord says,
Remember me in the demands upon your time,
seek my presence in the stillness.
Wait, and I will come to hold you,
to share the caring, the loving and the helping you are called
    to give.

Lord, sometimes I lose my way, and I forget where my life is
    going.
I set out with such clear convictions, with a genuine sense of
    purpose,
with a feeling of assurance in you, and my relationship with
    you.
But life has dealt me some hard knocks,
and left me feeling adrift from life, from you and from
    myself.

The Lord says,
Remember, I am the beginning and the end, the Alpha and
    the Omega,
the way, the truth and the life.
Wait, and I will lead you in paths of hope and peace
you have yet to know and walk in.

Lord, sometimes I am overwhelmed by the pain and
    suffering in your world,
I have an ache deep within when I hear or read
of how my fellow human beings treat each other.
Sometimes I am filled with despair
when I consider the damage we are doing to your creation
    and your creatures.

The Lord says,
My name is the Prince of Peace, the Light of the world, the
    Saviour of all.
Wait, and you will see that I hold all things in the palm of
    my hand.

Lord, sometimes I am aware of your presence
in a way too deep to put into words.
I feel I could reach out and touch you.
I long to know your arms around me,
to be known as your precious child and your valued
    possession.
Sometimes I am conscious of a void between us
and I am unable to reach you—and I am bereft.

The Lord says,
See my hands and my feet—they carry the marks of my
saving grace.
Wait, receive again my love—
that will never let you off, never let you down, and never let
you go.

Lord, sometimes I consider my life, and I think about my
walk with you.
I am only too painfully aware of the hurt I have caused to
those I love most,
and the way, time and time again, I have failed you.
Sometimes I wonder just how long your patience with me
will last
and I am afraid to turn to you, in case my appeal for
forgiveness is turned down
and I am sent away empty-handed.

The Lord says,
But you are my precious child.
I have promised forgiveness to all who come to me with
honesty and openness.
Wait, I am coming to lift you up, and to heal you.
Look not only at the emptiness of your life
but also at the fullness of my grace.

Sometimes when I compare myself with others I feel
inadequate—
I seem able to do so little.
You call me to be a witness for Christ
to show his light and his love to the whole world;
I feel challenged by the call to love my neighbours
when I am unable even to like them.
Sometimes I feel like giving up and giving in—
the task you have laid upon me is too great for me to cope
with.
It's all too much, beyond my meagre resources.

The Lord says,
I never said it would be easy,
but I never said you should do it all on your own or in your
    own strength.
Wait, and you will see that I have an all-sufficiency of grace
    to meet your need
and I will make you a channel of my grace for all.

Sometimes, just sometimes, I feel I can trust you completely.
Sometimes, just sometimes, I feel I could walk with you
to the end of time and beyond.
Sometimes, just sometimes, I simply know that you are there
and I can do all things in the strength of your love
and in the power of the Holy Spirit.
But Lord, it is just sometimes, not all the time.

The Lord says,
I will never leave you or forsake you.
I am with you always—even when you find it hardest
to know, to feel, to trust, that I am there.
Wait, I am coming to you, and for you.
Wait, it will not be long—trust me, just for today, just for
    now.
Then tomorrow, I will give you the power to trust me all
    over again.

Sometimes I love you with all my heart, with all my soul,
with all my mind and with all my strength! Lord, make it all
    the time.

The Lord says, Trust me, and I will. Amen.

410   LORD, I AM WAITING

Lord, I spend my life waiting.
I wait to be served at the checkout; to be seen by the doctor;
to be met by a friend.

I wait in the traffic queue; nothing is moving and there is
    nothing I can do.

Like the other drivers I just sit and stare.
I wonder sometimes why I set out on this snail-like journey.
Just waiting …

I was safe in my mother's womb—but all the time I was
    waiting
to begin; to be born; to enter the world; to start the journey
    of my life.
Waiting to learn and to grow; to give and to love.

But my waiting was not in vain. It wasn't an empty void.
Even as my parents awaited my arrival, I was growing and
    developing;
I was receiving nourishment and love;
I was preparing to step out onto the road of life
and the pathway of discovering what it would mean to be
    me.

Lord, I am waiting—waiting at the school gate; waiting to
    learn to be friends;
to share and live with others, to learn about your world,
to fill my mind with ideas and information
that's just waiting to be written on the blank pages of my
    mind.

When I entered your world, my understanding was like a
    blank disk
waiting to receive knowledge of things, of people and of
    places;
waiting to log into my memory faces I need to know,
things I want to remember, experiences I must not forget.
I am waiting.

I need to learn to wait, and not to waste
those precious moments that come each day, those
    unplanned spaces,
and to use them to wait for you.

Lord, I am waiting; waiting in the queue; waiting for my
    turn;
waiting for healing; waiting for health and wholeness.

I am waiting to continue my journey; waiting to make
    progress;
waiting to arrive; waiting, waiting for something to happen.
Waiting for friends to arrive; for the meal to be ready;
for someone to call; for the phone to ring.

I am waiting to know if the news will be bad or good.

But I am not simply waiting, just filling in time.
I am living; I am sharing the journey with others;
I am discovering a different pace of life;
I am still learning what it means to be me.

Lord, I am waiting, always waiting; waiting to know you;
to know you are there; to know you more.

I am waiting for you to break into my life;
to change who and what I am; to transform my words and
    deeds;
to renew my relationship with you, and with others I meet
    each day.
I am waiting; I am discovering a new value in simply
    learning to be;
to allow my whole being to be free;
to allow you time and space to speak—and for me, for once,
    just to listen.

Lord, I am waiting.
As life drifts by, and each day rolls past,
it feels as if I am trying to catch my life in a sieve
and it is all slipping through the fingers of my hopes and the
    grasp of my dreams.

Lord, am I simply here just to wait; to while away time; to
    pass time?
Am I here just to wait to die?

Am I waiting to say—finished; to know it's all over?
Am I simply waiting for no purpose, no reason at all?

But what is the point? Why make a journey with no
    direction, no hope?

Why wait to die? Sometimes I simply wonder why I set out
on a pathway that some tell me leads nowhere but simply
    ends.

But, Lord, you point me to Christ,
who came to tell me that the journey is worthwhile,
that he is the way, the truth and the life.
He makes the waiting important
and is himself the Alpha and the Omega, the beginning and
    the end.

My child, I too am waiting; waiting for you and all my
    creation,
waiting for you to trust me; waiting for you to respond to
    my love.
I am waiting for you to know me as I always meant you to;
waiting to enter your life, to make you whole,
to make you alive, to make you my precious possession.

But you must learn to use all your moments of waiting
to know that I am waiting too;
waiting for you to fall in love with me,
and to know the depth of my love for you.

My child, I am waiting, and I will wait—now, and to the
    threshold of eternity;
I will wait to break into your heart,
and then you will know just how much you have broken
    mine.

My child, waiting is good—but arriving is better!
Come, wait with me.
I will wait with you, and for you, now and until all waiting is
    over. Amen.

Lord, you are calling me to listen, to be still, to be quiet;
to make time to pause, just to be,
to sit in your presence and become more aware that you are
    really there.
You call me to listen—even when I'm too busy,
when I don't want to, when there are too many other voices,
saying different things, making different claims upon me and
    my time.
You call me to listen, to listen to you.

The Lord says, I have the words of eternal life, so listen to
    me.

Lord, you call me to giving.
You are calling me to begin to discover something more
of what it really can mean for me to give.
You call me to give my time. You require me to give myself.
You ask me to give myself to my neighbour.
You long for me to give to my enemy.
Lord, I thought giving meant some money in a charity
    envelope;
loose change I wouldn't miss; some coins I did not want,
that I gave to the young man who was sleeping rough.
It made me feel good—but you did not recognise my gift.
I thought my weekly gift, purposefully put on the plate and
    carefully gift-aided,
would pass your test—but I was mistaken.
Lord, you hold up your hands and you show me your feet—
I did not want to look because I did not want to know.
But you insisted, and I discovered the true meaning of
    giving.

The Lord says, I know what you give and I know what you
    keep—
giving means everything, or it means nothing at all.

Lord, you are calling me to serve, to go in your name

to lift the broken, to heal the sick, to weep with the
    sorrowful
and to walk with the lost and the fearful.
But Lord, you are asking too much.
You know I am too busy—already I have too much to do.
I have held every office in the church, and I am always first
    to volunteer—
if I have time, if it is something I want to do, if I'm not too
    busy.
So why are you calling me to serve at times and in ways
in which I feel so ill-equipped to respond?
Why are you asking of me what you know I am so reluctant
    to give?
Why should I serve in ways that only you will see
and where only you will say 'thank you'?

The Lord says,
My child, my call is to trust me—and to obey me.
I am making myself strangely dependent upon you
for the care and compassion I must show to my world.

Lord, you are calling me to speak, to share my faith in you.
You know that speaking does not come easily to me.
I would much rather live out my life as a silent witness.
Why can't my life of faith speak for itself?
I know you will tell me that you gave me speech
that others might hear of the love of God.
But it is so hard, Lord, and it is dangerous.
I feel others will laugh at me.
I will face their pity, their ridicule or questions I can't answer.
I will also have to live up to what I have said I believed
about your love being for all.
Lord, can't I be the exception to your rule—
can't I be your one silent witness?
Yet I know deep down that
to be silent about Jesus is a contradiction in terms.
How can I be silent about the love of Christ
and still claim that he died for me?

The Lord says,
Speak up and speak out; speak gently, lovingly;
speak of my love, my presence is with you—my Holy Spirit
will enable you.

Lord, you are calling me to love.
I like that, Lord, for everyone needs to know they are loved,
and you are the God of love.
It's just that I find it so hard to like everybody—
and to love them is asking the impossible.
How can you expect me to have warm and tender feelings
for people I don't like, for those who say and do such terrible
things?
Surely you don't really expect me to show your love to
strangers,
to the lost and the broken?
It's too demanding to love those facing injustice
and those who are the cause of it.
How can I love those who are not my kind of people?
But you tell me that love is the heart of the matter
and that, if I want to be loved, I must become a channel of
your grace.

The Lord says,
I loved the world so much that I gave and go on giving to all
without exception—including you, my child.

Lord, you are calling me to trust.
You want me not only to believe in you but to believe you,
to take you at your word!
I do not find this easy.
I can recite the words of the creeds with conviction.
I can sing hymns with great feeling.
I can even try to pray unceasingly and serve you
any time, any place and with any person.
I can seek to give until it hurts, and to go on giving.
I can even try to love those I don't like and those who are
different.

But to trust you, to expect you to be present,
and to act, to rely on you utterly and completely—
I am finding this so very, very hard.
You see, Lord, I prefer to be in control,
to be the one who makes the decisions.
But you are asking me to hand the control of my life into
    your hands.
Lord, I will trust you; help me where my trust falls short.

The Lord says,
Trust me in small things and in small ways.
Trust me for today.
Trust me with part of your life now.
Then I will help you to give me the rest of your life when I
    need it.

412   GUIDED SILENCE FOR WATCH NIGHT

Think of the year that is past—
the things you have done, and the things you have failed to
    do.

Think of the year that is past—
the things that have been important to you
and for which you want to give thanks and praise.

Think of the year that is past—
the things you want to leave behind,
the things that have hurt you too deeply for words.

Think of the year that is past—
those moments when you knew he was with you
giving you courage, peace and a love whose depth cannot be
    measured.

Think of the year that is coming—
the uncertainty of what it holds, and what it will mean for
    you and your life.

Think of the year that is coming—
the hopes you have and the good things you are longing for
    God to do in your life.

Think of the year that is coming—
the opportunities for witness and service
and the promise of the Holy Spirit to equip us for giving,
    caring and loving.

Think of the year that is coming—
this is the moment to thank him for it,
and to place it firmly in the hands of the one who is
    almighty. Amen.

413   THE GOD WHO CALLS—VOCATIONS

Lord, I had no idea that you might mean me.
I have heard how you called others, but I never expected you
    would call me.
I have read how you called people like Abraham, Moses,
    Jeremiah and the prophets,
but I did not think you would speak my name.
But you have spoken, and I am trying to listen and respond.

Lord, I had assumed that when you called,
it would be in a clear, unmistakable voice.
I hoped that if a call to serve ever came,
there would be no doubt or uncertainty.
Those who spoke of your call always seemed so definite.
But your voice to me seems only a faint whisper;
an echo that I strain to understand.

Lord, I knew that you called the most unlikely of men and
    women
to serve you in the most unlikely of ways.
But my gifts are so few. I feel so unworthy and extremely
    uncertain.
Can you really mean me?
Surely, this time, Lord, you are making a big mistake!

But your challenge rejects all my excuses,
and your promise to equip me gives me hope.

Lord, I don't really want to be called.
But, then, you already knew that, when you touched my
    heart and my mind.
You knew I would have my reasons just to say no,
and they would be fully primed for use!
I am quite comfortable as I am, and where I am.
I don't want to change, or be changed.
But neither can I ignore you,
nor can I ever be at peace until I let you disturb me,
and I say, however weakly, 'Yes, Lord, yes.'

So, Lord, I say yes!
Yes, not really knowing what my yes means.
Yes, wishing I could say no.
Yes, knowing I must trust you in a way I have never trusted
    you before.
Yes, not knowing the cost, or what will be demanded of me,
or even where it will lead.
Yes, knowing I am saying yes to the one who, in Christ,
always says yes to me.
Yes, Lord, here I am—you can call even me. Amen.

Prayers before a Service

The links to the calendar in this section's headings are optional.

414   1ST SUNDAY IN ADVENT

Lord, we come to worship you with hope and joy.
We ask that by your Holy Spirit you will use our worship
to prepare us for the coming of Jesus.
May the words of Scripture we hear read
and the word of hope that is proclaimed
fill our lives with joy and give you all the glory.
Through Jesus Christ our Lord. Amen.

415   2ND SUNDAY IN ADVENT

Lord, we come with our broken lives and our faltering
    faith;
we come from our world of darkness
and with empty hands and empty lives.
We come with nothing that will earn your love
and with everything that should receive your condemnation.
We pray for ourselves and the whole congregation
that your grace will make us whole.
We pray for [*leader/speaker*] who has been sent by you:
May s/he proclaim only your Word and do so with grace and
    truth.
In Jesus' name. Amen.

416   3RD SUNDAY IN ADVENT

Sovereign Lord, you are the God of grace, and you are King
    over all creation.
We wait in silence as we seek your presence.

Silence

We pray for ourselves and your people everywhere.
May our words and our thoughts, our hymns and our
    prayers bring you glory.
May we so worship you here that our songs of praise
will bring joy to the world and hope of freedom to many.
Through Christ our Lord. Amen.

417   4TH SUNDAY IN ADVENT

Lord, you are the high and the holy one
but you dwell in the hearts of those who love you.
Lord, you are sovereign over all things
yet you wait for Mary and her yes of faith.
We pray that the worship we offer and the words we use
will open our hearts and minds to your will.
We pray for [*leader/speaker*],

that her/his words may be filled with your love and offered
with your power.
We ask this in Christ's name. Amen.

418 CHRISTMAS EVE

Lord, we have come, we have come to wait with expectation.
This is your time, and Christ's coming is your plan.
We have come to wait in hope,
for you are coming to touch and change our lives.
We pray: Come, meet us at your table,
come to us as we receive the bread and wine,
the symbols of your coming to be our Saviour.
We pray for [*leader/speaker*] and the whole congregation,
that our worship together may prepare us to announce your
coming to all the world.
Come, Lord Jesus, come! Amen.

419 FIRST SUNDAY OF CHRISTMAS

Lord, as the wise of every age have done, we come to
worship you.
As those seeking truth come to you,
so we have come to open our minds, that we may learn of
you.
As those who long for life come to you,
so we have come to open our lives to your presence.
As those who long for meaning, peace and love come to you,
so we open our hearts to receive your grace and to give you
glory.
We pray for ourselves, for the whole congregation
and the one who is to lead our praises
that together we may come to you, the one who first came to
us. Amen.

420 SECOND SUNDAY OF CHRISTMAS

Lord, so mighty, you inhabit eternity.
Lord, so humble, you live in our hearts.

Lord, so holy, you are far beyond us.
Lord, so loving, you come to us in Christ.
Lord, so worthy of our praises.
Lord, so ready to forgive our failings.
Lord, you are worthy of the praises of heaven and earth.
Prepare each of us to sing your praises, and to live for your
glory.
In the name of Christ our Lord. Amen.

421   COVENANT SUNDAY

Lord, on this Covenant Sunday we give thanks for your
commitment
to your people of every age and place.
We praise you that you long for our commitment to you in
return.
For all our worship, witness and service
we confirm our dependence on the grace of the Lord Jesus
Christ,
the love of God and the fellowship and power of the Holy
Spirit. Amen.

422   SUNDAY BETWEEN 7TH AND 13TH JANUARY

Lord, our finest words can't reach the height of your throne.
By your Holy Spirit, take our feeble words and actions
and by your grace transform them into that which will
honour your name.
Lord, by your Holy Spirit, equip and enable the
congregation to worship you,
and [leader/speaker] to lead us all to the throne of grace.
Amen.

423   SUNDAY BETWEEN 14TH AND 20TH JANUARY

Lord, we have gathered to praise you so often before.
We have come to sing and to pray, to listen to your Word
read and proclaimed.

And yet we have not worshipped you, but we have tried to
    please ourselves.
Holy Spirit, come, move among us and within us,
that when we leave we may know we have been in the
    presence of the living God.
Lord, empower your servant to preach the good news with
    power,
and may your people respond with heartfelt praises. Amen.

424   SUNDAY BETWEEN 21ST AND 27TH JANUARY

Lord, your people are gathering for worship.
We come with all our differences:
our differences of colour, ability, gender and age,
our different needs of healing and hope,
our different longings for forgiveness and peace,
our different desires to express our thankfulness and praise.
Lord, we ask that the words we use, the songs we sing and
    the prayers we offer
may unite us all in Christ.
We pray for [*leader/speaker*], that the power of your Holy
    Spirit
may empower her/him to lead us closer to you. In Jesus'
    name. Amen.

425   SUNDAY BETWEEN 28TH JANUARY AND 3RD
       FEBRUARY

Lord, we come in our foolishness to receive your wisdom;
we come with our emptiness in order to be filled;
we come in our weakness that you may make us strong;
we come knowing everything of little value
to receive a little more of what matters for all eternity;
we come to kneel at the foot of the cross, that we might
    name him Lord.
We hold [*leader/speaker*] in our prayers
and ask that s/he will be held in your grace. In Jesus' name.
    Amen.

426 SUNDAY BETWEEN 4TH AND 10TH FEBRUARY

Lord, we are here, preparing ourselves
to worship you as King of Kings and Lord of Lords.
We know that no words we use will be worthy of you;
no song we sing will truly declare your praise;
no prayer we offer will ever reach the height of your throne
unless it is touched, moved and empowered by your Holy
      Spirit.
Lord, in the silence, open our hearts, our minds and our lives
to your loving presence.

Silence

Now Lord, go with us; receive our thanksgiving
and fill our praises with your glory. Through Christ the Lord.
      Amen.

427 SUNDAY BETWEEN 11TH AND 17TH FEBRUARY

Lord, we have come to hear your Word, to sing your praises,
to be nurtured in our faith and to learn more of you.
But though we call you Lord, your greatness is beyond our
      understanding;
your truth exceeds the reach of our minds;
your love far outstrips anything we have known as love
      before.
We pray for [*leader/speaker*],
that you will empower her/him to bring your greatness near,
to declare the truth of your Son and the depth of your love.
We pray for your people,
that together we may receive all that you are longing to give.
In Jesus' name. Amen.

428 SUNDAY BETWEEN 18TH AND 24TH FEBRUARY

Lord, you designed your church for worship and witness;
you created your people to make your love known;
you made us after your own image,
that as your body we might reveal your living presence.

Your Word tells us that we are your field and we are your
    building—
designed to bear fruit for your praise, and to be a living
    witness to your glory.
In the name of Christ. Amen.

429 SUNDAY BETWEEN 25TH AND 28TH FEBRUARY

Lord, we come to worship you, the Judge of all the earth.
We have come to confess that all things belong to you—
the past, the present and the future.
We pray for the congregation and for ourselves,
that all we share in this act of worship will lift our eyes from
    earth to heaven.
We pray for [*leader/speaker*],
whom you have sent to lead us in praise and thanksgiving,
in song and in prayer, and in hearing the good news of Christ.
Fill her/him with your Holy Spirit, that s/he may be filled
    with power
for the task you have laid upon her/him. In Christ's name.
    Amen.

430 SUNDAY BEFORE LENT

Lord, we have come to meet with you, to give you thanks
    and praise.
Too often we come for the wrong reasons
and the worship we offer is unworthy of you.
But in your grace, receive our poor offering
and by your Holy Spirit transform it into a celebration of
    your glory.
As your disciples climbed the mountain of transfiguration
we ask you to give us a glimpse of your glory.
We pray for [*leader/speaker*];
we thank you for her/his call to preach your Word.
May all that is said and done lead the whole congregation to
    the throne of grace.
In the name of Jesus. Amen.

431 FIRST SUNDAY IN LENT

Lord, we live in a fallen world.
Each day we are tempted to turn away from you and
to worship our gods of selfish ambition, self-sufficiency and
    self-centredness.
We rejoice that, though he was tempted just as we are,
Christ remained faithful to you.
We have come to worship the one who was truly human
and who brought your divine nature close to every one of us.
Speak through [*leader/speaker*],
that through our worship we may lift up Christ
so that all people might be drawn to him. In his name.
    Amen.

432 SECOND SUNDAY IN LENT

Lord, you are the God of truth and grace.
You alone know what is in all our hearts and minds.
You know where we have fallen short of living lives that
    bring you glory.
We have come to praise you for the promise of new birth.
Fill your servant [*leader/speaker*] with your Holy Spirit,
that we may all have the joy and the power to begin again.
In Christ's name. Amen.

433 THIRD SUNDAY IN LENT

Lord, we come from a world in turmoil
and we live and work among those without hope or purpose
    in their lives.
We come to you to celebrate the wonder
of your glory, your power and your love.
We rejoice that you offer us a peace that, in our own
    strength,
we cannot win, deserve or achieve.
Through Christ we can know what it means to be at peace
    with ourselves
because he has made peace between ourselves and you.

May the worship we offer declare the peace that passes all
    understanding,
the peace that finds its origin in the heart of God and at the
    foot of the cross.
We ask this for the sake of your glory. Amen.

434   FOURTH SUNDAY IN LENT

Lord, we come as those who are blind and longing to see.
We come as those who are empty and seeking to be filled.
We come as those who are deaf
that we may hear your gentle voice of love
and the cry of our neighbours in their brokenness.
We thank you for [*leader/speaker*]
and that you have called and equipped her/him to proclaim
    your Word.
We pray that you will open our eyes, our ears and our hearts
to receive what you are longing to give. In Jesus' name. Amen.

435   MOTHERING SUNDAY

Lord, from before we are born you surround us with your
    love;
from before we could understand you have been our God;
and even before we were ready to respond
your grace has been sufficient for our need.
We come on this Mothering Sunday
to celebrate not only the love of parents
but the privilege of belonging to your church.
May our worship today reflect your fatherly goodness,
your motherly compassion and the joy of knowing your Son
    as our brother.
We thank you for [*leader/speaker*], whom you have sent to
    lead our worship.
Help us to avoid vague sentimentality
and infuse our praises with the presence and power of the
    Holy Spirit.
In the name and for the sake of Christ the Lord. Amen

436 FIFTH SUNDAY IN LENT

Lord, we are aware that we can sing our hymns, say our
     prayers
and listen to your Word, but still not have worshipped you.
We can come for friendship, fellowship or just out of habit,
and find that our hearts are far from you
and our worship has been a dried-out and empty reflection
     of the real thing.
Come, Holy Spirit, and breathe new life into all our hearts
     and lives.
We thank you for [*leader/speaker*]
as we look forward eagerly to receiving the message you have
     given her/him.
By your Holy Spirit equip us all to offer the praises you
     deserve:
worship set on fire by the power from on high! For your
     glory's sake. Amen.

437 SIXTH SUNDAY IN LENT (PASSION SUNDAY)

Man of sorrows! What a name
For the Son of God, who came
Ruined sinners to reclaim!
Alleluia! What a Saviour!
Philip Bliss (1838–76)

Lord, on this Passion Sunday
we gather to hear again the message of the cross.
Though we have heard it so many times before
may we hear it today with wonder, amazement and joy—
as if we were hearing for the very first time.
We pray for [*leader/speaker*], who is to lead our worship
and for the congregation that has come to give praises.
Make us aware of the cost of healing our relationship with
     you.
Teach us the cost of forgiveness, show us the depth of your
     love,

reawaken our desire to kneel at the foot of the cross
and challenge us by the sacrifice of your Son. In his name.
Amen.

438   SEVENTH SUNDAY IN LENT (PALM SUNDAY)

Hosanna, save us now!
Lord, on this Palm Sunday we join with the disciples
who followed Christ into Jerusalem
and we walk with your pilgrims who led the way.
You came as the Prince of Peace, but we still want you to be
    our King!
You came to suffer and die,
but we would still prefer you to punish our enemies.
You came for your coronation,
but we still want to choose the kind of Saviour you will be.
Ride on, ride on—not only into Jerusalem, but into our
    hearts and lives.
We pray for [leader/speaker] and the whole congregation.
May the worship we offer today bring you glory,
and may the praises we bring echo through the rest of our
    lives,
change all our relationships and ring through eternity.
Let us praise the King of Glory. Amen.

439   EASTER SUNDAY

This is the day of the Lord's victory!
Let us be happy, let us celebrate!
Psalm 118:24 GNB

Lord, we celebrate today not only that you rose from the
    dead
but that you are our living Lord!
We praise you for the empty tomb
and we celebrate your victory over life and death.
We call you Friend and Brother, and we name you Saviour
    and King …
but today we declare that you are Lord!

We come with our hymns of worship and our prayers of
    praise.
We come to give you the honour, the thanks and the glory
    you deserve!
We pray that the power that raised Christ from the dead
will transform our lives, our witness and our worship
for the glory of your name. Amen.

440   SECOND SUNDAY OF EASTER

Lord, the disciples hid behind locked doors because they
    were afraid.
They had seen you die and couldn't believe that you are alive.
They had heard the story of the empty tomb
but they hadn't experienced its life-changing power.
So come to us as we gather, hidden away from the world,
perhaps feeling trapped in our doubts and fears,
and set us free, give us new life,
as we experience your living presence in our midst.
We pray for [*leader/speaker*]:
Touch her/him with your resurrection power
that our worship might declare that you are our Lord and
    our God.
In Jesus' name. Amen.

441   THIRD SUNDAY OF EASTER

Lord, we journey together as those two disciples did on the
    Emmaus Road.
We journey from faith to faith,
weighed down with our questions, our uncertainties and our
    not knowing—
just longing for certainty, needing hope.
Lord, we journey together, and you come and share our
    journey
because you are the answer to all our questions,
the solution to our uncertainties and the way through to
    beginning again.

Lord, our worship is part of the journey.
We pray for [*leader/speaker*],
whom you have sent to make your will and your presence
known.
May our worship be the moment when each member of the
congregation
begins a new journey to you and with you—a journey from
time to eternity.
In Christ's name. Amen.

442   FOURTH SUNDAY OF EASTER

Lord, we all come as servants of Christ.
We all come that your light can shine in our darkness.
We come as those with no right to judge each other;
we come in faith and trust before the Judge of all the earth.
Search all our hearts, test all our motives;
and may [*leader/speaker*], whom you have sent to lead our
worship,
be equipped by your Holy Spirit to bring your word of hope.
In Christ's name. Amen.

443   FIFTH SUNDAY OF EASTER

Lord, your name is holy; your will for us is perfect;
and your loving presence fills every corner of our lives.
We know that the riches of your love expose the poverty of
our lives.
So easily are we tempted to please ourselves,
to see even worship as something for our own personal
blessing;
to be offended when we are not thanked and praised.
We pray for [*leader/speaker*], that all that is said and done
might draw us all closer to Christ
and make us more ready to be servants of the Servant King.
Amen.

444 SIXTH SUNDAY OF EASTER

Lord, we know you by many names.
We call you Creator, Sustainer, Saviour,
Friend, Master, King and Sovereign Lord.
Most of all we know you as love.
We have come to praise you for that love
that holds everything and holds us;
for that love that accepts us as we are
and enables us to become what you meant us to be;
for that love that comes from above and empowers us to
    begin again.
We pray for [*leader/speaker*], that s/he may be so filled with
    your Spirit
that we may receive your word of love through her/him. For
    Christ's sake. Amen.

445 SEVENTH SUNDAY OF EASTER

Lord, we fill our hearts and minds and lives with so many,
    many things
that we hope will bring us peace and fulfilment.
But we are left feeling empty and alone.
We have come to worship you
because we believe that Christ is the Bread of Life
and that true fulfilment is only found in him.
We pray your blessing on [*leader/speaker*],
whom you have sent with your message of hope.
Open our minds to be attentive to your word of grace
and our hearts to the Spirit of Christ. Amen.

446 PENTECOST

Lord, we believe that you have called us here
and we have come to hear the Word of Life
and to respond to the truth of Jesus.
By your Holy Spirit, transform our formal act of worship
into a joyous celebration of your love.

May our praises overflow with love as on the day of
    Pentecost.
In the name of Jesus, may our worship honour you
here and everywhere and for ever.
We pray for [*leader/speaker*] and the whole congregation,
that your Holy Spirit will empower our praises for your glory
and infuse our discipleship with the presence of the living
    Christ. Amen.

447   TRINITY

Lord, we feel like the disciples
when you walked with them on the Emmaus Road
and they did not recognise your presence.
You came to them on the sea shore
when their work was fruitless and they felt they had failed.
You had spoken to them about your death and resurrection
but they hadn't understood.
They hid behind locked doors because they hadn't received
    your power.
Lord, by your Holy Spirit, speak the word we need to hear
and open our lives to receive it.
May our worship, witness and service reflect the love of God
    the Father,
the grace of God the Son and the power of God the Holy
    Spirit. Amen.

448   SUNDAY BETWEEN 24TH AND 28TH MAY

Lord, every day we are confronted by pictures of a world in
    need.
We see the anguish and pain on the faces of those around us;
we too carry our own damaged memories of a past that still
    hurts,
the doubts and uncertainties we face today
and the hopes and fears of the unknown tomorrow.
Forgive us when we are tempted to try to leave all these
    things behind

and use worship as a time to hide from the world.
We come bringing the brokenness of life with us
to lay it at your throne of grace.
By your Holy Spirit speak through [*leader/speaker*] your word
of hope, joy, courage, healing, and forgiveness. Amen.

449   SUNDAY BETWEEN 29TH MAY AND 4TH JUNE

Lord, when we feel surrounded by darkness
you call us to enter the light of Christ.
When we feel crushed, insignificant and forgotten
you lift our eyes to see your glory.
When we are alone, defeated, and we have lost our way,
you declare yourself to be the way, the truth and the life.
May the worship we offer bring you glory.
May the songs we sing come from hearts overflowing with
    your love.
May our prayers reach to the throne of your grace
and may the commitment we make bring you joy, and
    ourselves peace. Amen.

450   SUNDAY BETWEEN 5TH AND 11TH JUNE

Lord, we thank you for your presence with us
and we praise you for your glory that reaches the heavens.
We thank you for your people who meet to worship in every
    time and place.
We praise you for the millions of your people
who have faithfully met to sing your praises
and for those all over the world who turn to you today.
We thank you that you have invited us to join with your
    people,
in time and eternity, to give you glory. Amen.

451   SUNDAY BETWEEN 12TH AND 18TH JUNE

Lord, we are sometimes afraid when we come to worship
    you.
Whenever we are aware of your almighty presence

we feel utterly overwhelmed by the power of your love.
Though it strengthens and encourages us
we know that it is your love that calls us to witness and to
service.
It is your love that sends us out into all the world.
It is your love that touches and changes us,
and, as with Abraham, sends us on a journey of faith and
obedience.
Your love both calls and sends us,
and it is only when we listen for your call, and respond to
your sending
that we can possibly reach the destination which,
by your grace and through your Holy Spirit, you are leading
us towards. Amen.

452   SUNDAY BETWEEN 19TH AND 25TH JUNE

Lord, the psalmist sang for joy when he entered the courts of
your house—
he shouted for joy to you, the Lord of all the earth.
His praises sprang from a heart filled with great gratitude
and from his knowledge of your worth and your glory.
We have come, as generations of your people have come,
to offer you heartfelt thanks and praise.
May our praises be directed to you, the Lord of heaven and
earth,
and may our thankfulness find its mainspring
in the empty cross, the empty tomb and the 'emptying out'
of the Holy Spirit.
We pray for the whole congregation, and for [*leader/speaker*],
that together we may offer worship that is worthy of your
holy name. Amen.

453   SUNDAY BETWEEN 26TH JUNE AND 2ND JULY

Lord, we know that you are with us everywhere, every day.
But you have promised that when your people gather for
worship

you will be in the midst of them.
We claim your presence and we seek your power.
We come as the poor and needy into the presence of their
    King,
we come as the weak and uncertain have always come,
longing for your protection and mercy.
Lord, may we experience the joy of your service,
the liberation of your forgiveness and the extravagance of
    your love.
We pray for [*leader/speaker*] and the whole congregation,
that your Spirit might fill us up and send us out,
so that all the world might know that there is no God like
    you,
no other god besides you, and come to worship you.
In Jesus' name. Amen.

454   SUNDAY BETWEEN 3RD AND 9TH JULY

Lord, when we come to worship, you call us to look in
    different directions.
When we look up ... to offer hymns of adoration
and praise you in prayer and bless your name,
you direct our gaze within,
to the anger and selfishness there, and to the hurt and pain
that our thoughtless words and deeds have brought to our
    neighbours.
We know our need of your forgiveness.
When we look within ... you redirect our eyes to the needs
    of your world
and the brokenness of those around us.
When we come bearing the needs of your world ...
you direct us to bring our thanks for what we have received.
Lord, when we come—you meet us.
Hold us, and through your servant [*leader/speaker*]
lift our eyes to see your glory. Amen.

Lord, we have come to worship you; you have touched and
    changed our lives.
You are our reason for being here—you are our reason for
    being!
Lord, there is no greater task to which you call us
than to offer praises to your name.
There is no higher ambition that can fill our hearts and minds
than to lift up the King of Kings.
There is no deeper love we can experience
and no wider mercy on offer anywhere
than that which we find at the foot of the cross.
We pray for [*leader/speaker*]
and all your people who have gathered for worship, here and
    around the world.
May your Holy Spirit set us free from mere formality
and empower us for worship, full of free grace. Amen.

456   SUNDAY BETWEEN 17TH AND 30TH JULY

Lord, we confess that everything belongs to you!
We praise you because you hold the whole world in your
    hands,
but we worship you because you hold us!
We have come to give you glory, to welcome the King of
    Glory
and to invite the Lord of Glory
to be at the heart of our worship and the centre of our lives.
We also confess that we have no right to be here,
that there is nothing in our lives that makes us worthy
to be welcome in your presence,
no reason why you should love us or forgive us.
You are the King of Glory; you are also the Prince of Peace.
You are the sovereign Lord; you are also the God of grace.
Speak through your servant [*leader/speaker*],
that our praises may flow from this place in songs of joy
and lives lived for your glory. Amen.

457   SUNDAY BETWEEN 31ST JULY AND 6TH AUGUST

Lord, you are everywhere and you know everything.
There is nothing you do not know,
and there is nothing you do not understand.
There is no place we can hide from your searching gaze.
You know our thoughts and our dreams, our hopes and our
    fears.
We can fool everyone else, even ourselves, but we can never
    fool you.
You are sovereign! You are Lord! And there is no other!
We have come to worship you for your greatness,
but we have come to praise you that your greatness is clothed
    in lovingkindness.
We pray for [*leader/speaker*],
and we ask that you will speak through her/him the word we
    need to hear.
By your Holy Spirit, enable us to respond. Amen.

458   SUNDAY BETWEEN 7TH AND 13TH AUGUST

Lord, our hearts are simply longing to worship you.
We are filled with thankfulness
for all the blessings we have received at your hand.
We stand amazed at the sheer extravagance of your love.
We try to comprehend something of your grace towards us,
but again and again your love for us in Jesus takes our breath
    away.
Lord, you are great, you are worthy of praise.
Your majesty, power, authority and glory are simply beyond
    our understanding.
We do not have the words that will truly declare who and
    what you are.
We have brought our hymns and our prayers, our speaking
    and our listening,
our celebration and our silence;
by your Holy Spirit use these poor vehicles for the glory of
    your wonderful name. Amen.

459   SUNDAY BETWEEN 14TH AND 20TH AUGUST

Lord, we have come to hear again the story of your love for
    us, and for all the world.
We come to celebrate that, in the face of your Son, we have
    seen your love.
Thank you that on the cross he demonstrated once and for
    all
your grace that is at the heart of all creation.
By that same grace search all our hearts,
renew our lives and transform our worship.
We pray for [*leader/speaker*], believing you have sent her/him
with a message of life and of hope, of challenge and change,
    a message of Christ.
May the power of the Spirit apply your Word to our life
    together here
and our lives for you in the week to come. Amen.

460   SUNDAY BETWEEN 21ST AND 27TH AUGUST

Lord, we have come to praise you for your faithfulness to
    your people
down the centuries and across the world.
We have come to remember all you have done for us,
changing our lives, renewing our relationship with you
and, by your grace, making us your people.
We have come to give you thanks, to sing your praises
and to acknowledge that you are Lord!
We pray for those who have gathered for worship,
and for [*leader/speaker*], whom you have sent to lead our
    prayers and our praise.
May your name be honoured and lifted high here and
    everywhere. Amen.

461   SUNDAY BETWEEN 28TH AUGUST AND 3RD
       SEPTEMBER

Lord, we come as your people made one in Jesus Christ,
    your Son, our Lord.

We remember that you meant us to live in harmony with
you and with each other.
May the worship we offer be a celebration of our fellowship
in you.
Break down the barriers we erect against each other
and remove the difficulties we encounter as we approach
a deeper trust, peace and love between us.
We pray for [*leader/speaker*]
and ask that together our prayers and our praise may draw us
closer together
and bring joy to the heart of our God. Amen.

462   SUNDAY BETWEEN 4TH AND 10TH SEPTEMBER

Lord, it is a joy to be in your presence,
it is an awesome experience to know you as the living God.
Though you hold all creation in your hands
you have promised to hold us in your love.
Though you are great enough to inhabit eternity
you have promised to live in the hearts and lives of those
who put their trust in you.
Though you are worshipped by all the hosts of heaven
you have promised to receive the worship of broken, contrite
hearts.
We pray: Make your presence known,
and may our praises be empowered by the Holy Spirit.
Amen.

463   SUNDAY BETWEEN 11TH AND 17TH SEPTEMBER

Lord, so often we are tempted to come here not to worship
you,
but to find fellowship for ourselves.
We confess that we come seeking to receive a blessing
rather than to lift up the name of our God.
By your Holy Spirit transform our words and our actions,
our songs and our prayers, our listening and our waiting,
into a celebration of your glory.

We pray for [*leader/speaker*]: May s/he and all your people
be filled with your grace and worship you in Spirit and in
truth. Amen.

464   SUNDAY BETWEEN 18TH AND 24TH SEPTEMBER

Lord, all your people of every time and place
have longed to give you the worship that you deserve.
We praise you, our King, whose name will be praised for
    ever and ever.
You are our Lord, whose greatness will outlast all our
    generations.
We honour you—Father, Son and Holy Spirit.
Our minds cannot comprehend you, our thoughts cannot
    contain you,
our lives are a poor reflection of your holiness, glory and
    love.
Lord, may our worship declare your mercy, may our praise
    confess your worth
and may our prayers demonstrate your trustworthiness and
    love.
We pray for [*leader/speaker*], that the Holy Spirit
might equip her/him to lead us to the throne of grace.
    Amen.

465   SUNDAY BETWEEN 25TH SEPTEMBER AND 1ST
       OCTOBER

Lord, you tell us that the whole earth is a picture of your
    glory,
that everything we see and hear is specifically designed
to make you known and your presence a reality.
Compared to the mirror of creation
the words of our worship can seem too formal—almost
    empty, unrevealing.
Yet we long to worship you, to draw closer and closer to you,
and to know you—a living reality at the centre of our lives
and at the heart of our worship.

By your Holy Spirit, enable us to lift up Christ
and to lift up our voices and our lives in his praise. Amen.

466   SUNDAY BETWEEN 2ND AND 8TH OCTOBER

Lord, you call us to come to you just as we are.
You declare that when we come with open hearts and with
    open lives
you will never turn us away.
Yet we also know that, only as we focus our hearts and minds
    on your will
and allow you to infiltrate every corner of our lives,
will we truly be able to worship you.
We long to experience your renewing Spirit,
your healing grace and your empowering love.
We pray for this congregation
and for [*leader/speaker*], whom you have sent to bring your
    Word to us,
that we might walk in the way of your truth and love. Amen.

467   SUNDAY BETWEEN 9TH AND 15TH OCTOBER

Read Psalm 91

Lord, though we often find the world to be a frightening
    place
that drains our hope, stultifies our joy and robs us of our
    peace,
we rejoice in the promise that, in the midst of the storm,
everyone who stands close to you
will find freedom and security, peace and protection.
Lord, we have come to thank you for being present when we
    are tempted,
strong enough to hold us up when we were falling
and loving enough to stand by us,
forgiving us and helping us to begin again.
We bring our prayer in Jesus' name. Amen.

SUNDAY BETWEEN 16TH AND 22ND OCTOBER

Lord, we come to you, the source and centre of all our hope.
We come to you, longing to trust you more,
ready to confess the poverty of our faith.
We come to wait patiently, to be still in your presence.
We come, that your love and your kindness, your truth and
     your holiness,
might touch and change our lives.
We come, that in our worship our coming might be a
     confession
that you first came to us and for us.
We come, and our coming is in itself a prayer of
     commitment.
We pray for [*leader/speaker*],
whom we believe you have sent with the message of life,
     faith and peace.
Speak to us, Lord, that we may speak in your name. Amen.

469   SUNDAY BETWEEN 23RD AND 29TH OCTOBER

Coming into your presence, Lord, is like coming home!
It is here that we first found you, or rather you found us.
It is here that, again and again, we have met with you,
rejoiced in your love and found the strength to continue our
     journey.
Again and again your majesty, your glory and your power
overwhelm us and outstrip anything our tiny, finite minds
     could hope to comprehend.
Again and again you remind us that
you are not confined by time or place or eternity.
Lord, speak to us the word that will sweep away our doubts,
strengthen us in our weakness and provide that opportunity
     to begin again,
which we so long to have. Amen.

470 SUNDAY BETWEEN 30TH OCTOBER AND 5TH
NOVEMBER

Lord, we have come to worship you,
to bring our songs of joy and our words of thankfulness.
We long for our worship to be more than mere words
and our thanksgiving more than an act of the moment.
May the worship we begin here last the whole of our lives
and our praises ring through eternity.
We come to you, because you have promised to set us free,
to fill our lives with the blessings you have always given to
your faithful people.
We come to you because you are our Creator, Sustainer and
Sovereign Lord.
We thank you for [*leader/speaker*] who has brought your
Word for us.
By your Holy Spirit equip her/him with the power to share
that Word. Amen.

471 SUNDAY BETWEEN 6TH AND 12TH NOVEMBER

Lord, we prefer to come to worship you with words we know
and love
and with songs that make us feel comfortable.
But you are the God who makes all things new!
You are the one who speaks in words and ways that we can
understand.
We bring our new songs—
not those whose words appear on the written page
but the words of new songs written by your grace
on hearts and lives made new by your Holy Spirit.
May all we say and do and offer bring glory to your name
and a song that flows from hearts being renewed by your
love. Amen.

472 SUNDAY BETWEEN 13TH AND 19TH NOVEMBER

Read Psalm 123

Lord, you are our Lord;
your majesty and your power are beyond our understanding
and your mercy takes our breath away.
We know we should look up to you with the whole of our
    lives
and lift up our voices for your glory;
yet too often we come with limited expectations
and with our minds focused on ourselves
and our inadequate hopes and dreams.
Lord, we pray for [*leader/speaker*], and the whole
    congregation,
that you will prepare us to worship you in the way that you
    deserve
and glorify you here, and everywhere, and for ever. Amen.

473   SUNDAY BETWEEN 20TH AND 26TH NOVEMBER

Read Psalm 95

Lord, you call us to worship you with joy and thanksgiving.
You summon us to give you glory and to honour your name.
You remind us that you are our Maker
and that through you we may enter all that life was meant to
    be.
We come to confess that you hold us
and you hold all things in the palm of your hand.
And we would worship you.
Too easily our praises are restricted by our self-centredness
and our prayers by our self-interest.
We come to sing, to laugh and to rejoice in your presence.
By the power and presence of your Holy Spirit,
transform the formality of our praises, and renew the
    experience of your glory.
Lord, we kneel before you—
our hearts and lives lie open to your searching sight.
By your grace enable us to speak of your love
and to commit our very lives to sing of your glory. Amen.

Prayers with Pictures

In this section the text that is intended to appear on the screen over each picture is given in a different font; words for speaking are in roman. Instructions for suitable pictures are in italics. Copyright-free photographs can be uploaded from a digital camera, or downloaded from many sites on the Internet. You can display these by means of projection software such as PowerPoint, or an overhead projector, or large prints. It is helpful to insert a blank slide at the beginning and at the end as this allows better control of the presentation.

474   WATER OF LIFE

Slide: *Picture of the moonlight (on water)—*
Caption: Light of the world

Lord, we praise you because you are the light of the world.
Your mysterious light breaks into our darkness
and the warmth of your grace touches deep into our lives.
We pray for those whose lives are cold and empty.

Slide: *Picture of the turbulent sea—*
Caption: God's energy at the heart of life

Lord, you are the energy at the heart of life,
your unceasing activity disturbs our self-satisfaction
and your incessant power calls us to obedience, hope and
        trust.
We pray for those whose faith is weak
and whose ability to trust has been damaged.

Slide: *Picture of the birds with their young—*
Caption: you provide for our needs

Lord, your love holds us with unimaginable strength
and each day you provide for our needs;
you nurture us with an open hand
and gently lead us to the safety of your peace.
We pray for those who work for peace in your troubled world.

Slide: *Picture of the the seashore—*
Caption: your grace finds its way

Lord, the water of your grace finds its way to the shores of
    our need,
and the limitless expanse of your mercy laps with gentleness
    and love
on the sands of our emptiness and despair.
We pray for those who find it hard to love or be loved.

Slide: *Picture of the waterfall and the rainbow—*
Caption: your promise of hope

Lord, like the water of a mighty cascading torrent,
you reach down in the refreshing grace of Christ,
and your promise of hope is declared in the rainbow,
the empty cross and the empty tomb.
We pray for those who find it hard to trust in God.

Slide: *Picture of the reflection (on a lake or pool)—*
Caption: the reflection of your love

Lord, in the deep waters of your holiness we see the
    reflection of your love.
In the still waters of your grace we find the way to the peace
    we long for.
We pray for those we know to be in any kind of need: Give
    them your peace.

Slide: *Picture of the horizon—*
Caption: we look away from ourselves

Lord, you call us to look away from ourselves, to look to
    your horizon,
to discover that you are holding all the waters of eternity in
    the palm of your hand.
We pray for those in need of healing.

Slide: *Picture of the headlands—*
Caption: you have promised

Lord, your mercy surrounds us on every side,
your forgiving love touches and changes us;
you have promised never to leave us or let us go,
and your Spirit goes on reaching out to us with your joy.
We pray for strength to forgive and to be forgiven.

Slide: *Picture of the waves and rocks—*
Caption: barriers we put in our way

Lord, there is nothing that can ultimately withstand the
　　waters of your will.
The mighty waves of your truth are always seeking to
　　overcome
the obstacles we allow in our lives, and any barriers we put in
　　your way.
We pray for parents, teachers, those in the media and all in
　　positions of influence,
that they may guide and support us when obstacles seem to
　　bar the way.

Slide: *Picture of the waterfall—*
Caption: overwhelming love

Lord, the waters of grace crash down upon us in an endless
　　torrent of joy.
Your overwhelming love longs to saturate us with hope and
　　mercy
and your endless power takes our breath away.
We pray for those who make God real for us.

Slide: *Picture of the sunset—*
Caption: the sunset of our dreams

Lord, you light up our world with your truth
and you enrich our lives with your beauty.
You colour everything with the love of Christ
and your light brings hope as you shine on the waters of the
　　sunset of our dreams.

Lord, come refresh our lives with the living water of the
   Holy Spirit,
that by your grace we may become channels of hope and
   signs of your presence.
We ask this in the name of Jesus,
the one who is always seeking to renew our lives. Amen.

475   IN THE NEWS

*Set up a series of twelve PowerPoint slides which will be
moved on manually. These prayers work best using two voices
alternating between the stanzas of the prayers.*

Slide 1   Blank—launch slide

Slide 2   Title: Prayers for today's world

Slide 3   Picture of the earth

Lord, you gave us the earth as our home
and you have filled it with beauty and many good things.
Forgive us, that by our foolish self-interest
we are destroying your precious gift for future generations.

Slide 4   Picture of a terrorist bombing

We pray for those whose minds are filled with hatred
and whose hearts have no room for compassion;
for those whose anger is fuelled by the injustices they believe
   they are suffering.

Slide 5   Picture of a disaster

We pray for those whose lives have been torn apart
by the [*current disaster*] they have suffered;
for those who have lost home and family
and everything that gave value and meaning to their lives.

Slide 6   Picture of the local hospital

We pray for those who care for others;
for those who daily offer healing, hope and kindness

to people placed in their care;
for doctors, nurses and all the staff in our local hospital(s);
for any we know who have asked for our prayers.

Slide 7   Picture of a television or newspaper

We pray for those who work in the media;
for journalists writing in newspapers and reporters on radio
     or television;
for those whose words can bring hope or despair to millions
and for those who, in their concern for truth and justice,
have lost sight of the human tragedies they are trampling all
     over
in their focus on news that is bad.

Slide 8   Picture of starving people

We pray for those who, in this world of plenty,
are starved of the food and the medicines they need;
for those turned into homeless refugees by civil war
or their government's corruption and bad management;
for [*aid agencies*] who give voices to the voiceless and bring
     hope to the dying.

Slide 9   Picture of the police

We pray for the police, and for all those who work to keep
     us safe;
who spend their days responding to
those whose homes have been burgled, or their bodies
     attacked,
and lives wrecked by those with no sense of love and
     compassion;
for those driven to crime to support the addictions they
     cannot break.

Slide 10   Picture of your church

In the silence we hold in God's presence the life of our
     church

and those for whom we are concerned;
our life together in Jesus; our fellowship, worship and
mission.

Slide 11

Leader: Lord, in your mercy …
Response: **hear our prayer. Amen.**

Slide 12 *Blank*

476 ONE WORLD—A MEDITATION

Set up a series of twenty-one PowerPoint slides with a fifteen-second delay between slides. These prayers work best with music, either from a disk or played live.

Each picture is faded in, with the caption faded in after a one- or two-second delay. After a further fifteen seconds the picture and caption are faded out simultaneously.

Slide 1 *Blank—launch slide*

Slide 2 *Title: One world*

Music is launched

Slide 3 *Picture of the stock market*
Caption: When the money markets crash …

Slide 4 *Picture of a group of unemployed Africans*
Caption: … why do we feel the pain?

Slide 5 *Picture of happy school children [from behind]*
Caption: It's easy to laugh and have fun when you've got
food in your stomach and you have a chance to
live …

Slide 6 *Picture of a single hungry black boy*
Caption 1: … but think of the money spent on chocolate in
this country in just one year …

Caption 2: … it would clear Africa's debt in one go.

Slide 7 **Picture of a healthy farm animal**
Caption: He looks healthy …

Slide 8 **Picture of battery hens/animals in poor conditions**
Caption: … but will we never learn the true cost of our food?

Slide 9 **Picture of a bluebell wood**
Caption: When we neglect God's world and take it for granted…

Slide 10 **Picture of a mudslide or flash flood**
Caption: … someone always gets hurt.

Slide 11 **Picture of the earth from space**
Caption: We can rise above the heavens and look down on the earth …

Slide 12 **Picture of concentration camp**
Caption: … we can sink as low as Auschwitz.

Slide 13 **Close-up of a flower**
Caption: God's beautiful world …

Slide 14 **Picture of terrorist bombing**
Caption: … so why do people plant bombs that kill and maim?

Slide 15 **Picture of a person relaxing on the beach**
Caption: I need to get away from it all, to relax and have fun…

Slide 16 **Picture of homeless refugees**
Caption: … we have been driven from our home, and we just want somewhere to live.

Slide 17 **Close-up of a person crying**
Caption 1: My tears speak of my loneliness …

Caption 2: … and of a world that doesn't care.

Slide 18 **Picture of a crowded street**
Caption 1: Jesus says, 'There is room for all …

Caption 2: …in my kingdom of love.'

Slide 19   Picture of Earthrise from the moon
Caption 1: The earth is the Lord's …

Caption 2: … and everything in it.

Slide 20   Picture of the cross
Captions:
Leader: Let us praise the Lord of all the earth …
*Response: **And live to the glory of his name. Amen.***

Slide 21   Blank

477   THE FRUIT OF THE SPIRIT

Set up a series of thirteen PowerPoint slides which will be moved on manually. These prayers work best using two voices alternating between the stanzas of the prayers.

Slide 1   Blank

Slide 2   Title: The Fruit of the Spirit

Slide 3   Picture of caring hands
Caption: Love

We pray for those who feel unwanted and unloved;
for those excluded by the colour of their skin, by their
          gender or their age;
for those who long to know the healing touch of God's love
          upon their lives
and those for whom the church is a barrier to overcome
instead of the doorway to grace that God planned it to be.
May the Spirit's presence in our lives
bear fruit for God's glory.

Slide 4   Picture of a hug
Caption: Joy

We pray for those who are hurting deep inside;
for those whose days are filled with worry, fear and anxiety;
for those who live by themselves

and for those whose lives are coloured by their experience of
    aloneness;
for those weighed down by their burden of responsibility
and for those whose every moment is empty and joyless.
May the Spirit's presence in our lives
bear fruit for God's glory.

Slide 5   Picture of someone alone
Caption: Peace

We pray for those who pass their days with no real sense of
    their own worth;
for those who are searching for a purpose and for a way to
    make sense of the journey;
for those who once walked in faith but have wandered far
    from the path to life;
for those who are lost, and for those who simply long to be
    found;
for those with no peace in their hearts
and for those with an ache that nothing will heal.
May the Spirit's presence in our lives
bear fruit for God's glory.

Slide 6   Picture of an angry crowd
Caption: Patience

We pray for those whose hearts are filled with anger
and for those whose minds are in turmoil and despair;
for those whose frustrations boil over and cause pain and
    anguish to others;
for those whose cause is just and right
and who seek hope, peace and freedom for all;
for those whose words and deeds bring division and erect
    barriers
and for those who are driven by hatred and greed.
May the Spirit's presence in our lives
bear fruit for God's glory.

Slide 7   *Picture of someone in tears*
Caption: Kindness

We pray for those whose lives are in turmoil
and for those who must rely on the help of their neighbours;
for those who have lost everything in war, or through famine
    or drought;
for those with no one to care
and who have no one who will listen to their cry of despair;
for those who receive kindness and love beyond their wildest
    hopes and dreams.
May the Spirit's presence in our lives
bear fruit for God's glory.

Slide 8   *Picture of concentration camp*
Caption: Goodness

We pray for those who show the way to rise above the hatred
    and bitterness of others
and for those who shine like a beacon in the darkness of evil
    and lust;
for those who are enabled to speak words of hope to the
    hopeless,
to offer comfort and love to the desperate,
to be the sign of God's presence
in the face of a holocaust of unspeakable suffering and pain.
May the Spirit's presence in our lives
bear fruit for God's glory.

Slide 9   *Picture of a wedding*
Caption: Faithfulness

We pray for those who have made promises to God and to
    each other
and for those who have found them impossible to keep;
for those who through no fault of their own
have been made to feel guilty and ashamed;
for those whose unfaithfulness has added
to the pain and brokenness that daily colours God's world;

for those who have found that the path of discipleship is not
  easy and broad
but grows narrower the closer we walk with the Lord.
May the Spirit's presence in our lives
bear fruit for God's glory.

Slide 10   Picture of a baby being held
Caption: Gentleness

We pray for those who are ill or in hospital
and for those who may never recover;
for those who visit and care, and for those who share the
  tears of others;
for those who are forgetful and confused
and for those who no longer remember their name;
for those facing the weakness that comes with age
and for those who feel forgotten by a society
designed for those it counts able and successful.
May the Spirit's presence in our lives
bear fruit for God's glory.

Slide 11   Picture of a packet of cigarettes
Caption: Self-control

We pray for those who are trapped by an addiction they can't
  break,
and for those whose lives are ruled by the very things that are
  spoiling their lives;
for those whose goals are designed by the demands of their
  materialistic world,
and for those who are enslaved by the desire to please
  others—no matter the cost;
for those whose only purpose is to fill each day
with everything that has no ultimate value
and who find no space for that which matters for all eternity.
May the Spirit's presence in our lives
bear fruit for God's glory.

Slide 12   Picture of a dove
Caption: Worship

We pray for those who are discovering
that the only way to finding the real fruit of life
is through the presence of the Holy Spirit at work within.
We pray for ourselves, that we may demonstrate in all we say
    and do
the fruit of the Spirit's power.
May the Spirit's presence in our lives
bear fruit for God's glory.

Lord, in your mercy,
hear our prayer.
In the name of Christ. Amen.

Slide 13   Blank

478   PRAYERS OF THANKS AND PRAISE 1

*Set up a series of sixteen PowerPoint slides with a fifteen-second
delay between slides. These prayers work best with music either
from a disk or played live.*

*Each picture is faded in and the caption faded in after a one- or
two-second delay. After fifteen seconds the picture and caption
are faded out simultaneously.*

Slide 1   Blank—launch slide

Slide 2   Title: We say thank you to God and praise him for …

Music is launched.

Slide 3   Picture of a butterfly
Caption: new beginnings

Slide 4   Picture of parent and new baby
Caption: new life

Slide 5   Picture of a panda (or other endangered species)
Caption: our threatened neighbours

Slide 6   *Picture of DNA*
Caption: discovery

Slide 7   *Picture of Brazilian rain forests*
Caption: limited resources

Slide 8   *Picture of an operating theatre*
Caption: healing and hope

Slide 9   *Picture of sunset/sunrise*
Caption: the end — or the beginning?

Slide 10   *Picture of a space shuttle*
Caption: achievement

Slide 11   *Picture of Remembrance poppies*
Caption: human sacrifice

Slide 12   *Picture of Christ with a crown of thorns*
Caption: divine sacrifice

Slide 13   *Picture of daffodils*
Caption: life made new

Slide 14   *Picture of an empty cross*
Caption: resurrection

Slide 15
Captions:
Leader: For all your gifts, we thank you, Lord,
Response: **and we praise your holy name for ever and ever.
Amen.**

Slide 16   *Blank*

479   PRAYERS OF THANKS AND PRAISE 2
*Set up a series of sixteen PowerPoint slides with a fifteen-second
delay between slides. These prayers work best with music either
from a disk or played live.*

Each picture is faded in and the caption faded in after a one- or two-second delay. After fifteen seconds the picture and caption are faded out simultaneously.

Slide 1   Blank—launch slide

Slide 2   *Title:* We give thanks and praise

Music is launched

Slide 3   *Picture of the world*
Caption: God's world—our temporary home

Slide 4   *Picture of an insect*
Caption: the delicate wonder of God's world

Slide 5   *Picture of a loaf of bread*
Caption: our daily bread

Slide 6   *Picture of a computer*
Caption: for minds to think and skills to use

Slide 7   *Picture of a beautiful flower or scene*
Caption: the ability to enjoy beautiful things

Slide 8   *Picture of sunset or sunrise on still water*
Caption: for times just to be still

Slide 9   *Picture of a rainbow*
Caption: the promises of God

Slide 10   *Picture of a snow scene*
Caption: God's holiness and purity

Slide 11   *Picture of a powerful waterfall*
Caption: power, might and majesty

Slide 12   *Picture of parent and child*
Caption: joy and responsibility of parenthood

Slide 13   *Picture of a microscope*
Caption: God's gift—the search for knowledge

Slide 14   Picture of the world
Caption: God's world — our temporary home

Slide 15
Captions:
Leader: We give thanks to the Lord
Response: **and we bless his holy name. Amen.**

Slide 17   Blank

480   PRAYERS FOR A WORLD IN NEED

Set up a series of thirteen PowerPoint slides which will be moved on manually. These prayers work best using two voices alternating between the stanza of the prayers.

Slide 1   Blank

Slide 2   Title: Prayers for a world in need

Slide 3   Picture of the earth

Lord, we thank you for our world which you gave us to care
    for
but which each day we are gradually destroying.
We pray, help us in the choices we make
that we may demonstrate our love for you
in the way we protect your creation.

Slide 4   Picture of a flower

We thank you for the beauty we see all around us.
We pray for those who can't see
and for those who look, but are blind to the handiwork of
    God.

Slide 5   Picture of a drought or a desert

We pray for those who are facing times of drought and
    despair
and for those who see their hopes and their dreams
lying in the dust of the earth.

Slide 6   Picture of a tiger or other endangered species

We thank you for the incredible variety of animals all around
      our world.
We pray you will help us to change the way we live,
that each may have the chance to live.

Slide 7   Picture of a child in tears

Lord, we thank you for the joy we receive
through the laughter and play of our children.
We pray for those who abuse others
and those who have been or are being abused,
that they may yet find the healing they need and long for.

Slide 8   Picture of aid workers

We thank you for the work of [*aid agencies*] and all who offer
      aid in your name.
We pray for those with the power to make poverty history.

Slide 9   Picture of a local hospital or operating theatre

Lord we thank you for the care, the skill and the commitment
of those who care for others.
We pray for all who work in the health service
and hold up before you any we know to be in need of
      healing and hope.

Slide 10   Picture of a bee or butterfly or other small creature

We thank you for our world in all its intricate design.
We pray for those who today are making plans and decisions
that will impact on the delicate ecobalance for all our
      tomorrows.

Slide 11   Picture of a terrorist or place that has been attacked

Lord we pray for those who by their words and deeds
seek to terrorise and kill and maim,
and for those whose hopes and dreams are destroyed
by the hatred and fanaticism of others.

Slide 12   Picture of your church

In the silence we hold in God's presence
the life of our church and those for whom we are concerned.

Slide 13   Blank

Lord, in your mercy,
hear our prayer. Amen.

481   WHAT IS IMPORTANT

Project suitable pictures to illustrate the prayers.

Picture of money

We pray for those for whom money is the most important
        thing in their lives
and for those who think that, if they only had more of it,
        they would be happy.
We pray that God will open their eyes to the things that
        really matter in life.
The Lord hears our prayer.
Thank you, Jesus.

Picture of someone at work

We pray for those for whom work matters more than
        anything else;
for those who find their work gives them no joy or sense of
        fulfilment.
We pray that God will open their minds to the wonders of
        his love.
The Lord hears our prayer.
Thank you, Jesus.

Picture of a local hospital

We pray for those for whom being fit and healthy
is the most important thing in their lives; for those who are
        ill,
and for those whose strength has gone with the years,

making them feel empty and useless.
We pray that God will fill them with hope.
The Lord hears our prayer.
Thank you, Jesus.

Picture of possessions (retail catalogue)

We pray for those for whom possessions matter more than
    anything else,
those for whom all the things with which they fill their
    homes and their days
provide a way for them to feel important.
We pray that God will show them just how important they
    are to him.
The Lord hears our prayer.
Thank you, Jesus.

Picture of a family

We pray for those for whom their own family
is the most important thing in their lives;
for those who have concern for their own family
but too easily forget those families around them in need of
    love and care.
We pray that God will open their ears to the cry of the poor.
The Lord hears our prayer.
Thank you, Jesus.

Picture of pleasure park

We pray for those for whom the pleasure of the moment
matters more than anything the future may hold,
for those who have thoughts and concerns only for today
and for their own personal pleasure
but who give no thought to those in pain or sadness.
The Lord hears our prayer.
Thank you, Jesus.

Picture of a cross

We pray for those who are looking for the meaning of life,
for those who are wanting to know what it's all about,
for those who find the answer in Jesus.
We thank you for showing us that there is nothing wrong
with getting fun out of pleasure, enjoying our work, loving
our family,
being concerned for our health,
or having lots of money or many possessions—
just so long as Jesus is at the hub of our lives
and all these things revolve around him.
The Lord hears our prayer.
Thank you, Jesus.

We ask our prayers in the name of Jesus, the true source of
life. Amen.

482   OUR PRAYERS FOR OTHERS

*Set up a series of fifteen PowerPoint slides with a fifteen-second
delay between slides. These prayers work best with music or a
song (I used "You Raise Me Up" by Josh Groban). The prayers
are based on Matthew 25:31–46. I used two pictures on each
slide which faded in. The two captions come in one after the
other with a two-second delay between. After fifteen seconds the
pictures and captions are faded out together.*

Slide 1   Blank—launch slide

Slide 2   The cross and person praying

Music is launched

Slide 3   Title: Our prayers for others

Slide 4   Pictures of starving people
Captions: I was hungry
            and you gave me what you didn't need

Slide 5   Pictures of drought and deserts
Captions: I was thirsty
            and you said you were sorry

Slide 6   *Pictures of people crying and being comforted*
Captions: I was a stranger
                and you hoped I wouldn't bother you

Slide 7   *Pictures of the homeless or living in cardboard boxes*
Captions: I was in need
                and you pretended I wasn't there

Slide 8   *Picture of sick person and HIV ribbon*
Captions: I was sick
                and you said is was my own fault

Slide 9   *Picture of person behind bars and the gates at*
                Auschwitz
Captions: I was in prison
                and you tried to turn a blind eye

Slide 10   *Picture of Christ carrying his cross*
Captions: Whatever you did not do for one of the least of
                these
                you did not do for me

Slide 11   *Picture of the cross*
Captions: *(each caption on this slide appears one second after*
                the next)
                Our calling is to
                worship
                learning and caring
                service
                evangelism

Slide 12   *Picture of your church*
Captions: We have no mission
                but to serve!

Slide 13   *No picture for this slide, but each caption appears*
                one second after the next
Caption: In the silence let us hold before God
                those who made God real for us in the past,

fresh expressions of being church tomorrow,
those for whom we are concerned today.

Slide 14   Blank
Captions:
Leader: The Lord hears our prayer.
Response: **Thanks be to God. Amen.**

Slide 15   Blank

483   OUR SOVEREIGN GOD (ADORATION)

*Set up a series of twenty-five PowerPoint slides with an eight-
second delay between. These prayers work best with gentle music
(e.g. Agnus Dei) either from a disk or played live.*

*The list below is simply a suggestion and other pictures may be
thought more appropriate.*

Slide 1   Blank—launch slide

Slide 2   Title—Give praise to our Sovereign Lord

Slide 3   Earthrise from the moon

Slide 4   Close-up of Everest

Slide 5   Close-up of a bee on a plant

Slide 6   Snowy forest scene

Slide 7   Coral Reef

Slide 8   Ice landscape

Slide 9   Close-up of dandelion 'clock'

Slide 10   Lakeland scene or Canadian Rockies

Slide 11   Glacier

Slide 12   Close-up of an orchid

Slide 13   Close-up of frozen ferns

Slide 14   Autumn tints

Slide 15   *Sunset or sunrise*

Slide 16   *Colorado landscape*

Slide 17   *Sea surf and rolling breakers*

Slide 18   *Volcano erupting*

Slide 19   *Purple flower covered with ice crystals*

Slide 20   *Close-up of Niagara Falls*

Slide 21   *The galaxy*

Slide 22   *Close up of newborn baby*

Slide 23   *Empty cross*

Slide 24
Captions:
Leader: We give thanks to the Lord
Response: **and we will praise his name for ever and ever. Amen.**

Slide 25   *Blank*

484   PRAYERS OF CONFESSION 1

Set up a series of fifteen PowerPoint slides with a twenty-second delay between. These prayers work best with gentle music either from a disk or played live.

Slide 1   *Blank—launch slide*

Slide 2   *Title—We have come to say we are sorry*

Slide 3   *Picture of rubbish in the streets*
Caption: our pollution spoils your world

Slide 4   *Picture of a forest with many trees cut down*
Caption: we take everything—and leave nothing

Slide 5   *Picture of a desert*
Caption: we create barrenness by our exploitation

Slide 6   *Picture of a homeless person*
Caption: we leave him nowhere to call home

Slide 7   *Picture of violent scene of conflict*
Caption: we create hatred and hostility

Slide 8   *Picture of a traffic jam*
Caption: we abuse your world

Slide 9   *Picture of a starving child*
Caption: we have plenty—they have nothing

Slide 10   *Picture of an injured child (or child-line poster image)*
Caption: what are we doing to our children?

Slide 11   *Picture of an elderly person*
Caption: isolated and forgotten because they are old

Slide 12   *Picture of black and white hands held together*
Caption: how can we start again?

Slide 13   *Picture of a cross*
Caption: help me to remember the cost

Slide 14
Captions:
Leader: *Lord, forgive.*
Response: **Christ, forgive. Amen.**

Slide 15   Blank

485   PRAYERS OF CONFESSION 2

Set up a series of twenty-two PowerPoint slides with a three-second delay between. These prayers work best with music either from a disk or played live.

Each picture is faded in and then the caption faded in after a half-second delay. After three more seconds the picture and caption are faded out simultaneously.

Slide 1   *Blank—launch slide*

Slide 2   *Title: Lord, we confess*

Music is launched

Slide 3   *Picture of Earthrise from the moon*
Caption: you gave us our world

Slide 4   *Picture of traffic jam/fumes*
Caption: but we have polluted it

Slide 5   *Picture of the moon landing*
Caption: we have achieved great things

Slide 6   *Picture of a pile of money*
Caption: and made our own gods

Slide 7   *Picture of a newborn baby*
Caption: you gave us life

Slide 8   *Picture of a drug addict injecting himself*
Caption: but what have we done with it?

Slide 9   *Picture of fresh vegetables*
Caption: there is plenty for all

Slide 10   *Picture of a starving boy*
Caption: if we learn how to share it

Slide 11   *Picture of a mobile phone*
Caption: we could communicate better

Slide 12   *Picture of a soldier and a young child*
Caption: but we prefer to fight

Slide 13   *Picture of a lake*
Caption: we love your beautiful world

Slide 14   *Picture of rubbish in the street*
Caption: so how come we spoil it?

Slide 15   *Picture of caring hands*
Caption: we can offer love and compassion

Slide 16   *Picture of a tearful person*
Caption: but we can break each other's hearts.

Slide 17   *Picture of a single rose*
Caption: a single rose is a precious thing

Slide 18   *Picture of an isolated, homeless person*
Caption: so why does he feel so alone?

Slide 19   *Picture of happy children*
Caption: a happy child is such a joy

Slide 20   *Picture of a child hiding her/his face in fear*
Caption: so why do we steal their smiles?

Slide 21
Captions:
Leader: *Lord, forgive.*
Response: · **Christ, forgive. Amen.**

Slide 22   *Blank*

Prayers of Intercession

486   TIME TO PRAY

Set up a series of fourteen PowerPoint slides with a twenty-second timed delay between. These prayers work best with gentle music (I used Quanta Qualia by Patrick Hawes) either from a disk or a flute or other musical instrument.

Slide 1   *Blank—launch music*

Slide 2   *Title—It's time to pray*

Slide 3   *Picture of a person on her/his own*
Caption: for those who are lonely

Slide 4   *Picture of Earthrise from the moon*
Caption: for the way we damage planet Earth

Slide 5   *Picture of starving mother and child*

Caption: for those for whom the next meal may be too late

Slide 6   *Picture of rubbish*

Caption: throwing away the world's resources

Slide 7   *Picture of William Wilberforce*

Caption: for those who are still slaves today

Slide 8   *Picture of mother and son crying*

Caption: when the tears just won't stop

Slide 9   *Picture of a current accident*

Caption: are we in too much of a hurry?

Slide 10   *Picture of a newborn baby's hand holding an adult's finger*

Caption: for those weighed down with responsibilities

Slide 11   *Picture of cherry blossom*

Caption: our God turns our ends into his new beginnings

Slide 12   *Picture of praying hands*
The following captions appear with a delay of 15 seconds between each:

Caption: Pray for those whom God has laid on your heart.
             Pray for yourself.
             Give thanks to God for all he has given you.

Slide 13   *The cross*
Captions:
Leader: The Lord is good to all
Response: **and we will praise him for ever and ever. Amen.**

487   GIVE THANKS FOR THE HARVEST

Set up a series of twelve PowerPoint slides with a twenty-second delay between. These prayers work best projected or spoken over gentle music either from a disk or a flute or other instrument.

Slide 1   *Blank*

Launch music

Slide 2   Picture of fields at harvest time
Caption: Give thanks for the harvest
Prayer: Lord, we come today to give thanks to you

Slide 3   Pictures: Different kinds of fruit
A series of pictures of fruit can be set to appear at one-second intervals on a single slide—and then held for around fifteen seconds.

Caption: the goodness of fruit
Prayer: for fruit that comes to us from our own country and from all around the world.

Slide 4   Picture of various kinds of flowers
Caption: the beauty of flowers
Prayer: for the burst of colour that wild and cultivated flowers add to our lives.

Slide 5   Picture of bees and butterflies
Caption: all creatures great and small
Prayer: for all creatures great and small—those that buzz and those that fly.

Slide 6   Picture of mountains and sunsets
Caption: God's wonderful world
Prayer: for God's beautiful world of hills and valleys, for rivers and streams and for sunsets that take our breath away.

Slide 7   Picture of each of the seasons
These should appear on the screen with a one– or two–second delay between.

Caption: for each of the seasons that make up our year
Prayer: for each of the seasons spring and summer, autumn and winter, that lead us through a year of thankfulness.

Slide 8   *Picture of pizza and salad, cup of tea, glass of orange juice*

Caption: the things we eat and the things we drink

Prayer: for the food we eat and the drinks we enjoy that
give us strength to learn and to play, to care and
to serve.

Slide 9   *Picture of farmers and fishermen*

Caption: all who bring us our food

Prayer: for those who work on the land or the sea, and
for those around the world whose daily labour
brings food to our tables.

Slide 10   *Picture of Christian Aid, Tear Fund and other charities*

Caption: for those who work for a fairer world

Prayer: for those who work for a fairer world
and for those who will not allow us to forget
that our concern for justice for others
is how God measures our thankfulness today.

Slide 11   *Picture of praying hands*

Leader: We give thanks to the Lord.

Response: ***And we praise his name. Amen.***

Slide 12   *Blank*

488   YOU GAVE US HANDS

*Set up a series of eleven PowerPoint slides which can be moved
on manually. Display pictures that feature hands in ways
appropriate for each prayer. The words are to be spoken.*

Slide 1   *Blank*

Slide 2   *Hands that share*

Lord, you have given us hands.
Thank you for those who use their hands to give and to
share; to love and to care.

Slide 3   Hands that hold

Lord, you have given us hands.
Thank you for those who use their hands to touch and to
    hold;
to deal gently; to enable others to trust.

Slide 4   Hands that serve

Lord, you have given us hands.
Thank you for those who get their hands dirty in the service
    of others.

Slide 5   Hands that pray

Lord, you have given us hands.
Thank you for those who use their hands in their
    commitment to the ministry of prayer.

Slide 6   Hands that heal

Lord, you have given us hands.
Thank you for those who use their hands to heal and to
    bless,
to offer wholeness to those who are broken.

Slide 7   Hands that care

Lord, you have given us hands.
Thank you for those whose hands speak of self-forgetfulness
and their lifetime of caring for others.

Slide 8   Hands that lead

Lord, you have given us hands.
Thank you for those who lead friends and neighbours
to become brothers and sisters in Christ.

Slide 9   Hands that obey

Lord, you have given us hands.
Thank you for those who use their hands to serve you by
    serving others

and for those who are ready to use their hands
when, where, how and with whom you choose.

Slide 10   Praying hands

In the name of him who placed himself in our hands
we praise the Lord. Amen.

Slide 11   Blank

489   PRAYERS FOR LEARNING

Display suitable pictures for each prayer.

Slide 1   Picture of the world

Lord, we pray for your world, our home,
where we can live and enjoy the beauty of all that you have
    made.
Lord, we pray: Help us to do all we can to care for your
    creation,
and may nothing we say or do or plan spoil what you have
    made.

Slide 2   Picture of learning

Lord, we thank you for every opportunity to learn more
about ourselves, your world and your glory.
We pray for our school, and all the schools in this area,
for colleges and universities,
for all who teach and use their gifts to help us to learn.

Slide 3   Picture of outer space

Lord, we simply cannot imagine just how utterly immense
    the universe really is.
We thank you for the work of all scientists and their
    discoveries
which amaze us and give us even more reasons to give you
    our praise.
We pray that, as we learn more about the vastness of space,

we will remember you hold everything, even us, in the palm
    of your hand.

Slide 4   Picture from the Internet

Lord, we thank you for the World Wide Web
and for all the good things that it can be used for,
for information shared, for help given, good messages
    received.
We pray for all who misuse the Internet
and for those who use it to spoil people's lives
by what they see, and by what they are led to do.

Slide 5   Picture of drugs

Lord, we pray for those who misuse drugs,
for those who spoil their own lives and the lives of others
by the things they allow into their bodies, their minds and
    their lives;
for those whose lives are being damaged
by the things to which they are addicted;
and for those who push illegal drugs on children and young
    people
without any concern for the damage done to people's lives.

Slide 6   Picture of someone in hospital

Lord, we pray for doctors, nurses and for all who work in the
    health service;
for those who seek cures for new diseases
and for those who care for the sick and the dying,
and for those who may never recover.
We pray for anyone we know who needs God's healing
    touch,
to feel his hand of love upon their lives.

Slide 7   Picture of the world

Lord, we praise you for the joy and the wonder of being alive
    in your world,

for all the things we can learn and the exciting things we can
  discover.
We pray: By your Holy Spirit go on touching and changing
  our lives,
that we may be empowered to serve you, and use the gifts
  you are giving us,
to bring hope to the hopeless, joy to those who are hurting
and your love to all who have lost their way.
Lord, in your mercy,
hear our prayer. Amen.

490   WE GIVE THANKS 1

Set up a series of seventeen PowerPoint slides to be moved on manually. These prayers work best using two voices alternating between stanzas.

Display appropriate pictures for each prayer.

Slide 1   Blank

Slide 2   *Title:* We give thanks

Slide 3   *Pictures of vegetables, pizza and fruit*
Prayer: We give thanks for our food that helps us to grow.

Slide 4   *Pictures of orange juice and a cup of tea*
Prayer: For things to drink that quench our thirst.

Slide 5   *Pictures of playschool, dressing up, swimming*
Prayer: For games to play.

Slide 6   *Pictures of school*
Prayer: For those who teach us and for things to learn.

Slide 7   *Pictures of children and teenagers*
Prayer: For friends to have fun with and laughter to enjoy.

Slide 8   *Pictures of flowers, trees*
Prayer: For beautiful flowers and trees all around us

Slide 9   *Pictures of a glacier and an ocean*
Prayer: For majestic glaciers and powerful oceans.

Slide 10   *Pictures of a rainbow*
Prayer: And for the rainbow's promise of hope.

Slide 11   *Pictures of spring, summer, autumn and winter*
Prayer: For each of the changing seasons that run round
            through the year.

Slide 12   *Pictures of mother and baby, older person and
            family*
Prayer: To know we are loved and that there are those
            who care for us.

Slide 13   *Picture of a Bible and praying hands*
Prayer: For the Bible that brings us God's Word and for
            the gift of prayer when we can express our praise
            and our needs.

Slide 14   *Picture of person being embraced*
Prayer: For times to say sorry and mean it, and to know
            what it means to be forgiven.

Slide 15   *Picture of the cross*
Prayer: For the cross of Jesus where new life, hope and
            peace begin.

Slide 16
Captions:
Leader: For all his gifts
Response: **we praise the Lord. Amen.**

Slide 17   *Blank*

491   WE GIVE THANKS 2

*Set up a series of eighteen PowerPoint slides with a fifteen-second
timed delay between slides. These prayers work best with music
inserted into the slide show, either from a disk or played on an
instrument. Fade each picture in and then fade the caption in*

*after a one- or two-second delay. Then after fifteen seconds fade
the picture and caption out together.*

Slide 1   *Blank*

Slide 2   *Title:*   *We give thanks ...*

Music is launched

Slide 3   *Picture of the earth*
Caption: for God's beautiful world

Slide 4   *Picture of a river*
Caption: for the rivers of life

Slide 5   *Picture of mother and newborn baby*
Caption: for moments of sheer joy

Slide 6   *Picture of a sunrise*
Caption: for times of peace and tranquillity

Slide 7   *Picture of a coral reef*
Caption: for depths of wonder and a world we cannot see

Slide 8   *Picture of a garden of flowers*
Caption: for the ability to enjoy God's world

Slide 9   *Picture of a bench on a woodland path*
Caption: for places—just to be

Slide 10   *Picture of hands*
Caption: for hands that care for us

Slide 11   *Picture of a satellite above the earth*
Caption: for the desire and the will to reach up and beyond
            ourselves

Slide 12   *Picture of Everest*
Caption: for peaks to conquer

Slide 13   *Picture of a sunset on still water*
Caption: for times of stillness and understanding

Slide 14　*Picture by Monet of poppy fields*
Caption:　for those who help us to see your world in new ways

Slide 15　*Picture of the cross*
Caption 1:　for the place to begin ...

Caption 2:　... and the one who helps us to begin again.

Slide 16　*Picture of the earth*
Caption:　for each new day

Slide 17
Captions:
Leader:　For all your gifts
Response:　**We thank you, Lord. Amen.**

Slide 18:　*Blank*

492　PRAYER OF THANKS AND FORGIVENESS
Display suitable pictures.

Lord, we thank you for—

Slide 1:　*Picture of the World*
Prayer:　Lord, we thank you for the world in which we live and for all the wonder of your creation

Slide 2:　*Pictures of Niagara and a beach*
Prayer:　For powerful waterfalls that take our breath away, and for quiet bays that offer a time of peace.

Slide 3:　*Pictures of an elephant and a caterpillar*
Prayer:　For all creatures great ... and small ...
that make your world such a wonderful place in which to live.

Slide 4:　*Pictures of a bird and a butterfly*
Prayer:　For the beauty of birds ...
and for butterflies with delicate wings that speak of your care and design.

Slide 5:	*Pictures of a dandelion and an orchid*
Prayer:	For flowers of all shapes and sizes—those that are common ... and those that are rare— and for the way they enrich our lives.

Slide 6:	*Pictures of bright colour and a painting*
Prayer:	For a world full of colours ... and for those who paint wonderful pictures and for the pleasure we receive from the use of their gifts.

Slide 7:	*Pictures of a baby and an elderly couple*
Prayer:	For newborn babies that bring us laughter and hope and joy ... and for those who have seen many years and for the wisdom they offer.

Slide 8:	*Pictures of friends and family*
Prayer:	For friends ... and for families who love us and help us and care for us, even when we don't deserve it.

Slide 9:	*Pictures of a house and small town*
Prayer:	For our homes where we feel safe ... and for the place where we feel we belong.

Slide 10:	*Pictures of prayer and worship*
Prayer:	For the gift of prayer when we can talk to our heavenly Father ... and for times when we long to give praise to Jesus who makes God so real.

Slide 11:	*Picture of a cross*
Prayer:	For Jesus, who died on the cross and was raised from the dead ... and is with us today—and every today of our lives.

Slide 12:   *Picture of the world*

Prayer: For the world in which we live
and for God's promise that he holds everything in
his hands.

Captions:

   Leader: For all your gifts

   Response: **we thank you, Lord.**

*For the following I used appropriate pictures of the cartoon
character Homer Simpson.*

Captions:

          Lord, we admit –

          that we are lazy and we let you down

          that we only love those who love us

          that we spoil each other's lives by what we say and
          by what we do

          that we think we are more important than other
          people

          that we think we can sort out our own lives without
          putting our trust in you.

Captions:

   Leader: We have come to say we are sorry,

   Response: **Forgive us, Lord. Amen.**

Slide 13:   *Blank*

Prayers for Repentance and Renewal

493   FREEDOM IN REPENTANCE

*Use appropriate pictures and perhaps a sung response such as O
Lord, hear my prayer.*

Slide 1:   *Blank*

Slide 2:   *Picture of the world*

Prayer: We pray for your world, which is your precious
gift to us all.

Help us to change the way we live, that your
world might be renewed.

Caption: O Lord, hear my prayer ...

Slide 3:   *Picture of money*
Prayer: We pray for those who think they are rich but are
paupers in your sight.
Forgive our trust in material things, and renew
our hope of heaven.

Caption: O Lord, hear my prayer ...

Slide 4:   *Picture of drugs*
Prayer: We pray for those who long to live but whose
addiction to drugs is killing them.
Forgive our neglect of those who are hurting
and renew our commitment to help and to care.

Caption: O Lord, hear my prayer ...

Slide 5:   *Picture of slavery*
Prayer: We pray for those enslaved today, and for those
still longing to be set free;
for those involved in the trafficking of people
and for those trapped by their poverty in
dangerous and degrading conditions.

Caption: O Lord, hear my prayer ...

Slide 6:   *Picture of gambling*
Prayer: We pray for those whose whole lives are a gamble
and for those who cannot see God's hand of
grace;
forgive our society that takes risks with people's
lives
and renew our faith in the healing love of God.

Caption: O Lord, hear my prayer ...

Slide 7:   *Picture of poverty*
Prayer: We pray for those on the margins of life
and for those for whom poverty is still not
history;

forgive us for stealing the bread of your children
and renew our commitment to justice for all.

Caption: O Lord, hear my prayer …

Slide 8:   *Picture of local churches*
Prayer: We pray for all the churches in [*local area*],
            for our witness, worship and service.
            Forgive our failure to speak of our faith in Jesus
            and renew our obedience to Jesus our Lord.

Caption: O Lord, hear my prayer …

Slide 9:   *Picture of local congregation*
Prayer: We pray for ourselves and our walk with Christ
            and for our daily experience of his living
            presence.
            Forgive our neglect of opportunities for renewal
            and renew our openness to the work of the Spirit.

Caption: O Lord, hear my prayer …

Slide 10: *Picture of a dove*
Prayer: Lord, we came to the empty cross and we found a
            Saviour;
            we went to the empty tomb and we received our
            Lord.
            Now pour out your Holy Spirit, that we might
            repent and our lives be renewed.
            We ask our prayers in the name of Jesus, Saviour
            and Lord. Amen.

Prayers for a Memorial Service

494   MEMORIAL SERVICE—PREPARATION

Lord, you have given to us the gift of memory.
We use it to hold pictures in our minds
of those we have loved but see no more.
We have come, not only to remember

but to receive again your promise that you will hold us, help
us and love us,
now and for evermore. Amen.

495   MEMORIAL SERVICE—PRAISE

Lord, we praise you, our Creator God;
your almighty power is the source of our lives
and gives us meaning and purpose
to the beginning and the end of all our journeys.

Lord, we praise you, our merciful God;
your overwhelming love is something we can never deserve
but is at the heart of everything that is of ultimate worth.
It is your love that enables us to stand when we might have
fallen
and to begin again when we could see no way forwards.

Lord, we praise you, our God of peace;
your gentle touch lifts the fallen; brings victory to the
defeated;
and restores the broken-hearted.
It is your peace that transforms our darkness with your light
and it is your presence that promises a joy that is beyond
words
and a hope that nothing can end.

We praise you in the name of Christ,
who is our peace and our reason for worship. Amen.

496   MEMORIAL SERVICE—CONFESSION

Lord, where we have gone wrong, set us again on the right
path;
where we have said hurtful things, help us to say we are
sorry;
where we have made mistakes, enable us to start again;
where we have caused pain and suffering to those around us,
show us how to make amends;

where we have failed to love you, and our neighbours as
    ourselves,
fill us with your love;
where we have lost sight of you, and thought only of
    ourselves,
forgive us, Lord, that your love might make us whole. Amen.

497   MEMORIAL SERVICE—THANKSGIVING

Father, we thank you for being our light in the darkness
and our peace when sadness had all but crushed the life out
    of us,
for being there when no one else could
and for sharing our grief when no one else wanted to.

Father, we thank you for every memory we have
of those we have loved and who have loved us;
for those whose voices we miss
and whose ways are for ever etched on our minds.

Father, we thank you for the laughter and the tears we
    shared;
for the things they said and did that made them so special;
for particular moments that made them, and our memories
    of them, so special.

We bring our thanks to you in the name of Jesus,
whose endless grace sustains and guides us. Amen.

498   AN ACT OF THANKSGIVING

*As the congregation enters the church, they are invited to write
the name of the person they will be remembering on a slip of
paper and to place it in a basket.*

The congregation stands.

*The basket containing the slips of paper is brought forward and
placed at the front of the church.*

Lord, we thank you for those we have come to remember,
for all they meant to us, for all they have added to our lives
and for all they have done to make your love real.

In a moment of silence we bring our personal memories with
thanks and praise.

Silence

Father, so understanding, so patient;
Jesus, self-giving Saviour, all-sovereign Lord;
Holy Spirit, our enabler, our strength and the presence of
God within us.

In this moment of remembering we ask you to comfort and
to help us;
to hold us and heal us; to guide us and change us;
to love us and to be our Saviour, Friend and Lord. Amen.

499 MEMORIAL SERVICE—INTERCESSIONS

Lord, we pray for those who are hurting
and for those whose pain is deep inside;
for those whose sense of loss is so great
they are finding it hard to put their lives back together again.
Lord, hold them in the hollow of your hand,
that your peace and grace may hold them.
God of all peace and hope,
hear our prayer.

Lord, we pray for those who are really lonely,
for those who miss the friendship, the laughter and the love
they have lost;
and for those who long to see a friendly face and feel a loving
touch.
Lord, hold them in the hollow of your hand,
that your peace and grace may hold them.
God of all peace and hope,
hear our prayer.

Lord, we pray for those who are angry
and for those whose emotions are stretched to breaking point;
for those who experience an emptiness that nothing seems to
    fill;
for those who are filled with remorse
because of what they said or did, or failed to say or do.
Lord, hold them in the hollow of your hand,
that your peace and grace may hold them.
God of all peace and hope,
hear our prayer.

Lord, we pray for those who have lost hope
and for those for whom each day is a burden;
for those whose faith is being severely tested
and for those who are finding that their pain is bringing
    them closer to God;
for those who find that they cannot cry
and for those who are discovering that you share their tears.
Lord, hold them in the hollow of your hand,
that your peace and grace may hold them.
God of all peace and hope,
hear our prayer.

Lord, we pray for those who want to know that you are real
and that you do understand their pain;
for those who long to put their faith in the risen Christ
and to find their hope in him;
for those who are discovering that you are the one
who promises to walk with us now and to the end, and
    beyond.
Lord, hold them in the hollow of your hand,
that your peace and grace may hold them.
God of all peace and hope,
hear our prayer.

We bring our prayers in the name of Jesus Christ,
who died and rose again that we might put our trust in him.
    Amen.

May the grace of the Lord Jesus Christ hold you;
may the love of the Father enfold you;
and may the presence of the Holy Spirit uphold you.

Go in peace and be assured that God's peace, love and
    presence
will be with you now and for evermore. Amen.

Index

Key to categories of prayer. Numbers indicate prayers not pages.

ad = adoration 10–29
all = all-age worship 160–229
bef = before service 414–473
call = call to worship 1–9
com = commitment 283–299
con = confession 134–159
dis = dismissal 300–335
fu = funeral 371–382
heal = healing service 356–361
int = intercession 230–282
med = meditation 383–413
mem = memorial service 494–500
off = offertory 336–355
pic = with pictures 474–493
pr = praise 47–106
prep = preparation 30–46
th = thanksgiving 107–133
wed = wedding 362–370